THE LANGUAGE

of

ETHICS

THE LANGUAGE

of

ETHICS

Carl Wellman

1961

HARVARD UNIVERSITY PRESS

Cambridge, Massachusetts

Distributed in Great Britain by
Oxford University Press, London

Library of Congress Catalog Card Number 61–8843
Printed in the United States of America

PREFACE

This book is a considerably revised version of my doctoral dissertation. It is only fitting, therefore, that I begin by acknowledging my indebtedness to my two thesis advisors, Professors C. I. Lewis and Morton White. That I ever reached the point where I was able to undertake such a project successfully I owe to the stimulating guidance of all my Harvard professors. A particular debt of gratitude is due to Professors Aiken and Bugbee under whom I took courses in ethics. It is also appropriate to mention the very helpful discussions I was privileged to have with Professors Broad, Wisdom, and von Wright as well as Doctor Ewing while my ideas were germinating in the fruitful atmosphere of Cambridge.

Once my ideas had grown into their written form, I received both aid and comfort from the two readers known officially only to the press; their suggestions have been of great help in improving the manuscript. The friendly and expert efforts of all those connected with the Harvard University Press who have guided this work from manuscript to book have been invaluable. Finally, let me thank Mrs. Ruth Lesselyong, whose prompt and efficient typing has reproduced my ideas stage by stage.

The subject of this book is the meaning of ethical sentences, a subject which belongs to the epistemology of ethics. It will be apparent that my general epistemological viewpoint owes more to the thought of C. I. Lewis than to any other. At the same time, my approach to language has been deeply affected by the writings of Ludwig Wittgenstein. In addition, of course, I have

PREFACE

acquired many specific insights from my readings in the contemporary literature of ethics. I have refrained from detailed acknowledgements in the form of footnotes only out of pity for my reader and the printer. But let me partially remedy this breach of courtesy by here publicly acknowledging my unpaid debts.

If my writing can claim any originality, it is not because it owes nothing to other writers. My ideas are not all my own in this sense. While I have not consciously stolen anything from others, I have learned a great deal from them. This distinction is a subtle, but genuine, one depending upon the fact that what one thinker borrows from another becomes modified and reoriented in becoming assimilated into his own thought. It is my way of thinking, my way of systematically interpreting the meaning of ethical sentences, which I would claim to be my own. My primary purpose in writing this book is to explain and defend this way of thinking about the language of ethics.

CARL WELLMAN

Appleton, Wisconsin
August 1960

CONTENTS

CONTENTS

CONTENTS

CONTENTS

THE LANGUAGE

of

ETHICS

— I —

Introduction

Unlike the penguin or the dodo, the ethical sentence is neither an unusual nor an extinct species. In fact, the ethical sentence has something of the same pervasiveness in the English language that the sparrow has in the English countryside. The questions one asks oneself, the discussions one enters into with his acquaintances, the advice one receives from his friends, the sermon one hears from the pulpit, the editorial one reads in the paper, all abound with sentences such as these:

Ought I to give up teaching and find a better-paying job?
Euthanasia is wrong.
You really should give up smoking.
Divorce is a wicked rebellion against God's will.
Democracy is better than Communism.

These, and sentences like them, are ethical sentences. But

exactly what is one asking when he asks himself what he ought to do? It is not clear what one is saying when he says that an action is right or wrong. People disagree heatedly over the nature of wickedness and betterness and, therefore, over what it means to apply the adjectives "wicked" and "better." Although ethical sentences are very common, their correct interpretation poses many difficulties. What do ethical sentences mean? It is this question which I shall attempt to answer in the following pages.

1. *The Nature of the Question*

Before trying to answer this question it would be well to notice what kind of a question it is. Although the question is about ethical sentences, the question itself is not an ethical one. Historically ethics has been primarily concerned with determining what things are good or bad and what acts are right or wrong. Perhaps one should include an investigation of the nature of value and obligation in the core of ethical theory as well. Epistemology, on the other hand, is concerned with the possibility and nature of knowledge. It must decide which statements are meaningful and which are meaningless. This leads to an investigation of the nature of meaning and the kinds of significance sentences can possess. While ethics deals with problems of value and obligation, epistemology deals with problems of knowledge and meaning. Thus the problem of whether stealing is wrong belongs to ethics; the problem of what it means to say that stealing is wrong belongs more properly to epistemology. The latter problem, however, is hardly irrelevant to ethics. Perhaps the true relation can be best suggested by speaking of the epistemology of ethics. Similarly, to ask "What do ethical sentences mean?" is to ask an epistemological question about ethical sentences. Therefore, the problem with which I am concerned is one in the epistemology of ethics.

To fully understand this question, however, one must do more than locate it in the appropriate branch of philosophy. Questions like this one have become so common in contemporary philosophy, which is preoccupied with epistemology in general and semantics in particular, that one is inclined to forget how unusual the question really is. In fact, it is a most peculiar question indeed. To realize this, one must notice how very different it is from everyday questions which arise about the meaning of a sentence.

When a person hears or reads a sentence which he does not understand, he usually wonders how he is to interpret it. If his interest is sufficient and the opportunity is present, he may ask "What does this sentence mean?" This question is about the meaning of a single given sentence. Although this same sort of question can be asked about a group of sentences, it would normally be a group of sentences which occur together in a particular paragraph or within a single linguistic context. One asks this question because he is perplexed by the particular bit of language he has just met; he is not sure what the speaker or writer intended to say with the sentence. This may be because the sentence is in a foreign language, or because it uses an unfamiliar word or grammatical construction, or because it uses a familiar word in an unfamiliar way. In any event, the hearer is at a loss to fathom the speaker's meaning; he cannot figure out what the speaker wishes to communicate.

The obvious way to answer this kind of question is to give another sentence which says the same thing in other words. This answer will be satisfactory only in case the questioner understands this new sentence. At times, however, one cannot think of any synonymous sentence which the hearer can interpret. Then one has to use a more roundabout method of answering the question; one must teach the language to the person who does not understand it. How one teaches the language depends, of course, upon the kind of language involved and the linguistic abilities of the questioner. One teaches words like "red" and "soft" quite differently from words like "it" or "not." Definitions are a useful teaching device only when the pupil has a sufficient grasp of the language used in the definition. If the questioner succeeds in learning the language, he will cease to be puzzled by it. Now that he can interpret this particular bit of language, he will no longer ask "What does this sentence mean?"

It is not this sort of question, however, which the philosopher is asking when he asks "What do ethical sentences mean?" His difficulty is not that he has just met some particularly unintelligible sentence which happens to be ethical; much less is it the case that he is at a loss when it comes to interpreting all ethical sentences. The philosopher finds it no harder to understand someone when he talks ethics than when he talks politics or physics. He has long since learned the language of ethics. He finds speaking and hearing, reading and writing ethical sentences no more difficult than using any other kind of language. There is no point, therefore, in trying to answer his question as one would answer a question about the meaning of some particular sentence.

It is not very helpful, for example, to say the same thing in other words. The philosopher is already prepared to suggest numerous synonymous sentences. That this is not what he is asking for can be readily seen by the fact that he would not be satisfied if he had such a translation. Any sentence with the same meaning as the original would, presumably, have the same kind of meaning; and it is the *kind* of meaning which disturbs our philosopher. It is not this particular sentence, but ethical sentences in general which perplex him. Although translations do not directly attack the basic problem, I would not say that they are entirely useless. It may be that one way of making an ethical remark brings out what one is doing better than another. There is some gain in translating particularly misleading expressions into those which reveal the intent more clearly. One is not in a position to know which formulation is in fact preferable, however, until after he discovers what one is really doing when he uses an ethical sentence. Reformulation may remind us of the true meaning of ethical sentences, but it cannot tell us the meaning in the first place.

The other method of answering the question "What does this sentence mean?" is equally inappropriate to the question "What do ethical sentences mean?" Since the philosopher already knows the language of ethics, he would probably not be very grateful to anyone who tried to teach him words like "good" or "wrong." He knows how these words are used as well as, although not much better than, any other adult who has learned the language. It is possible that in the course of his investigations into the epistemology of ethics he will come to know the language a little better even in the ordinary sense of knowing a language; he may become more sensitive to the finer points of usage with respect to these particular words. He is not asking to be taught the language, however, for it was no lack of mastery of the skills of using and interpreting ethical sentences which prompted him to ask his question. He is not puzzled about how to use ethical sentences, but about how to fit them into his philosophical theory.

It begins to be evident that the question which I wish to discuss is not to be confused with everyday questions of meaning. Normally when a person asks "What does this sentence mean?" it is because he is unable to interpret some particular bit of language with which he is confronted.

Such ordinary semantical problems can be solved either by offering a synonymous sentence which the questioner can interpret or by teaching him the bit of language which he cannot understand. But when a philosopher asks "What do ethical sentences mean?" he is not puzzled in the same way. The philosopher knows very well how to use ethical sentences and how to understand others when they use them. In this sense of knowing the meaning of a sentence, he already knows the meaning of ethical sentences. It is in another sense that he does not know what ethical sentences mean; he has no theory which will give him a grasp of the kind of thing one is saying when he utters an ethical sentence. His problem is not *in* the using of language but *about* the using of it. His perplexity arises out of the peculiarities of ethical language. When the distinguishing features of ethical sentences are noticed, these sentences seem unusual or even queer in some way. What is needed is a theory of ethical sentences which will dispel this sense of queerness.

So far I have spoken of *the* question "What do ethical sentences mean?" Perhaps this can be legitimately interpreted as a single question, for it seems to concern one class of sentences and to call for a unified theory to explain this species. If one wants to consider it a single question, however, then he should admit that this one question expresses a variety of distinct problems. Someone who is convinced that all words stand for ideas derived from experience cannot identify any quality of virtue in his experience. What, then, do sentences about virtue mean? Someone who is convinced that the meaning of a sentence is its method of verification cannot discover any possible way to confirm or disconfirm sentences about our obligations. How, then, can sentences about obligation be more than meaningless gibberish? Someone who supposes that to say something is to describe some object cannot see that ethical words add anything to the description of an object. What, then, are we saying when we use ethical sentences? All of these problems arise because certain features of ethical language seem to conflict with one's conception of the nature of language in general.

There are, however, other problems which arise when two features of ethical language itself seem in conflict. How can ethical sentences both express emotions and have objective validity? Why do we continue to argue about the truth of ethical sentences when we never seem able to settle these arguments? Why are ethical sentences formulated in the indicative mood when they seem just as normative as imperatives?

No doubt additional problems will arise when one tries to reconcile his theory about ethical sentences with the rest of his philosophy. If knowledge by itself has no motivational power, how can ethical judgments be normative? If ethical sentences state facts, what are normative facts? If Platonic realism is unacceptable, what are nonnatural characteristics? If ethical sentences are true, with what do they correspond?

Perhaps it would be unkind to belabor my point further. The question "What do ethical sentences mean?" is a philosophical question, and like most philosophical questions it arises within a theoretical framework. It is only when seen against the background of some theory about the nature of language, or the nature of truth, or the irrationality of the emotions, for example, that ethical sentences seem particularly questionable. What disturbs one about ethical sentences depends upon the general preconceptions with which he approaches them. Ethical sentences pose many different problems when thought of in terms of different philosophical perspectives or when related to different parts of a single philosophical theory. The question "What do ethical sentences mean?" hides a teeming multitude of problems.

Any complete answer to this question would have to solve all these problems. Since there is an almost unlimited diversity of preconceptions with which one might approach ethical sentences, the sources of perplexity are close to infinite. One is unlikely to resolve all the problems which might conceivably arise over the nature of ethical language. If completeness is unattainable, what one can strive for is something approaching adequacy. A helpful answer to the question should explain at least (a) what similarities lead us to classify these sentences as ethical, (b) how ethical sentences differ from other types of sentence, (c) how ethical sentences differ among themselves, and (d) what the purpose or purposes of using such sentences are. To explain this much in such a way as to resolve the more important problems raised by recent discussions will be my aim.

2. Which Sentences are Ethical?

Since my goal is a theory explaining the nature of ethical language, the logical way to begin my investigation, it would seem, would be to define my subject matter. What is an ethical sentence? Until I know how to recognize an ethical sentence when I meet one, I literally do not know what I am writing about. At the same time, it appears to me that there are grave difficulties in the attempt to define precisely what it is to be an ethical sentence. Probably there is no one feature essential to all ethical sentences and lacking in all nonethical ones.

Instead of pretending to give a real definition of an ethical sentence, let me give only some rough indication of my subject matter. For my limited purposes, an ethical sentence is any sentence which states either a judgment of value

8

or a judgment of obligation. I cannot here explain in more detail the nature of either type of judgment, for to do that I would have had to have completed the investigation which I am just beginning. What I can, and should, do is to warn the reader that I interpret both very widely. Thus any judgment which asserts that something is good, bad, or indifferent I consider a judgment of value. Likewise any judgment that asserts that someone ought or ought not to do something is, for me, a judgment of obligation. When I write of ethical sentences, therefore, I shall be writing of sentences like the following:

Sally is a wicked woman.
This ice cream is very good.
That is a fine painting.
Every citizen has an obligation to pay his taxes.
You ought not to have killed your father on his birthday.
If you want to be popular, you really should go on a diet.

To some it will seem that not all of these are really ethical sentences. Not all judgments of value are ethical judgments; we must distinguish clearly between moral value and other kinds of value such as esthetic satisfactoriness or practical utility. Similarly, not all judgments that someone ought to do something are genuinely ethical. Although the burglar ought to break in quickly and silently, one would hardly say that this was a moral obligation on his part. Only those sentences which deal with specifically moral values or obligations, it could be contended, are ethical in the strict sense.

I would not wish to deny that one should distinguish carefully between specifically moral judgments and related nonmoral ones. There certainly is a difference between asserting that a person is virtuous and asserting that steak is nice. There is an equal disparity between saying that a businessman ought to advertise widely and that he ought to advertise honestly.

Although I recognize the reality of the distinction between the specifically moral and the nonmoral, I wish to use the terms "ethical sentence" in a way which is broad enough to include both. In large measure, this is because I feel that, important as the differences between moral and nonmoral judgments of value or obligation are, the similarities are more basic. To say that a person is virtuous is not, of course, exactly like saying that a steak is nice; but it is to say something of fundamentally the same kind. The prudential and moral oughts are distinct, but they are two variations on a single underlying theme. Naturally I cannot expect anyone to agree with me on these claims unless I can support them in the course of my analysis. Even if I am wrong, however, it does not appear that any great harm will be done. The fact that I choose to investigate the genus does not exclude, but rather necessitates, a consideration of the species. After describing the generic traits of ethical sentences in this broad sense, I shall go on to specify the distinguishing features of the narrower class of specifically moral sentences. I hope that these few remarks will placate those who feel that my conception of ethical sentences is too broad.

To others it will seem that my conception is too narrow. There are many kinds of sentence which have as good a claim to be considered ethical as those which express judgments of value or obligation. Ethical theories normally contain statements about the nature of the self, the possibility of free will, and the existence of God. Also statements about the meaning of ethical words or the ways of knowing ethical truths abound in ethical treatises. Moreover, there are two sorts of sentences, promises and ascriptions of responsibility, which recent discussion has shown to have distinctive features and which have clear ethical implications. It would appear that the class of ethical sentences is far, far wider than I have been willing to admit.

I do not, however, wish to imply that judgments of obligation and judgments of value are the only two kinds of sentence which are genuinely ethical; I am confident that they are not. Promises and ascriptions of responsibility, for example, may well have an equal claim to membership in the class of ethical sentences. I am not at all sure how many other kinds of sentence can claim membership in the class as well, but I suspect that there are several. I do not pretend to be writing about all ethical sentences, but only about two species of the genus.

There are several reasons for picking these particular species as my subject matter. For one thing, they are obviously important kinds of sentences. However they may be labeled, they deserve to be studied in detail, and I hope to give them something like the attention they deserve. For another thing, these are the two kinds of sentence which have been most frequently taken as typically ethical by recent writers in ethics. By restricting myself to these it will be easier to apply the insights of previous theories to my own investigation. Finally, there is some reason to think that these two types of sentence are central to systems of ethics. By and large, ethical theories have been primarily concerned with problems of value and obligation. Metaphysical, epistemological, and scientific statements seem to be included in ethics only insofar as they contribute to the solution of questions about value or obligation. Thus, although theoretical ethics includes much more than judgments of value and obligation, these may be considered central to it.

I shall, therefore, take as my subject matter sentences which express judgments of value or judgments of obligation. Since it is somewhat inconvenient to write "sentences which express judgments of value or judgments of obligation" several times on each page, I shall refer to these simply as "ethical sentences." This abbreviation does not appear entirely inappropriate, for these seem clearly to be species of ethical sentences. It is important to bear in mind, however, that I do not pretend to be writing about all ethical sentences; my analysis is concerned only with some ethical sentences. Nor do I wish my remarks about judgments of value and obligation to be assumed to apply to all other kinds of ethical sentence. I leave it an open question whether these species are typical of the genus.

3. *The Importance of the Question*

My present aim is to give a systematic account of the meaning of judgments of value and obligation. Nor am I alone in my interest in the meaning of ethical sentences. It would not be too much to say that this has been the primary concern of ethicists, at least in the English-speaking world, for the past half-century. When G. E. Moore published his *Principia Ethica* in 1903, he set the problems which were to be central in the following decades. At that time he contended that the question of how the word "good" is to be defined is "the most fundamental question in all Ethics." Since then the question has been broadened to include other words like "right," "ought," and their contraries. This broadened question of the meaning of ethical words in general has probably received more attention in the past 57 years than any other single problem in ethics. It is as solutions to this problem that the main contemporary theories of ethics (naturalism, intuitionism, and emotivism) have argued their cases.

In the light of this continued and concentrated attention, one may wonder whether this particular question deserves any further consideration. There are, in fact, some signs that many philosophers feel that greater progress can be made by bypassing this issue and approaching directly the problem of ethical reasoning. However, I am of the opinion that the question of the meaning of ethical sentences has a genuine and lasting importance.

For one thing, the way in which one interprets the nature of ethical reasoning depends upon his concept of the meaning of ethical sentences. If ethical sentences refer to non-natural characteristics, we can know them only by intuition. If they refer to empirical characteristics we might be able to establish them by the scientific method. If they have only emotive meaning, perhaps it is pointless to look for any ethical reasons in the strict sense. We cannot know what the reasons for or against an ethical sentence are until we know what it means. I do not wish this "until" to be interpreted temporally; I do not intend to forbid anyone to begin his investigation with the problem of ethical reasoning. After all, one must begin somewhere. I desire merely to make the logical point that the two problems are interdependent; the two issues can only be finally resolved together. Perhaps, therefore, continued attention to the nature of ethical language is particularly appropriate at a time when others are turning to the nature of ethical reasoning.

One reason why questions of meaning were discussed with such interest early in this century was their relative novelty. Philosophical questions are seldom really answered, they are simply forgotten. After a time it becomes very hard to think of anything original and interesting to say on a given question. At the turn of the century the problems which had attracted the attention of ethicists for the past few centuries were losing their provocativeness. Here in the meaning of ethical words was a whole new range of issues which lay invitingly unexplored. After a half-century of intensive discussion, however, the novelty has rather worn off. Although one cannot reasonably hope for an entirely new answer at this late date, it does not follow that the question has lost its significance. In fact, the question has gained in significance because the recent discussion has brought out more clearly the nature of the problems it raises. Also, existing theories contain many unclarified presuppositions and suggest many unexplored interpretations of ethical language. Most important, a really detailed and systematic analysis of ethical language remains to be done.

It seems quite possible that the interest, almost an obsession, with such questions of meaning arose in large part as a reaction against the Idealisms which predominated at the end of the nineteenth century. To many of the younger thinkers the writings of the Idealists seemed like very large volumes of very long sentences on very obscure topics. Gradually the impression grew that these sentences were either completely meaningless or at least unnecessarily obscure. The desire to avoid such empty pomposity led to a preoccupation with explaining clearly and simply exactly what one did mean by any philosophical term. It may well be that the Idealists wrote more significantly than this reaction suggests; but the ideal of clarity, however it may have arisen historically, seems genuine enough. It is one of the fundamental responsibilities of any philosopher to make clear the meaning of his central conceptions.

If the ethicist fails in this responsibility, the analyst will probably hint darkly that his entire theory is nonsense. One of the most common suggestions in contemporary epistemology, one which can be supported by various theories of meaning, has been that certain kinds of sentence are literally meaningless. Once the possibility that one is talking nonsense is taken seriously, it becomes important for any philosopher to show that the statements he wishes to make are genuinely significant. If he cannot or will not do this, he is apt to be dismissed without a hearing on the grounds that he really is not saying anything anyway. Since ethicists are particularly susceptible to such attacks from hard-headed analysts, it is particularly important for the ethicist to show that he is not talking nonsense. But this can be done best by explaining what in fact his sentences do mean.

In meeting this challenge of the analysts, the ethicist will be doing more than protecting his theories from a premature dismissal; he will actually be doing these epistemologists a favor. One of the goals of epistemology is to work out a general theory of the nature of meaning and the conditions of meaninglessness. If such a theory is tenable, it must apply accurately and informatively to all significant discourse. Clearly one of the important tests for such a theory is whether or not it can explain ethical sentences plausibly. An insight into the nature of ethical sentences will provide some measure of the adequacy of any general theory of meaning which might be considered. The investigation of ethical sentences might, moreover, reveal features of these specific sentences which would suggest some modification in one's general epistemological position.

Finally, one's answer to the question of the meaning of ethical sentences may have important implications for ethical issues. It is often contended that metaethics has no relevance for ethics itself, but I am dubious of this claim. No doubt many ethical questions remain unaffected by one's interpretation of ethical sentences; but some real, if indirect, relations exist. If it turned out that "good" means "pleasant," for example, this would have an important bearing on deciding what things are in fact good. If "right" means "according to the code of one's society," this will help one to determine what he ought to do. If "ought" stands for a metaphysically real nonnatural relation, then obligation is more than a feeling in our minds. At least some interpretations of the meaning of ethical sentences, therefore, are relevant to the nature of goodness and obligation and, perhaps, indirectly relevant to specific judgments of value and obligation as well.

In short, there are many reasons to consider the problem of the nature of ethical sentences a genuine and important one. The extensive discussions of this question have not exhausted its fruitfulness; rather they have supplied the material with which it can be discussed much more incisively and profitably in the future. Let us not turn away from this question just when we begin to grasp its full significance and to discover what we must expect of any adequate answer.

4. *The Road Ahead*

The question which I intend to discuss, therefore, is "What do ethical sentences mean?" I have tried to explain something of the nature, subject matter, and importance of this question. Now it is time to decide upon a plan of attack. Perhaps it would be wisest to approach such a difficult question indirectly. I shall begin by examining the main types of answer which have been given to the question. Then I shall distinguish and characterize the main types of meaning which seem relevant to the interpretation of ethical sentences. Finally, I shall try to show how these kinds of meaning illuminate the nature of ethical language.

There are four existing answers which deserve careful attention. Ethical naturalism is the view that ethical sentences can be considered as one class of empirical descriptions. It is quite right in maintaining that the ultimate evidence for our judgments of value and obligation is experience. I shall argue, however, that it is a mistake to infer that ethical sentences merely describe experience. Ethical intuitionism is the theory that ethical sentences describe a realm of nonnatural qualities and relations. The great merit of this theory is in insisting that ethical sentences differ radically from empirical descriptions; its fault lies in the inability to realize how radical this difference is. Ethical sentences are not primarily descriptions at all, not even of some special realm. The emotive theory of ethics contends that ethical sentences are not primarily descriptive, but that they express and evoke our emotions. In breaking with descriptivism this theory has performed a great service to the epistemology of ethics. However, its own view of emotive meaning is far from clear and its interpretation of ethical sentences fails to do justice to their claim to rationality. The ordinary language approach suggests that ethical sentences are *sui generis* and cannot be reduced to any other sort of sentence. Although I cannot accept either the presuppositions which lie behind this approach nor the interpretations it has produced, I do believe that it points the way towards a much more adequate analysis of ethical language. Its most important contribution is the realization that language functions in many different ways, each of which must be understood in its own terms. My first task will be to present detailed arguments to show that none of these points of view provides an adequate analysis of ethical language.

Probably the main lesson to be learned from a critical examination of existing theories is the need for a more adequate conceptual framework for analysis. Before turning to my own analysis of ethical sentences, therefore, I shall try to discover those different kinds of meaning which might have some bearing on the question at hand. I shall distinguish and characterize five kinds of meaning: descriptive, emotive, evaluative, directive, and critical. Descriptive meaning is the use of language to classify objects according to their similarities and dissimilarities. Emotive meaning is the use of language to express some emotion which the speaker does or might have. Evaluative meaning is the use of language to assert an attitude toward some object. Directive meaning is the use of language to prescribe or prohibit some action. Critical meaning is the use of language to make, modify, press, challenge, reaffirm, or withdraw the claim to rationality. I do not guarantee that these are the only kinds of meaning important for ethics; much less do I suggest that they are the only kinds of meaning sentences can possess. What I do insist upon is that at least these kinds of meaning must be thoroughly understood before one can make sense of ethical language.

After I have characterized as best I can some of the ways in which we use language, I shall apply this conceptual framework to the language of ethics. I shall show how the use of certain key ethical words can be clarified in terms of these kinds of meaning; for this purpose I shall discuss the words "good," "right," "ought," and their contraries. It will appear that each of these words can be used with different kinds of meaning in varying contexts. "Good" does not always formulate a value judgment, and "ought" need not formulate a judgment of obligation. Sentences which do formulate value judgments stand somewhere between descriptive statements and emotive utterances; they assert or deny an attitude. Although they put some pro or con feeling into words, they also claim that this feeling can be rationally justified. Sentences which formulate judgments of obligation are neither a special class of evaluations nor a peculiar type of imperative; they are that species of critical judgments which deal with action. They affirm, challenge, press, withdraw, or concede the claim to rationality implicit in some act or class of acts. After characterizing the uses of a few ethical words, I shall go on to see whether anything interesting can be said about ethical sentences in general.

This book will fall into three main parts. The first section is critical; in chapters II through V, I will examine the four existing answers to my question and argue that none is fully adequate. The second section is constructive; in chapters VI through X, I will give a systematic account of various kinds of meaning. The third section is interpretive; in the final two chapters I will apply my semantical categories to the interpretation of ethical language.

Ethical Naturalism

In the wide sense of the term, ethical naturalism is any theory which interprets value or obligation in purely natural terms. "Natural" in this context means pertaining to nature. While one would be hard pressed to give an exact definition of nature, it is safe to assume that it is to be identified with the world that is studied by the natural sciences. Nature need not be interpreted materialistically, however, for it is still an open question whether psychology and biology can be reduced to physics and chemistry. Ethical naturalism in the wide sense is primarily the rejection of the relevance of anything supernatural to ethics. It rules out an appeal to God, to an eternal soul, or to Platonic Ideas in explaining value or obligation. It is simply the insistence that ethical problems must be solved within the framework of a naturalistic metaphysics.

G. E. Moore gave a new and more restricted meaning to the term in his *Principia Ethica*. Generalizing his formulation slightly to accord with subsequent usage, we can say that in the narrow sense ethical naturalism is any theory which interprets ethical words as standing for natural characteristics. Moore never could explain to his own satisfaction just what he meant by a natural characteristic. Broad has tried to clarify the matter by giving an "epistemological description" instead of a logical definition. "I propose to describe a 'natural characteristic' as any characteristic which either (a) we become aware of by inspecting our sense-data or introspecting our experiences, or (b) is definable wholly in terms of characteristics of the former kind together with the notions of cause and substance." [1] In this light, let us reformulate our definition. Ethical naturalism is any theory which interprets ethical words as standing for empirical characteristics. This is probably what Moore really wanted to say; at any rate it seems to fit the theories to which the word has actually been applied during the past half-century. This definition also has the advantage that it brings out quite clearly the main issue between ethical naturalism and ethical intuitionism. Naturalism holds that our ethical knowledge is entirely based upon experience; intuitionism contends that ultimately ethics rests on the direct insight of reason. Ethical naturalism in the narrow sense is simply one way of solving the problems of ethics within the framework of an empirical epistemology.

We are now confronted with two different meanings for the term "ethical naturalism." In the wide sense of the term ethical naturalism is the view that value and obligation must be understood as belonging to the natural world; this is the application of a metaphysical naturalism to ethics. In the

---

[1] C. D. Broad, "Certain Features in Moore's Ethical Doctrines," in P. A. Schlipp, ed., *Philosophy of G. E. Moore* (Chicago, 1942), p. 62.

narrow sense of the term ethical naturalism is the view that ethical words refer to empirical characteristics; this is the application of an empirical epistemology to ethics. This latter view is concerned with the meaning of words like "good" and "ought," while the former view deals with the nature of value and obligation. The latter view seems to imply the former view, but the converse relation does not hold. Anyone who holds that we can experience the characteristics to which "good" and "ought" refer must admit that goodness and obligation are purely natural phenomena, unless he is prepared to admit that we experience some supernatural realm. It would be quite possible to interpret value and obligation as purely natural phenomena, however, without conceding that the words "good" and "ought" stand for empirical characteristics. The typical ethical emotivist is a case in point. Since my primary interest in this book is with the language of ethics, it is the narrow sense of the term which is important for my purposes. Therefore whenever I use the term "ethical naturalism" I shall, unless I indicate otherwise, use it to refer to the view that ethical words stand for empirical characteristics.

1. *Who Is an Ethical Naturalist?*

It is interesting to notice that the term "naturalism" was taken by Moore as a label for his opponents. There is real doubt, however, whether this term in the sense in which he used it really fits the philosophers whom he attacked as being naturalists. Consider Mill, for example. He is certainly an ethical naturalist in the wide sense of the term, but is he also an ethical naturalist in the narrower sense which Moore introduced? Mill clearly holds that pleasure is the good. But does he believe that the word "good" stands for pleasantness, or does he simply believe that pleasure is the one thing which is in fact good? It is not easy to know whether hedonism is analytic or synthetic for Mill. Nor can one readily tell why he felt so confident that the desired is desirable. Is it because the word "desirable" means being desired, or is it because we in fact desire what is desirable? Since Mill was not primarily concerned with linguistic questions, it is dangerous to classify him according to his theory of the meaning of ethical words. Any such theory, if he had one, would hardly be explicitly stated in his discussions of very different matters. The same can be said of the other traditional objects of the intuitionists' polemic, such as Bentham and Spencer. This confusion has also plagued more recent applications of the term. Are Köhler and Pepper ethical naturalists in the narrow sense? The label can be applied to such men only indirectly, if at all; for they are more concerned with the nature of value and obligation than with the meaning of ethical words. It is very doubtful whether everyone who has been called an ethical naturalist is so in the sense intended.

I do not wish, however, to give the impression that the intuitionists have been fighting with straw men only. Ethical naturalism has been ably represented by such men as Schlick and Perry. Westermarck, if one could pin down his careless writing, would probably turn out to belong in this category as well. Lewis is also an ethical naturalist in his theory of value judgments, although his interpretation of judgments of obligation is another story. The class of ethical naturalists is neither null nor negligible.

Perhaps it would be worthwhile to pause and consider another problem in the use of the term "ethical naturalism." How can one distinguish a naturalist from an emotivist in ethical theory? The difference seems clear enough when one considers only philosophers like Schlick and Ayer. For Schlick an ethical sentence states an empiral proposition about the existence of certain feelings. For Ayer an ethical sentence expresses certain feelings but asserts no proposition.

It is no accident that both men are logical positivists, for naturalism and emotivism seem to be the two alternatives left open by the verifiability theory of meaning. Either ethical sentences assert empirical propositions, or they are empirically meaningless and can have only emotive meaning.

The difference between naturalist and emotivist, however, does not seem so clear when one thinks of Perry and Stevenson. Perry would translate ethical sentences into empirical statements describing interests, but he admits that the language in which we talk about interests acquires a derivative moving appeal. Stevenson claims that the primary meaning of ethical sentences lies in their disposition to reenforce and modify interests, but he acknowledges that they also describe existing interests. Both men assert that ethical language describes interests and has an emotive force; their disagreement would appear to be largely a matter of emphasis. The issue seems to be whether this emotive force is part of the meaning of ethical language. This disagreement may be more about the nature of meaning than about the nature of ethical sentences.

How does one classify Philip Blair Rice? He maintains that ethical sentences have both a cognitive meaning, probably empirical, and a noncognitive meaning, apparently emotive. He places almost equal emphasis upon these two kinds of meaning. The existence of such borderline cases does not, I think, make the term "ethical naturalism" useless. We should remember, however, to be careful in our use of this label.

2. Principal Doctrines

Ethical naturalism, then, is the view that ethical words stand for empirical characteristics. The word "wrong," for example, might be said to stand for the property of being socially condemned. The word "good" might be said to stand for the quality of pleasantness or for the relation of being desired. Since there are many different characteristics of experience for which ethical words might stand, there are many versions of ethical naturalism. What they have in common is that they all interpret ethical language as having the same kind of meaning.

Since ethical naturalism is a theory about the nature of ethical language, it constitutes one answer to my central question, "What do ethical sentences mean?" The naturalist answers that they mean to describe objects or acts empirically. The meaning of ethical sentences is both descriptive and empirical. This need not imply that ethical sentences have no other function than empirical description; they might also express emotions and incite to action. But ethical naturalism contends that these other uses of ethical language are either derivative or incidental. The primary, although not necessarily the exclusive, use of ethical sentences is empirical description.

Associated with this central thesis of ethical naturalism are certain corollaries. One of these is that all ethical words are capable of empirical definition. This does not follow, to be sure, if one limits definition to the analysis of a whole into its constituents as Moore suggests. The ethical naturalist need not hold that the characteristics for which ethical words stand are always complex. But if one allows definition by synonym and ostensive definition, ethical naturalism would seem to imply that ethical words can be defined in terms of experience.

Another corollary is that ethical statements can be established in the same manner as any other empirical propositions. Allowing for the limited applicability of laboratory experiment and precise measurement, ethical truths can be verified by the same scientific method that has been so successful in the natural sciences. Ethics is simply one more branch of knowledge based upon experience, and all ethical questions are to be answered by an appeal to empirical evidence.

3. *Important Insights*

What can be said for ethical naturalism? We have noticed that it amounts to one application of an empirical epistemology to the problem of ethics. On the whole empiricists have tended to be suspicious of unnecessary presuppositions. Traditionally they have rejected any metaphysical assumptions which are incapable of empirical testing and have distrusted any appeal to a rational intuition that is not publicly confirmable. As one might expect, ethical naturalism attempts to free ethics, an area where tender-mindedness seems particularly attractive, from all unanswerable metaphysical problems and all unreliable epistemological assumptions. To define the key concepts of ethics in terms of experience is to make unnecessary, in ethics at least, any use of ontological extravagances or dubious insights. It seems to me that this distrust of speculation is healthy provided it is not carried to the point of ignoring those genuine ethical phenomena which happen to be difficult to explain empirically.

Another valuable contribution of ethical naturalism is its insistence that ethics should have a relevance to the world of experience. Surely the theory of practice can be required to remain practical. Yet ethical principles offer specific guidance in particular situations only if they have concrete implications for experience. Unless ethical principles contain some reference to empirically recognizable characteristics, how can one apply them to the situation in which he here and now finds himself? An ethics which centers around self-evident truths pertaining to a nonnatural realm is, therefore, apt to lose contact with our everyday lives. But if the words in which ethical principles are formulated must be empirically definable, then these principles can hardly avoid having implications for our experience. In this way ethical naturalism would appear to guarantee that ethics has at least some bearing on our lives and on the moral problems arising out of our everyday experiences.

The third and most important insight of ethical naturalism is that ethical judgments are grounded in experience. No doubt there are analytic truths in ethics which are not subject to empirical verification, but one could hardly claim that no ethical statement is synthetic. At least our more specific ethical judgments grow from and are responsible to the given. The evaluation of a painting, for example, is grounded in a direct confrontation of the work of art. One's objection to totalitarianism should come from an awareness of what it is like to live in a totalitarian state. Ethical judgment is irresponsible unless it is based upon an acquaintance with the object judged. A nonempirical acquaintance with the object does seem logically possible. But such rational intuition does not appear to be a sufficient basis for judgment, for even the intuitionists admit that one must also have a knowledge of the object's empirical properties upon which the ethical characteristics depend. Not only is some experience of the object a prerequisite to any reasonable ethical judgment, but the rational man is prepared to modify his judgments in the light of further experience. If one does not recognize the relevance of experience for ethical judgment, what fixed basis is there for the criticism of ethical opinions? The inevitable result would be to leave that area open to unassailable dogmatism. The only way to avoid irresponsible and dogmatic assertions in ethics is to recognize that ethical judgments are grounded in experience. Rational judgment should arise from and be tested by the facts of the case, and these are known through experience. I would agree with ethical naturalism that in ethics the ultimate evidence is empirical.

4. *An Unreal Advantage*

In spite of these very real advantages of ethical naturalism, the position seems untenable to me. Let me begin by explaining why I believe that one of the supposed advantages of ethical naturalism is illusory. To see this one must remember that there are two senses in which the term "ethical naturalism" is used. In the wide sense ethical naturalism is the theory that value and obligation are purely natural; in the narrow sense it is the theory that ethical words stand for empirical characteristics. It is understandable that an ethical naturalist in the wide sense should be sorely tempted to adopt ethical naturalism in the narrow sense. Suppose, to take a single example, that one had become convinced that the interest theory of value is true. Since dogmatism is not philosophically respectable, he would want to defend his position rationally. But how? It does not seems possible to establish ultimate ethical principles deductively. Many ethical statements can be deduced from more general principles, but the starting point in this chain of proofs cannot itself be proved. Nor does it seem any easier to establish fundamental ethical principles inductively from factual information; no survey of what is the case implies what ought to be the case. At the same time, one would be loath to admit that such basic ethical principles are arbitrary and without any rational support. Perhaps, the happy thought dawns, they are true by definition. If "*x* is good" means "interest is taken in *x*," the interest theory of value turns out to be analytic. Its truth can then be established by appealing to its very meaning. Analogous considerations would, of course, apply to any other version of ethical naturalism.

Adopting ethical naturalism in the narrow sense seems, therefore, a very convenient way to support ethical naturalism in the wide sense. It must be pointed out that the convenience of this gambit is no guarantee of its correctness. That it is not always easy to decide whether a given statement is analytic has been ably argued by Quine and White. Until we find some way to distinguish reliably between analytic and synthetic propositions, the claim to analyticity is a weak basis for establishing ethical naturalism. The claim that one's basic ethical principle is analytic rests on the possibility of supplying the appropriate definitions of the words in which the principle is stated. But how can one establish the fact that the suggested definition correctly reports the actual meaning of the word defined? One could say that he is merely proposing a new meaning for the word. How, then, could he show that he has not changed the subject and that his proposed definition is preferable to any other? It does not appear to me that adopting ethical naturalism in the narrow sense gives any real support to ethical naturalism in the wide sense of the term.

What such a move does accomplish is to produce needless confusion. It is important to remember that the same words can be used to formulate either an analytic or a synthetic proposition. An example would be "To have intrinsic goodness is to be pleasant." This sentence might express either an ethical insight into the goodness of pleasure or a linguistic insight into the meaning of "goodness" and "pleasant." Even if one should accept hedonism as a normative ethical theory, he would not be justified in concluding that "good" means "pleasant." The evidence which supports the former does not necessarily lend credence to the latter. To infer the truth of ethical naturalism in the narrow sense from considerations which really imply ethical naturalism in the wide sense is to commit the fallacy of irrelevant conclusion. Conversely, in rejecting the view that ethical words stand for empirical characteristics I am not necessarily repudiating the attempt to understand the nature of value and obligation naturalistically. In fact, I am inclined to accept ethical naturalism in the wide sense. Although they are not unrelated, let us not confuse linguistic questions with ethical issues. Until linguistic questions can be answered more conclusively, one does little to resolve ethical issues by defining ethical words in terms of empirical characteristics.

5. *The Claims of Empiricism*

There are some who adopt ethical naturalism, not as a convenient support for their ethical theory, but as a necessary consequence of their epistemological theory. It can, and has, been argued that the truth of empiricism logically implies that all ethical words refer to empirical characteristics. There are two ways in which this argument can be developed. One begins with the empirical theory of meaning; the other begins with the theory that synthetic propositions can be known only empirically.

The first version of this argument is direct and powerful. Clearly not all ethical sentences are meaningless. But any meaningful sentence must refer to empirical characteristics. It obviously follows that, in every meaningful ethical sentence, the ethical words must stand for empirical characteristics.

It would be hard to question the logic of this argument for ethical naturalism, but the premises are not beyond all doubt. For one thing, is it really so clear that ethical sentences are not meaningless? One must, I think, grant that they are not mere gibberish or strings of nonsense syllables. There is, therefore, some sense in which ethical sentences are meaningful. It does not follow, however, that they are meaningful in the sense provided for by the empirical theory of meaning. The word "meaningful" is highly ambiguous. Ethical sentences could be empirically meaningless and still have emotive meaning or some other kind of nonempirical meaning. The mere fact that ethical sentences are not sheer nonsense does not guarantee, therefore, that they have empirical meaning.

Again, the empirical theory of meaning might itself be rejected. Traditionally empiricism has maintained that all words derive their meaning from experience. This view presupposes that a word is meaningful only when it stands for some concept and that concepts are copies of previous experiences. Presumably ethical words acquire their meaning in the same way as any others. This position received its classic statement in the philosophy of Locke; today his psychology seems dangerously speculative. In particular his assumption that all conception involves images has been challenged by empirical evidence of the existence of imageless thinking. The philosophical difficulties contained in the notion of images to correspond to our general concepts have been evident since Berkeley. Besides, it is at least doubtful whether speaking or writing must be accompanied by a series of mental pictures to be meaningful. My own introspection show no exact parallel between the use of language and the flow of images, and Wittgenstein has shown that such a parallel would explain little even if it did exist. That all concepts originate in experience is equally dubious. It can be plausibly claimed that our concepts of redness and hardness are abstracted from past experience. But what of our concept of implication? We do not literally see that the premises of a given argument imply the conclusion; logical relations are not given in the same sense that sensations and even feelings are. Nor is it obvious how implication can be analyzed into elements which are themselves given in experience. The concepts of negation and existence have been equally embarrassing for empiricism.

More recently the emphasis in empirical theories of meaning has shifted from the psychological origins of our ideas to the logical implications of our statements. Today it is widely held that a sentence can be cognitively meaningful only if it is logically possible to verify it by future experience. This would seem to require that the predicative words of the sentence should refer to empirical characteristics; for if a sentence does not predict what future experiences will be like, how could these experiences possibly confirm or disconfirm it? This question is intended to be rhetorical; it is assumed that the only cognitive use of synthetic sentences is to make predictions. I suggest that this assumption should not be accepted without some evidence, and contemporary epistemologists have seldom presented any reasons to support it. The difficulties of interpreting historical statements on this assumption have often been pointed out. It seems to me that explanatory hypotheses do not fit the predictive model any better. The detective is not so much concerned with predicting new facts as with fitting together the known clues into an intelligible pattern. Statements can be used to make sense of experience as well as to predict it. At least in its usual formulations the empirical theory of meaning does not have a broad enough concept of knowledge. It does not seem to me that one is forced to adopt ethical naturalism in order to explain how ethical sentences can be meaningful.

There is, however, another way in which an argument

for ethical naturalism can be built upon empiricism. While some ethical statements are doubtless analytic, most of them seem to be synthetic. Now empiricism denies that there is any synthetic a priori knowledge. Yet we sometimes do know these synthetic ethical statements to be true. These ethical truths must, therefore, be empirical propositions, and surely empirical propositions describe the characteristics of experience.

The problem of synthetic a priori knowledge has a long history, and it is just possible that not all the evidence is on the side of empiricism. In fact, ethical propositions may be the very exception that disproves the rule. Until we are sure that ethical knowledge is either empirical or analytic, we must not rule out the possibility of synthetic a priori knowledge. There seem to be other examples of knowledge which is neither empirical nor analytic as well. How do we know that taller-than is a transitive relation? How do we know that orange is more like red than it is like green? How do we know that every cube has twelve sides? I wish I knew. Although I cannot answer these questions, I am not convinced that empiricism can answer them adequately either.

But even if ethical judgments are empirical knowledge, it does not follow necessarily that they are descriptions of experience. To say a judgment is empirical is simply to say that it is based upon experience. The denial of synthetic a priori knowledge implies that all knowledge of synthetic propositions must be supported by empirical evidence. If evidence must support a conclusion either deductively or inductively, then empirical statements would indeed have to make some assertion about the characteristics of experience. But perhaps this is too restricted a conception of evidence; there may well be kinds of reasoning which are neither deductive nor inductive. Toulmin and Nowell-

Smith, among others, have suggested that ethics has its own pattern of reasoning. If this is so, and I think that it is, then ethical sentences can be grounded in experience without being descriptions of experience. At least this possibility cannot be ignored. Until the empiricist works out his theory of evidence more fully, I am not prepared to say that the only way to explain our ethical knowledge is to adopt ethical naturalism.

It does not seem to me, therefore, that one is forced to be an ethical naturalist by such epistemological considerations. In neither of its basic forms is the empiricist's argument convincing. The empirical theory of meaning and the denial of synthetic a priori knowledge can both be questioned. What is more, neither of them, even if correct, requires that one accept ethical naturalism.

6. *Identifying Ethical Characteristics*

So far I have been explaining why one need not be an ethical naturalist. Now let me explain why one should not be one. Ethical naturalism claims that ethical words stand for one or more empirical characteristics. But which ones? As I consider my own experience I do not find any characteristic which could plausibly be identified with goodness or oughtness. It is impossible for me to argue the point in all its generality. I have neither the time nor the ability to consider all of the qualities and relations of experience one by one and to explain why each cannot be the one to which ethical words refer. Perhaps it will be enough to suggest the difficulties which I find in a few of the more likely candidates.

Pleasantness has often been claimed to be the quality which the word "good" names. There does seem to be an identifiable quality of pleasantness common to the experience of eating, drinking, relaxing on the beach, and sexual intercourse; but surely not all experiences of intrinsic value are such physical enjoyments. To avoid the suggestion that human life holds nothing better than animal satisfactions Mill introduced the distinction between higher and lower pleasures. But I am not at all sure that I can identify any single quality common to these two classes of goods; the word "pleasant" seems to lose its connotation when its denotation is extended too far. Lewis seems to have recognized the force of this phenomenological objection, for he prefers to speak of goodness as a dimension of experience or as a mode of presentation. This suggests that the word "good" is more analogous to "colored" than to "red." If this is so, there should be a range of qualities which fall along the dimension of goodness. Yet I am not able to identify such a range of qualities in my own experience.

Although such phenomenological considerations have convinced me that goodness is not a quality or set of qualities of experience, I must admit that they are far from conclusive. In particular, must goodness be a clearly identifiable quality? We tend to take qualities such as redness and hardness, which are readily distinguished and located, as typical of experience; actually the greater number of empirical characteristics are far more indistinct and elusive than these. I have, perhaps, been unfair in demanding that goodness should be clearly identifiable. On the other hand, if the ethical naturalist cannot point to some distinct quality, we can hardly be very confident that he is correct either.

There are forms of ethical naturalism which make a virtue of the fact that there is no clearly identifiable quality of goodness. For them goodness is not a quality but a relation. We imagine that it is a quality only because our attention is focussed on the object to such an extent that we overlook the relations peripherally contained in our experience. Some claim, for example, that the word "good" stands for the relational characteristic of being the object of interest. As long as one considers the speaker's state of mind at the moment he is speaking this view seems very plausible, for no one would call anything good unless he had some positive interest in it. The plausibility becomes less, however, when one considers the value judgments of another person. The mere fact that Mister Smith takes an interest in something does not confer value upon it. It is not merely that his interest does not give the object value for me; the object may not be good for him either. One may be mistaken in, not merely about, one's interests. Although this is most easily recognized in the case of others, reflection on one's own past evaluations drives home the same point. Nor is one interest criticizable only in terms of other interests; the nature of the object has a direct bearing upon the appropriateness of an interest.

Attempts to identify an empirical characteristic of oughtness seem to me to be even less successful. To say that someone is obliged to do something can hardly mean only that he feels obliged to do it. We condemn the morally insensitive person for failing to feel his obligations, and we condemn the moral fanatic who feels obligations where none exist. Although such condemnation may be misplaced, it is hardly self-contradictory. Felt requiredness has at times been put forward as another alternative, but it is not clear that this is a distinct interpretation. The feeling of being required can probably be analyzed in terms of one's feelings of obligation or one's awareness of his interests.

Another version of ethical naturalism analyzes obligation in terms of the mores of one's society. To speak about what someone ought or ought not to do is to speak about what is commanded or forbidden in his society. Since these social prescriptions and prohibitions can be studied empirically, obligation turns out to be an empirical characteristic. But to accept this view is to make all recommendations for social reform self-contradictory. Surely it is not meaningless to suggest that people ought not to follow the dictates of their society.

Among the currently popular varieties of ethical naturalism I can find none which satisfies me. No one has yet indicated to me that empirical characteristic for which ethical words stand. It is possible, of course, that tomorrow some ethical naturalist will point out a characteristic of experience which I will recognize as the subject matter of ethics. Considering the amount of energy which has already been expended on the attempt, however, I venture to predict that it will not be tomorrow morning. Although the line of reasoning I have been suggesting is by no means a conclusive refutation of ethical naturalism, it does seem to me to have some weight.

7. Teaching Ethical Words

Fortunately there is a second line of reasoning, suggested by Wittgenstein's approach, which seems to me to be considerably stronger. We do not teach the meaning of ethical words in at all the same way that we teach the meaning of those words which stand for empirical characteristics. This difference in the ways in which the words are taught would seem to imply that the two groups of words have different kinds of meaning.

We teach the basic words of the language in which we describe the experienced world by ostensive definition. We teach the child to use the word "red," for example, by repeating it when his attention is directed at something red. When he utters the word himself, we pick up or point to the nearest red object; where possible we point to several red things which differ in other respects. We also correct the child when he misapplies the word to things which are not red. In this way we gradually get the child to associate the word "red" with his sensations of redness. Words such as "sweet," "loud," "hot," and even "mama" and "dog" are taught in the same way.

The procedure by which we teach the child to use words which refer to subjective features of his experience, such as pain, is similar in principle although more difficult in practice. We use the word "hurts" when the child appears to be in pain, and we could even stick pins into him to help him get the point. We correct him when he says "it hurts" to have his face washed, but we agree that it hurts to fall down hard on the sidewalk. The only real differences between teaching the child those words which refer to experienced characteristics of external objects and those words which refer to characteristics of his inner experiences are that in the latter case it is harder to know when the child is having the experience and more difficult to direct his attention to it.

However, not all the words which stand for empirical characteristics are taught by ostensive definition. It would, for example, be difficult to teach the word "mermaid" in this manner. In such cases we use verbal definitions. We explain that "mermaid" means "a creature with the top half of a woman and the bottom half of a fish" or that "antiquated" means "as old as Uncle Louis."

As far as I can see there are only these two ways of associating a word with the characteristic of experience to which it is intended to refer. Either we associate the word with the experience directly by ostensive definition, or we associate it indirectly through other words which are already associated with experience. The use of pictures does not really constitute a distinct alternative. Since the visual presentation must be interpreted as a representation of the object referred to, pictures are just another variety of language. Now do we teach ethical words in either of these two ways? I do not believe so. Consider how we do teach words such as "good" or "wrong" to a child and I think that you will agree.

The word "wrong" brings this out most clearly. When the child does something which we think that he ought not to do, we tell him that it is wrong. (Notice that the occasion for teaching the word is not when the child is attending to something, as is the case in ostensive definition, but when he is doing something.) We tell the child that it is wrong to pull the cat's tail. We may explain that it hurts the cat. We probably frown and scold the child. Often we forcibly keep the child from continuing the action. We may even punish him.

All this might suggest that the word "wrong" simply refers to the fact of being forbidden, but this is not the case. To be sure, the words "wrong" and "forbidden" may sometimes be used synonymously. In such cases, however, one of the words is being used in a nontypical sense. This is shown by the fact that a child could learn the descriptive meaning of "forbidden" by watching others being told not to do things, but he can learn what "wrong" means only by being told to stop what he is himself doing. One teaches the meaning of "wrong" *in* the process of forbidding a child to do something; one teaches the meaning of "forbidden" by pointing *to* the process of forbidding.

The word "right" is taught as a negation of the word "wrong." When we see the child begin to do something and then hesitate with a look in our direction, we tell him that it is "all right" to go ahead. In this way we tell him that there is nothing wrong in what he is tempted to do. We will probably accompany the word "right" with smiles and may even help him to pat the kitty. Later on we may use the word as part of our efforts to encourage some pattern of behavior in the child.

It is not quite so clear that we teach the words "good" and "bad" without the use of ostensive definition, but I think that this is the case. One use of these words is to praise or blame the child and to encourge or discourage him in his activities. We teach these words much as we teach the words "right" and "wrong." The main difference seems to be that we apply the words "right" and "wrong" primarily to actions, while the words "good" and "bad" are applied primarily to the child and only secondarily to his actions. The word "good" is first taught as an emphasis of or substitute for smiles and rewards; the word "bad" is taught as a verbal extension of frowning and punishing. One teaches these words by using them in praising or blaming the child.

There is a related use of the words which we teach, not by calling the child "good" or "bad," but by applying these words to things which he likes or dislikes. When we feel that he is obviously enjoying his food, we say "good" as we give him another helping. When he spits out something in disgust, we admit that it might be "bad" food. We are more ardent in the former kind of linguistic education than in the latter simply because we wish to encourage the child to eat and hope to divert his attention away from the pastime of spitting. It might seem that in this sense, at least, value words are descriptive adjectives, for we seem to be classifying foods into the good and bad kinds. Reflection upon what we actually do, however, will dispel this illusion. Originally we do not apply the word "good" to foods which we think are actually good, but to those which the child enjoys. I am confident that bleu cheese is better than pablum. Yet I do not try to teach the word "good" to my child by attracting his attention to the goodness of bleu cheese. Rather I repeat the word "good" enthusiastically as he gobbles up the almost tasteless cereal which he seems to enjoy so much. In this way we teach the child to express his likes and dislikes towards things by the use of the words "good" and "bad." Later on we may express our own likes and dislikes with these words in the hope that the child will come to feel as we do, but this use of the words seems to presuppose that the child has already learned their meaning.

This somewhat sketchy survey of the way in which we teach the meaning of typical ethical words reveals that they are not taught by ostensive definition. First, the occasion upon which we teach these words is quite different from that in which we employ ostensive definition. The most opportune time to teach a word by ostensive definition is when the child's attention is fixed upon something. Then we repeat the appropriate word to give the child a label for the thing or its obvious characteristic. But we do not wait for this kind of opportunity to teach ethical words. Rather we teach the words when the child is doing something, hesitating to do something, or apparently liking or disliking something. Second, the activities of teaching the words are quite different. In ostensive definition we try to focus the child's attention upon some object or feature of experience while we repeat the word. We try to indicate other examples of the same kind of thing, something we seldom do in teaching ethical words. Correcting the child when he mislabels something is central to teaching words ostensively, but it is only incidental to teaching ethical words. Rather than pointing, producing examples, and correcting verbal mistakes, we forbid, encourage, praise, blame, and help the child to express his likes and dislikes when we teach ethical words.

Even if ethical words are not taught by ostensive definition, they might still refer to empirical characteristics. In this case they would be taught verbally by defining the words in terms of other words which had been ostensively defined. Although we probably do explain the meaning of some ethical words by verbal definition, those definitions make use of more basic ethical words already learned by the child. That we teach the basic vocabulary of ethics in this manner seems unlikely when one asks himself exactly what nonethical words he would use to explain to the child the meaning of "wrong" and "good." Those naturalistic definitions which have been suggested as analyses of the real meaning of our ethical words seem less plausible when one imagines himself using them to teach a child these words. In point of fact, we do not first explain the meaning of "wrong" and "good" and then use them in forbidding or approving the child; rather the child learns their meaning originally from the way in which we use them in concrete situations in which the child is involved.

Someone might object to drawing any conclusions about what ethical words mean to an adult from the way in which we teach them to a child, for a young child does not have the power of abstraction to enable him to grasp ethical concepts in their full meaning. To a child these ethical words may have only the rudimentary meaning I have suggested, but for the adult they have an additional descriptive content.

All right, then, let us consider an adult. Suppose one had to teach the meaning of our basic ethical vocabulary to an adult foreigner whose language one did not speak and whose knowledge of English was incomplete. How would one do it? In particular, is there any method one could employ which he could not use with very young children? The obvious way is to use definition by verbal example.

That is, we might explain that "wrong" meant acts like stealing, telling falsehoods, killing, hurting animals, and so on. It might be claimed that an adult could abstract from these examples a common feature of wrongness, while a young child might be unable to recognize what these examples had in common. One could go on to maintain that until the child has learned to reflect upon examples of wrong action and see what they have in common, he has not learned the full meaning of the word. Thus there is more to teaching and learning ethical words than my previous remarks would suggest.

Is this objection compelling? Well, it certainly is plausible. It seems as though one could teach ethical words by describing examples much in the same way one might define "skyscraper" or "skilled craftsman." And it would be hard to deny that the learner, such as someone speaking a foreign language, is learning by noticing what the examples have in common. Moreover, the fact that we do not normally use this method of teaching ethical words to young children could be explained by the fact, acknowledged by most psychologists, that the young child has very limited powers of abstraction.

Plausible as the objection is, I think that it fails to make its point. First, its explanation of the way in which an adult could learn ethical words is mistaken. He could not learn the meaning of the word "wrong" by noticing what the various examples of wrong actions have in common, for they have nothing in common. I base this claim on my own reflections upon these examples. If I, who already understand the word "wrong," can see nothing in common, it is unlikely that one unfamiliar with the word would perceive any similarity. That this technique works on the adult who speaks a foreign language is simply because these examples suggest to him the ethical words he already knows in his own language. But suppose that one had to teach our ethical vocabulary to an adult who did not know any other language and whose knowledge of English was complete except that, because of very peculiar upbringing, he had never learned a single ethical word. Assuming that he possessed no unverbalized ethical concepts, it would be impossible to teach him the meaning of the word "wrong" by describing examples of wrong action.

Second, the objection asserts that ethical words mean one thing to the small child and another to an adult. Why, then, do we use the same words? One can reply that this is because the new adult meaning is simply added to the previous meaning, which is retained. But, according to ethical naturalism, it is this additional meaning which is central to ethical language. Granted that there is some continuity between early and later uses of these words by the child growing into adulthood, if the *primary* meaning of ethical words is unintelligible to the child, why do we bother to teach these words to children? There are, after all, other ways of forbidding, rewarding, discouraging, and so forth.

Third, if ethical words mean more to the adult than to the child one could not teach the adult the full meaning of ethical words in the same way that one teaches these same words to the child. I will admit for the sake of argument that there are ways one can teach ethical words to an adult that one cannot use in teaching these words to children. But it seems to me that one could *also* teach them to adults in the very same ways one teaches them to children. Nor do I see that anything essential would be left out by this procedure.

I conclude, therefore, that the way in which we teach the meaning of ethical words is radically different from the way we teach the meaning of words that refer to empirical characteristics. This must be more than a remarkable coincidence revealing only two classes of descriptive words. The obvious implication is that ethical words do not stand for empirical characteristics and that their ethical naturalism must be rejected.

8. *The Naturalistic Fallacy*

Probably the objection which has most frequently been made to ethical naturalism is that it commits the naturalistic fallacy. If there is some fundamental mistake implicit in this position, this would constitute a third reason for rejecting it. But exactly what is this naturalistic fallacy? One would expect that he could find out by examining *Principia Ethica* where this charge against ethical naturalism was christened and elaborated. Unfortunately it is not at all clear which of the many errors with which Moore charges the naturalists is intended to be *the* naturalistic fallacy.

The name chosen to designate this terrible mistake would suggest that (1) it is a logical error. Surely the naturalistic fallacy, like its cousins the fallacy of undistributed middle or the *argumentum ad verecundiam*, must lie in some violation of the canons of deductive or inductive logic. Moore does claim that the arguments which the naturalists use to support their position are invalid.[2] One of his interpretations of Mill's proof of hedonism brings this out well:

That which is desirable (worthy of being desired) is good.
Pleasure is desirable (capable of being desired).
Therefore, pleasure is good.

The words in parentheses are, of course, Moore's additions intended to bring out the fallaciousness of the argument. If this is a typical example, it turns out that the naturalistic

[2] G. E. Moore, *Principia Ethica* (Cambridge, 1903), p. 19.

fallacy is one species of the fallacy of four terms in which some key word is used in both an ethical and a nonethical sense. The plausibility of the argument results from failing to distinguish these two senses.

Other passages suggest that (2) the naturalistic fallacy consists in defining the indefinable. Moore might be willing to admit that some ethical words could be defined in terms of other ethical words; but the fundamental ethical word, which he thought was "good," stands for a simple quality. Since all genuine definition requires the analysis of some complex into its constituents, it would follow that the word "good" could not be defined (p. 7). Therefore the attempt of ethical naturalism to define all ethical words in terms of empirical characteristics makes the mistake of trying to define something which is by nature indefinable.

Another interpretation is that (3) the fallacy really lies in the identification of two distinct characteristics or the confusion of two words with different meanings. Moore repeatedly states that the naturalists confuse goodness with the other characteristics which accompany it (p. 10). On this interpretation the naturalist fallacy is one form of what Frankena has called the definist fallacy.

Again, it might appear that (4) the mistake involves reducing the a priori to the empirical. The real error is not so much in defining ethical words as in defining them in terms of experience. This may be what Moore means when he objects to reducing ethics to one of the natural sciences (p. 11). Certainly the intuitionists object to any attempt to analyze ethical statements in such a way that they become part of empirical knowledge.

At other times one gets the impression that (5) the naturalistic fallacy consists in reducing the synthetic to the analytic. Moore insists that it is a mistake to treat the basic principles of ethics as analytic propositions (p. 7). The force of this objection is derived from his concept of analytic propositions. Analytic statements are merely verbal truths which make no assertion about reality. They are empty tautologies or, in the delightful terminology of Locke, trifling propositions. If the ethical naturalist defends his position on the grounds that it is analytic, therefore, he reduces the import of his position to mere conceptual analysis.

The most obvious interpretation is that (6) the naturalistic fallacy is the confusion of the nonnatural with the natural. Moore contends that the characteristics for which ethical words stand are fundamentally different from any natural characteristics (p. 13). The error of ethical naturalism is looking within nature for the ethical facts which actually belong to quite another realm of being.

The last hint which I can find in *Principia Ethica* is that (7) the mistake of naturalism lies in the reduction of the ethical to the nonethical. Ethical judgments properly belong to practical philosophy; any attempt to define the vocabulary of ethics in terms of experience will inevitably remove their practical significance. Moore suggests that ethical naturalism destroys ethics because it interprets ethical propositions in such a way that they cease to have any relevance for action (p. 12). Perhaps this is really the naturalistic fallacy. Yet, each of the other possibilities could be supported with numerous passages.

Whether or not the ethical naturalist makes each of these seven mistakes could, and should, be questioned. But for the moment let us not be tempted away from our purpose of uncovering the correct interpretation of the naturalistic fallacy. It is clear that Moore believes that ethical naturalism makes all of the alleged mistakes which I have mentioned. It is not so clear which one of them he intends to refer to as the naturalistic fallacy. The fact that he uses this label to stand for each of them in turn suggests that he is far from clear in his own mind about precisely where the fallacy lies. Which of these mistakes did he consider central?

Probably Moore thought that the crux of the naturalistic fallacy was the mistake of defining the indefinable. This is indicated both by the relative amount of space he gives to this in the important first chapter of *Principia Ethica* and by his own summary of that chapter. And in a certain sense this is the central error. For if Moore is right in contending that goodness is a simple and unanalyzable characteristic, it follows logically that ethical naturalism also makes most of the other errors which he mentions. If "good" is indefinable, any argument based on a definition of goodness must be unsound. The plausibility of any suggested definition must lie in confusing the simple quality of goodness with some other characteristic. No propositions about goodness could be analytic in the sense of those in which the predicate concept is part of the subject concept. Thus these four errors all hinge on the failure to see that goodness is a simple quality. The other three mistakes result from the failure to realize that this simple quality is nonnatural, nonempirical, and the only basic ethical characteristic. Given Moore's concept of the nature of goodness, then, it is easy to see why he laid such stress upon the indefinability of the word "good."

Still, I venture to suggest that he did intuitionism a disservice here. It does not seem to me that what the intuitionists in general, and Moore in particular, really object to in ethical naturalism is that it defines a simple quality. For one thing, they agree that the word "good" does not refer to the quality of pleasantness. Yet, if pleasantness is a simple quality, the hedonist need not hold that goodness is complex. For another thing, the naturalistic fallacy is supposed to have some peculiar relevance to ethics, but the mistake of defining the indefinable could be made in any area. The only interpretation which would explain the special importance of the fallacy for ethics is that it is the mistake of reducing the ethical to the nonethical.

This interpretation seems to be conclusively supported by the way in which the term has been used. Although there are many conflicting explanations of the nature of the naturalistic fallacy, there seems to be pretty general agreement on the application of the term. All intuitionists would agree that the attempts to identify goodness with pleasure is an instance of the fallacy, although there does not seem to be any analysis involved here. They would agree that the definition of "right" in terms of God's will is an example, although this is not a naturalistic analysis. Whatever they may have thought that they were doing, the intuitionists, including Moore, have in fact applied the "naturalist" label to all those who seem to deny the characteristically ethical nature of moral judgment and to no others. None of the other interpretations fits all and only those cases where the charge is actually leveled. Those other mistakes may accompany and compound the reduction of the ethical to the nonethical, but they are not the heart of the matter. What Moore was trying to say is that the fallacy implicit in ethical naturalism is that it destroys the ethical import of ethical sentences.

It is easy to make such a charge; it is not so easy to substantiate it. How can one show that ethical naturalism really does make the mistake of reducing ethical sentences to nonethical ones? This is supposed to be established by the open-question argument. One can always ask of anything which satisfies the definiens of any proposed definition of the word "good" whether it is in fact good. Presumably there would be a corresponding open question for each of the other ethical words, but let us concentrate upon this one. I would agree with Moore that we can always raise such a question about anything which the naturalist might define as good. My evidence for the claim that this question remains open no matter what empirical definition of goodness is proposed is simply that I have been unable to think of any definition which would close the question. Until I discover such a definition, the question remains open for me.

Suppose that the question does remain open. What does Moore think that this proves? As an example let us take the definition of "good" as "pleasant." We find that the question "But is pleasure good?" is still open. The question remains open in that the sentence "But is pleasure good?" remains significant in two senses: it is not a string of meaningless symbols, and it is not a pointless query. The fact that the question has any significance at all proves that the word "good" cannot be entirely meaningless. The fact that the question does not become trivial in the face of a proposed definition proves that the definition is mistaken. For if the definition of "good" as pleasant were correct, the question would amount to the pointless query whether pleasure is pleasant. The fact that the question remains open no matter what naturalistic definition is substituted for our example shows that all forms of ethical naturalism are mistaken. Moore's conclusion from all this is that goodness must be a simple quality.

By this time the reader will not be surprised that I am unwilling to accept this at its face value. For one thing, Moore's argument rests on the assumption that every meaningful word stands for some property. He argues that since "good" is meaningful it must stand for some property. Since all definitions of "good" are incorrect, it cannot stand for a complex property. Therefore, it must stand for a simple property. I am not willing to concede this theory of meaning. I doubt very much if every meaningful word, or even every meaningful adjective, stands for a property.

More important, on Moore's own interpretation the open-question argument loses most of its force. Moore uses the open question as a test for the correctness of some proposed definition. If the definition were correct, he contends, the question would cease to be open. The question would become pointless because, presumably, the answer would be so obvious that no one would bother to ask it. But are the correct analyses of our concepts always so obvious that no one bothers to question them? Indeed a fair share of philosophical controversy seems to center about the correctness of certain proposed analyses of important words. The fact that one can question a proposed definition does little to prove it incorrect; for the synonymy of definiendum and definiens may be, as Brandt puts it, covert. Once more Moore has missed the real point of what he is trying to say.

It is important to be clear about what the open question is and the sense in which it remains open. It seems as though the question is over the correctness of a proposed definition, but actually the question is not of this kind at all. When one asks "But is it good?" he is asking "But is it worth desiring?" (Strictly speaking, he could be asking any of a number of questions: "But is it worth desiring?" "But is it worth admiring?" "But is it worth approving?" "But is it worth liking?" and so on. I chose, of course, the one which brings out my point most clearly.) The problem posed in the open question is the problem of what attitude one is to take towards the object. One can always stipulate that something is to be labeled "desirable," but the question remains open of whether it is reasonable to desire it. Value judgments are concerned with the objects of desire and the goals of action. The question which any proposed definition of "good" poses is not "Is it verbally correct to call it good?" but rather "Does it deserve to be pursued?" The problem is simply the problem of choosing one's goals in life. It is primarily the question of choice that remains open no matter what definition is offered.

But in what sense does this question remain open? We are certainly able to make decisions on the basis of the available information; our knowledge of the alternatives is often sufficient to enable us to choose rationally. Suppose one included all the empirical information relevant to the choice of an object in a definition of "good." It might seem that it would then be pointless to ask of anything which satisfied the definiens "But is it good?" Yet this is not so. One's knowledge that the object possessed the characteristics mentioned in the definiens would enable him to answer the question, but no knowledge of such good-making characteristics removes the point of the question entirely.

The reason is that the selection of a goal of action involves more than an awareness of its properties; it includes a decision of the self to undertake action intended to produce the goal. Knowing what an object is like and choosing it as a goal remain distinct. No amount of knowledge of the nature of the chosen is the same as the choice itself; knowledge about the character of the alternatives remains distinct from commitment to one or another of them. The autonomy of ethics lies in this difference between a realization of the nature of an object and the choice of it as a goal of action. This difference is the basis of the distinctness of the question "What is it like?" from "Shall I choose it?" The answer to the first question may supply all the data necessary for an answer to the second; but no answer to the first could constitute an answer to the second. It is in this sense that the latter remains open. No amount of knowledge about the alternatives destroys the significance of the choice between them.

This point is worth belaboring because it is fundamental to our understanding of moral judgment. Ethics is concerned with criticizing conduct and setting goals. That this is basically different from our knowledge of the nature of such action and goals is the crux of the claim that ethics is autonomous and irreducible. In effect, this claim amounts to distinguishing between the theoretical and practical aspects of human life. As knowers we recognize the character of reality; as agents we choose between possible realities. In the one case reality is a datum to be mirrored in our knowledge and acknowledged as a standard of the acceptability of our thought; in the other it is an open possibility to be molded as we will and to take on a character determined by our thought. This distinction between the theoretical and the practical, the knower and the agent, is fundamental to our understanding of ethical language.

At last we are prepared to return to our consideration of ethical naturalism. This view stands charged with committing a very serious mistake, the naturalistic fallacy. The essence of this error consists in reducing the ethical to the nonethical. I believe that this charge is justified. Ethical naturalism holds that ethical words stand for empirical characteristics. If this is so, ethical sentences turn out to be simply one more form of empirical description. The statement that x is good, for example, asserts that x has a certain empirical characteristic; it describes the nature of the object x. Fine. Any inquisitive mind will be delighted to have this information about the nature of the object. But this knowledge of the nature of the object leaves open the question of whether the object is to be chosen. It is this practical problem of whether to choose the object which is the primary ethical problem. It appears that on the naturalistic interpretation of ethical sentences *no* ethical statement ever constitutes an answer to this central ethical question. To my mind this is an intolerable position and should be rejected.

I do not mean to imply that the problem of choice is the only genuinely ethical problem. Ethics also includes, among others, the problems of criticizing choices, adopting pro or con attitudes, classifying values and obligations, justifying judgments of value and obligation, and determining the conditions of responsibility. All of these problems, however, are broadly practical; they all bear directly or indirectly upon decision. Thus, if it is not the only problem in ethics, the problem of choice remains the central one about which all other ethical problems cluster. And together these practical problems go far beyond the theoretical problem of knowing what the world is like. It is not that factual knowledge is irrelevant to the problems of ethics, but that knowing is only a preliminary to solving many of these problems.

The mistake of ethical naturalism, therefore, does not lie in including empirical descriptions in the language of ethics. Such descriptions are essential to any responsible ethical inquiry. Its mistake lies rather in reducing ethical language to description. One cannot say that the only, or only important, kind of meaning which ethical sentences have is empirical description. To do this is to imply that the only serious ethical problem is to learn the truth about reality. Although the practical man will wish to know what the world is like, there is much more to practice than recognizing the nature of things. Just as the problems of practice go far beyond theory, so the language of ethics includes far more than description.

9. Recapitulation

In my opinion, then, ethical naturalism is an untenable position. It is no real help in establishing a naturalistic interpretation of value and obligation. It is not required by general epistemological considerations. It cannot point out any empirical characteristics which can plausibly be identified with the meanings of ethical words. It conflicts with the ways in which we actually teach the meaning of ethical words. And it destroys most of the ethical import of ethical sentences. For all these reasons I find ethical naturalism unacceptable.

10. *Recent Salvage Attempts*

Before leaving the subject, however, it is only fair to consider two attempts to modify ethical naturalism to meet recent criticism. The crux of the position is that ethical words stand for empirical characteristics. It is usually assumed that each word stands for a single characteristic. Edwards has suggested that actually ethical words stand indefinitely for several different characteristics.[3] Thus ethical sentences turn out to be vague descriptions. To say that I will arrive about four o'clock is to say that I will arrive at three fifty-five or at three fifty-six or at four one or four two, and so on. Similarly, to say that a steak is good is to say that it is tender and juicy or tender and flavorful or flavorful and nutritious, and so on. It is this vague and flexible meaning which allows the open question to remain open. Whichever set of characteristics one includes in his definition, there is always a question whether he has included too much or too little.

If my interpretation of the open-question argument is accepted, this attempt to meet it misses the point. The question is not about the correctness of the definition but about the choice of the object. No matter how various and indefinite the information supplied by a sentence, the

[3] P. Edwards, *The Logic of Moral Discourse* (Glencoe: The Free Press, 1955), ch. VII.

sentence still answers the question "What is it like?" Truly ethical sentences must answer some variation of the question "But is it good?" I think that reflection would show also that we do not teach ethical words in the same way that we teach the use of indefinite descriptive phrases. It does not seem to me that this modification of ethical naturalism meets the basic objections which can be made against it.

Another modification of ethical naturalism arises from the criticism of various versions of noncognitivism in ethics. Ethical naturalism holds that ethical words stand for empirical characteristics. This need not imply that ethical words have no other function, but only that any other functions are secondary. Rice has recently suggested that the naturalist should give more attention to these non-referential uses of ethical words. He interprets ethical sentences as having both empirical descriptive meaning and emotive matrix meaning.[4]

This view might placate some emotivists, but it does little to answer my objections. What are these empirical characteristics contained in the descriptive meaning of ethical words? Do we teach ethical words in such a way as to give them descriptive meaning? Why should information remove the open question when expressed in emotive language? Perhaps the key problem in any attempt to combine the merits of ethical naturalism with the emotive theory of ethics is the exact relation between the descriptive and the matrix meaning. Rice has not made it clear how they are related or how this particular combination avoids the objections which can be made to each of the parent theories.

I do not believe, therefore, that ethical naturalism can

[4] P. B. Rice, *On the Knowledge of Good and Evil* (New York: Random, 1955), chs. VI, VII.

be saved. The real trouble with ethical naturalism is not that it underestimates the ambiguity or emotiveness of ethical language, but that it misunderstands the functions ethical sentences perform. This is probably because it has failed to perceive the basic nature of ethical problems. Let us see if ethical intuitionism has done any better.

— III —

Ethical Intuitionism

Traditionally ethical intuitionism has maintained that we have a direct insight into the rightness or wrongness of certain actions without any consideration of the value or disvalue of their consequences. This position combines an epistemological view about the way in which we know what we ought to do with an ethical view about the nature of obligation. Epistemologically it holds that we have an immediate rational awareness of our duties; ethically it holds that the rightness or wrongness of an action is independent of the value or disvalue of its consequences. That these two theses are distinct does not seem to have been realized.

Sidgwick and Moore both wished to make it plain that they were not ethical intuitionists in this traditional sense. They agreed in rejecting the deontological theory of obligation in favor of a teleological one. It was their opinion that the value produced by an action does determine its rightness or wrongness. Since we must consider the consequences of what we do, we do not have any direct insight into our obligations. At the same time Sidgwick and Moore conceded that ultimately our knowledge of ethics does rest upon intuition. In effect this shift in ethical point of view modified the traditional ethical intuitionism in two ways; it separated the epistemological thesis from the theory of obligation and it generalized the epistemological thesis to include value judgments as well as judgments of obligation. In this way there arose a new and broader concept of intuitionism. Ethical intuitionism in this new and broader sense is the theory that ultimately our knowledge of ethical sentences is grounded in intuition. It is this broader theory that I wish to discuss here.

1. *Principal Doctrines*

The definitive thesis of ethical intuitionism is, then, that our knowledge of ethical sentences rests upon intuition. What is this intuition that is so important in ethics? It can, perhaps, be best characterized as intellectual apprehension. Intuition is, in the first place, intellectual. This implies that it is cognitive rather than affective or volitional; moral judgment does not lie with our feelings, emotions, desires, or decisions. To be sure Scheler and Hartmann have advanced a theory in which our ethical intuition is emotional, but this seems to be a deviation from the main stream of intuitionist thought. The English-writing intuitionists are unanimous that to admit emotion into our ethical judgment would be to undermine its validity. That intuition is intellectual also implies that it is nonempirical. Our moral insight does not rest on our sensation of external objects or the introspection of our internal states. If there is one thing upon which all intuitionists agree, it is that experience alone cannot tell us whether any ethical sentence is true or false. Intuition is, in the second place, a mode of apprehension. In intuition the intellect is directly aware of some content; something is given or presented to the mind. Intuition is, to use the typical metaphor, seeing with the mind's eye. The mind's eye is, of course, very different from the body's eye. For one thing, it does not make use of any bodily organ, unless the brain be considered such. For another, the objects of which it is aware are presumably very different from the physical objects or sense-data apprehended through our sense organs. The similarity lies in the fact that in both cases one is directly conscious of something which is immediately revealed for inspection. Intuition is the faculty of the intellect which enables it to apprehend such nonsensuous givens.

While the central thesis of ethical intuitionism is that such nonsensuous apprehension is central to ethical knowledge, the outstanding representatives of this position also agree on several additional doctrines. The first of these is that ethics is autonomous. In some way the knowledge of ethical truths is fundamentally different from other kinds of knowledge such as physics, mathematics, or even theology. Intuitionism tries to explain this difference by its theory of the meaning of ethical sentences. Ethical sentences describe objects and acts in terms of their nonnatural characteristics. Whether these are properties such as goodness and rightness or relations such as fittingness, they are different in kind from the properties and relations which the natural scientist describes. The peculiarities of ethical language turn out to reside in the special subject matter of ethics. On this interpretation ethical words stand for nonnatural characteristics. The distinctive features of ethical sentences are supposedly guaranteed by the insistence that ethical words cannot be defined in terms of natural characteristics. It is at this point that the battle with ethical naturalism is joined.

The second doctrine associated with ethical intuitionism is that our ethical knowledge is constituted by or rests upon synthetic a priori propositions. Probably ethics contains some statements which are merely analytic. No doubt at times it uses empirical information in the application of its principles. But the really fundamental assertions upon which everything else hinges are known synthetic a priori. Thus, that stealing is or tends to be wrong is neither an empty tautology nor an empirical truth. A fortiori it is not an emotive utterance with no cognitive meaning at all.

Thirdly, the intuitionists unite to defend the objective validity of moral judgment. Ethical sentences have a truth value and can be known to be true or false. Our ethical statements are correct or incorrect just as much, although not on quite the same basis, as scientific or logical statements. Any ethical truth has a claim upon the belief of all rational persons. Thus whenever two people disagree over an ethical question, at least one of them must be mistaken.

2. Important Contributions

Such are the main tenets of ethical intuitionism. What are we to say of this position? It has, I believe, some real contributions to make to the epistemology of ethics. One of these is the realization that ethical sentences differ in important respects from the sentences of physics or mathematics. Ethical sentences have certain peculiarities which set them off from other kinds of language. The intuitionists do not seem to have realized, however, just how different ethical language is. They have tried to defend the autonomy of ethics by insisting that any reduction of ethical sentences to descriptions of nature commits the naturalistic fallacy. This suggests that the difference between ethical sentences and scientific sentences is simply one of subject matter, much like the difference between biological and psychological sentences. Actually the peculiarities of ethical language do not lie in the fact that it describes a realm beyond nature but in the fact that it does not describe at all. Although I cannot accept their analysis of ethical sentences, I must thank the intuitionists for posing sharply the question of the meaning of ethical sentences.

Others have taken up this question posed by the intuitionists and have interpreted ethical sentences in terms of emotive meaning. They have tried to save the practical nature of ethical language by emphasizing the ways in which it differs from the language of science. The intuitionist will accept no such theory, however, if it saves the practicality of ethical judgment by sacrificing its objective validity. This recognition that ethical sentences have a claim to acceptance by every rational being is, it seems to me, another contribution of intuitionism. There are standards independent of the judger by which the correctness of any ethical judgment is to be determined. To make a moral statement is to claim that it cannot be denied without error by any other person. Ethical intuitionism stands opposed to all forms of ethical relativism or skepticism.

Whether or not ethical sentences can make good their claim to objective validity depends upon whether or not there are good reasons for and against them. If there are considerations which rationally determine the correctness of an agent's choice, ethical judgments are objectively valid; if there are no relevant reasons in moral questions, relativity cannot be denied. To have seen that the objectivity of ethics depends upon the existence of a genuinely practical reason is one more important contribution of intuitionism. Intuitionists have agreed that "the ought" defies any subjective or empirical analysis and that the concept of obligation is an essentially rational one. The suggestion that the key to the objective validity of ethical sentences lies in the nature of ethical reasoning has been developed in quite another way by Toulmin and Baier, but the suggestion itself was originally made by the intuitionists.

The intuitionists give us some genuine insights into the nature of ethical language. Ethical sentences are different in kind from the sentences of mathematics or empirical science. Even ethical sentences make a claim to objective validity. This claim rests upon the possibility of supporting these sentences with reasons.

3. *An Alternative to Naturalism*

Their insight, however, has been somewhat less than twenty-twenty. First let me try to explain why I believe that the reasoning which leads people to adopt ethical intuitionism is weak. One line of reasoning in support of this position is a slight variation on Moore's use of the open-question argument. Since ethical words are not meaningless, they must refer to some characteristic or characteristics. Since no naturalistic definition of ethical words is correct, they cannot stand for any characteristics of experience. Therefore, ethical words must stand for one or more nonnatural characteristics.

The assumption that ethical words can be meaningful only if they refer to characteristics could be questioned.

I shall argue shortly that the theory of meaning underlying this argument is mistaken. But for the moment let us grant the first premise and examine the second one instead. Is it so certain that no naturalistic definition of ethical words is correct? How does the intuitionist know this? If he relies on his sense of synonymy, the naturalist can counter that *his* sense of synonymy tells him that some such definition is correct. If he resorts to arguments similar to the ones I employed in the last chapter, he is apt to find that they apply against his own theory as well. The intuitionist argues that since there are no empirical characteristics to which ethical words refer, there must be some nonnatural characteristics for these words to refer to. It seems to me that the existence of these nonnatural characteristics is at least as dubious as the nonexistence of any empirical ethical characteristics. What is gained by substituting one uncertainty for another? If one insists on saying that ethical words stand for characteristics, it seems more plausible to say that they stand for empirical characteristics. Even the intuitionist is forced to admit the ethical relevance of empirical characteristics as good-making and right-making properties. Occam's razor would require that we do not postulate another realm of characteristics unless there is some strong positive reason to do so. By itself, the fact that one cannot think of any empirical definition of ethical words would seem insufficient to justify any such excursion into speculative metaphysics.

There is another line of reasoning which is closely related to the first. We often know ethical sentences to be true. Since they cannot be established by empirical evidence alone, there must be some other way to establish ethical sentences. Therefore we know ethical sentences by intuition.

Instead of arguing from the meaningfulness of ethical

sentences to their special kind of meaning, this argument proceeds from their knowability to a special way of knowing them. Noncognitivists would question the assumption that we can know ethical sentences to be true. Since I am not a noncognitivist in this sense, I will pass over this assumption. Rather I will question the second premise. Is it the case that empirical evidence is irrelevant to ethical conclusions? Although one cannot deduce an ethical conclusion from empirical information, I believe that there are other kinds of reasoning than deduction. Moreover, the intuitionist himself asserts that one must know the empirical facts of the case before he can intuit its ethical characteristics. One wonders why this empirical investigation is necessary as a psychological preparation if the empirical information is logically irrelevant to the ethical judgment. Even granting that one cannot give an adequate empirical account of our ethical knowledge, this does not prove that the intuitionist's account is any better. That the intellect can have a direct awareness of ethical facts is at least as dubious as the relevance of empirical evidence.

In short, it does not seem to me that one can make a case for ethical intuitionism on the basis of the implausibility of ethical naturalism. (1) It is not enough to assert that ethical naturalism is implausible. One must show why no empirical definition of ethical words can be given or explain why empirical evidence is irrelevant to ethical sentences. Without some rational argument to back up his feeling of implausibility, the intuitionist has no case. (2) Even proving ethical naturalism inadequate would not be enough. Perhaps ethical intuitionism is equally inadequate. No purely negative argument will suffice. One must go on to show that intuitionism can actually explain those things which naturalism leaves unexplained. (3) The supposition that ethical intuitionism is the only logical alternative to ethical naturalism results from the fact that the two positions share certain assumptions. Both assume that to be meaningful a word must stand for some characteristic and that we do have knowledge of ethical sentences. Once these assumptions are questioned, it appears that there are other alternatives to naturalism, such as the emotive theory of ethics. It seems to me, therefore, that the considerations which are often taken to establish ethical intuitionism are far from conclusive. The rejection of ethical naturalism does not force one to adopt ethical intuitionism, nor is it clear that there would be any advantage in doing so.

4. *Misinterpretation of Ethical Knowledge*

In fact, and this is my second objection to the position, I doubt whether ethical intuitionism can explain the actual nature of our ethical knowledge. How do the intuitionists say that we obtain our ethical knowledge? There seem to be two distinct models used by them. Some say that intuition is much like perceiving a physical object. It is the direct awareness of some particular moral fact. The only difference is that the awareness is intellectual rather than sensory. Thus Moore seems to hold that we intuit the goodness or badness of individual objects and Prichard claims that we intuit the rightness or wrongness of particular actions. Others say that intuition is more like perceiving the truth of a mathematical principle. What we are directly aware of is, for example, the universal proposition that promises ought to be kept. While our knowledge of the ethical characteristics of particulars is derivative, the general principles from which it is derived are self-evident. The "philosophical intuitionism" which Sidgwick defends and the "dogmatic intuitionism" which he rejects are both examples of this attempt to explain our particular ethical insights as deductions from universal principles. The main difference is that Sidgwick's "axioms" (note the mathematical term) are much more abstract than the relatively specific ethical rules taken to be self-evident by the "dogmatic" intuitionist. Although Ross leans heavily upon the model of mathematics, his conception of intuitive induction forces him to use both models at once. My contention is that neither model does justice to the facts of our moral cognition.

Let us take the first model first. The housewife sees the goodness of the lemon she selects with her mind's eye just as she sees its yellowness with her bodily eye. I do not think, however, that this view can explain the nature of ethical disagreement. If we are directly aware of the goodness of the lemon, one would expect that everyone would agree that in fact the lemon is good. It is very likely, however, that some would claim that it is bad instead. We don't disagree about whether lemons are yellow, for everyone can see that they are. If we see goodness with the same immediacy, why do we disagree about whether lemons are good?

Perhaps some of us do not see the goodness of the lemon. Often the intuitionist appeals to a kind of value blindness to explain ethical disagreement. But it should be questioned whether value blindness is really analogous to color blindness. For one thing, the value-blind person typically insists that the lemon is not really good, but the color-blind person seldom continues to argue that the lemon is not really yellow. Also, the person who just cannot see the value of lemons is quite able to see the goodness of classical music or even of mince pie. This is as though a person could not see that lemons are yellow but could perceive the yellowness of the sun without difficulty. This would be a most peculiar form of color blindness. It seems to me that the intuitionist who tries to explain ethical disagreement on the analogy of color blindness is on very precarious ground. We simply do not argue over the yellowness of lemons in the way that we argue over the goodness of things.

Nevertheless, we might well argue over whether a very pale orange is really yellow or orange in color. Where we do argue over sensory qualities is where one quality merges with another in such a way that it is hard to tell them apart. Such disagreements stem from a lack of color discrimination rather than a lack of color vision. This suggests a better analogy for the intuitionist to fall back upon. Ethical disagreements arise from the fact that one or both parties are unable to make the fine discriminations required to tell the various degrees of value or disvalue apart. Just as we do not argue over whether lemons are yellow, for they obviously are, so we do not argue over the goodness of obvious values. It is the borderline cases which occasion the genuine ethical disputes. While this way of interpreting our ethical disagreements seems stronger than appealing to a value blindness, it still seems to be inadequate. For one thing, disagreements over the exact shade of some color do not seem to be culturally dependent to the same degree that ethical disagreements are. No doubt different groups may classify colors in somewhat different ways. But since all normal human beings see colors in the same way, these differences are the exception rather than the rule. Moreover, in many cases a little explanation of the different color concepts will show that there is no real disagreement. But any discussion of the differing ethical concepts employed seems to underline rather than remove the disagreement in ethics. More important, it does not seem plausible to contend that cross-cultural ethical disagreements are limited to borderline cases. A missionary and an African native might disagree over whether human sacrifice was good or bad. Is it plausible to claim that their disagreement is caused by the fact that this practice has such slight value or disvalue that discrimination is difficult? I think not. Human sacrifice is either very good or extremely bad. Arguing over such a vast difference in value is hardly like arguing over a shade bordering on both orange and yellow. It does not seem to me that the intuitionist can explain our ethical disagreements as long as he uses sensory perception as his model.

Another difficulty with this first model is that so many people deny having any faculty of intuiting particular moral facts. Since one can hardly doubt the sincerity of these people, presumably they are not aware of intuiting the goodness of particular objects or the rightness of individual acts. But this throws grave doubt on whether they in fact possess this faculty. It would be peculiar if a person could see colors but was not aware of ever seeing colors or if someone with normal hearing honestly denied that he could ever hear anything.

This model will also have difficulty explaining why our direct awareness of moral facts does not seem immediate. One can look at a lemon and "just see" that it is yellow. It is not necessary to analyze the chemical constitution of the lemon's surface or to measure the frequency of the light emitted from it before one can be aware of the yellowness of the lemon. Although it probably does take some imperceptible length of time for the eye to focus, it seems as though one can see the color in a flash. One comes to see the value of something, on the other hand, only gradually as he thinks about it. Before one can know whether the lemon is a good one, he must make a preliminary investigation to determine whether it is ripe, firm, tangy-sweet, refreshing, and so on. One must collect the relevant information and balance one fact against another before he recognizes the goodness of the fruit. If one consults the actual process of making a moral judgment, it seems to be a far cry from judging the color of a given object.

The intuitionist has, I suppose, an answer for this. Seeing the value of something does require a preliminary investigation which is unnecessary in seeing the color of an object, but this simply reflects the fact that nonnatural characteristics differ in important respects from natural ones. In particular, ethical characteristics are resultant or consequential; that is, they depend for their existence upon the nonethical characteristics which the object or act possesses. Therefore, one cannot know whether the lemon is good until he has found out what good-making or bad-making properties it has. But why not? One can see the yellowness of the lemon without finding out about the physical structure of its surface, although the yellowness depends upon the nature of the surface. If we really were *directly* aware of goodness, it is not clear why we should not be able to intuit it without any preliminary investigation. The intuitionist can only say that what we are directly aware of is not simply the goodness of the lemon but the goodness as resulting from the good-making characteristics. What we really see is that certain natural characteristics possessed by the lemon imply its goodness. But to say this much is to abandon the first model for the second. This is not intuiting the particular lemon with its properties; this is intuiting the general principle that tangy-refreshingness implies goodness. The intuitionist is wise, I think, to give up the model of sensory perception.

Can the model of our perception of mathematical truths do any better? On this model we see that promises ought to be kept much as we see that equals plus equals are equal. Such general propositions are self-evident; they do not need to be supported with other evidence because to understand them is to be directly aware of their truth. Presumably we see the truth of these principles with our mind's eye; our direct awareness of the proposition reveals its truth to us. More specific ethical conclusions are derived from these universal insights much as the various theorems of Euclid are derived from his postulates and axioms.

The first thing that strikes one about this model is that there is one obvious difference between mathematical and ethical principles. A mathematical principle states the universally necessary relation of subject and predicate. An example would be that all plane triangles have interior angles equaling one straight angle. This relation of triangularity and interior-angles-equaling-one-straight-angleness is without exception. There is not and could not be any triangle without the latter property. An ethical principle does not seem to possess the same universal necessity. One cannot say that one ought always to keep his promises; sometimes circumstances arise which make it obligatory to break a promise. Thus the fact that one promised to do an act does not by itself imply that one ought to do it. The most one can say is that the fact that one promised tends to imply that one ought to do the act. One wonders how one can claim necessity for a principle which does not state a universal relation. I am not asserting that this difficulty cannot be explained away, but only saying that the intuitionist must explain how we can see tendencies to imply just as we see actual implications. At the very least this difference between mathematical and ethical truths suggests that the analogy between them may not be complete.

It is easy to see why the intuitionist is tempted to adopt

the model of mathematics. He wants a general principle from which he can deduce ethical conclusions about particular cases. Since one's ultimate premises cannot be proved, it appears that self-evidence is the only alternative to skepticism. But even if we grant the intuitionist his general principles, they will not do the job he wants them to do. Let us see how this works out in a typical practical syllogism:

Acts of promise-keeping are right.

This act is an act of promise-keeping.

Therefore, this act is right.

The intuitionist hopes to be able to establish his ethical conclusions by such logically impeccable reasoning. Unfortunately, as we have seen, the premise of this practical syllogism is false. It is not always right to keep one's promises. One can, if he wishes, counter that it always tends to be right to keep one's promises. But when this new premise is substituted in the original syllogism, the original conclusion no longer follows. All one can conclude is that this act tends to be right. This new conclusion poses two problems for the intuitionist. How can he explain clearly what it means to say that a single act tends to be right? How can he explain how one can determine what is actually right from a knowledge of what merely tends to be right? Therefore it seems to me that the intuitionist cannot explain our knowledge of value or obligation in particular instances by using the model of mathematical knowledge.

The intuitionist assumes that the knowledge of universal principles is logically prior to the knowledge of particular cases. One is directly aware of the truth of some ethical generalization, and then he applies this rule to the case at hand. Reflection on my own ethical thinking suggests that this puts the cart before the horse. I do not reach my conclusions about particular cases by deduction from universal premises but by considering the various features of this particular instance. Moreover, I do not recognize the truth of an ethical principle by peering directly at it with my mind's eye but by comparing it with my convictions about various actual or imagined instances to which it might apply. Often I even modify my general principles in the light of new cases. This is exactly the opposite of what one would expect on the mathematical analogy. I never give up the general principle that the interior angles of a plane triangle equal one straight angle on the grounds that this triangle I have just measured carefully seems to have 182 degrees.

Another difficulty in applying the model of mathematics to our ethical knowledge is that we sometimes feel that we have more reason to accept one ethical principle than another. In mathematics either a principle is necessarily true or it is necessarily false. One may, of course, not know whether a given principle is true or false, but one never has reason to think it merely probable. On the intuitionist's view this should be equally true of ethics. If I see the truth of an ethical principle, I can be sure that it is correct; if I do not see the truth of the principle, I have no reason at all to accept it. Since all evidence is irrelevant to self-evident principles, our knowledge of them must be either complete or nonexistent. It seems to me, however, that my knowledge is never so complete that my ethical principles are not subject to revision in the light of further evidence. Also I often have some reason to accept an ethical principle even though my knowledge falls short of certainty. If I am correct in suggesting that some of my ethical convictions are more reasonable than others, then the model of mathematics does not fit our ethical knowledge.

My conclusion is that intuitionism is unable to explain our knowledge of ethical sentences. In trying to explain how we can intuit ethical facts, the intuitionist makes use of two models. Either we intuit particular values or obligations much as we perceive particular physical objects or we intuit ethical principles much as we perceive the truth of mathematical propositions. Whichever model one considers, there are several features of our ethical knowledge to which it cannot do justice. Unless the intuitionist can suggest another model, his position is inadequate.

5. *The Appeal to Intuition*

Why does the intuitionist model his explanation of ethical knowledge after the example of seeing? It is because he is convinced that ethical knowledge involves an essential rational element and that reason is a kind of direct awareness. Clearly the models which the intuitionist attempts to apply to ethical knowledge are borrowed from his general epistemology. Here arises my third major objection to this position. It is a mistake to conceive of reason as intuition.

It is easy to see what would lead one to this mistaken position. Reason is our faculty of reasoning. In the activity of reasoning we infer the truth of some statement from some given evidence. For example, we pass from the truth of the premises of a syllogism to the truth of the conclusion. Drawing a conclusion is an act of the human mind which might lead us astray. In fact, our inferences are sometimes mistaken. What justifies our confidence in our powers of inference? How can we know when the conclusion we draw really does follow from the evidence at hand? There must be some fixed logical relations between propositions which exist independently of our mind but which we can discover in some way. But how can we be aware of these implications? Clearly not by sense experience. We cannot see or hear either propositions or the relations between them. Therefore, the mind must have some other way of being aware of logical relations. This nonsensuous kind of awareness is intuition. The acceptance of intuition is, then, the only alternative to skepticism; for if we could not intuit the real relations between propositions, we could never know whether our inferences were correct.

Tempting as this escape from skepticism is, I cannot accept it. At the onset there are certain phenomenological difficulties with the conception of nonsensuous apprehension. It does not seem to me that when I inspect my own reasoning processes I find any nonsensuous givens. I find some images, mostly verbal, but they are empirical in content and hardly to be identified with propositions. If I am aware of propositions, at least I am not aware of any such awareness. It is hard to know how much weight to give to this consideration. Other people assert confidently that they find propositions when they examine their own reason phenomenologically, and I am not anxious to admit that my mind and theirs work in basically different ways. Their phenomenological reports do not seem to fit my own reasoning; yet I cannot be positive that it is not my own introspection which is at fault. This uncertainty over the correct description of my reasoning is in sharp contrast to confidence with which I hold certain logical truths. The very sharpness of this contrast indicates strongly that the intuitionists are mistaken, for how could my confidence in my reasoning depend upon an awareness of which I am so exceedingly dubious?

In addition to these phenomenological reservations, I have some ontological misgivings about intuitionism. Where there is awareness there is something of which one is aware. If we intuit the logical relations between propositions, therefore, there must be propositions and relations between them. But what is the nature of propositions and logical relations?

75

And what sort of ontological status are we to give them? The principle of parsimony would be sufficient to make us reluctant to admit such nonnatural objects into the furniture of reality if we could.

In addition to the desire to keep one's ontological commitments to the minimum, there is the feeling that propositions and logical relations have certain ontologically embarrassing features. We know universal propositions and some of the relations between general concepts. But what is a universal entity? It seems perilously close to being an individual which is somehow not limited to individuality. Moreover, our reason knows of possibilities which are not actual. It is rather disconcerting to discover that that which is not actual has being. Even though they do not actually exist, possibilities really exist. To some it sounds better to say that possibilities do not exist at all; they merely subsist. This distinction between existence and subsistence does little to reassure me, however, for we are also aware of certain impossibilities. "Round square" is not mere babbling as is "etmas gind"; and our realization that there could not be a round square is rational understanding. If reason is intuition, there must be impossibilities for us to intuit. But if we admit logical impossibilities into the realm of subsistence, in what way does correspondence with this realm of being guarantee the logical correctness of our reasoning? Nor is it any clearer how a being composed of incompatibles could subsist than how it could exist. Finally there is an example of particular relevance to ethical intuitionism. If judgments of obligation are to be rationally grounded, this theory requires that there be norms to be intuited. Yet the same theory insists on a sharp distinction between ought and is. Then how can the ought be?

When faced with the problem of justifying our acts of reasoning, the intuitionist postulates the existence of a host of nonnatural entities to be directly apprehended by our reason. Even if this postulation would solve the epistemological problem, it brings with it so many ontological problems that it seems hardly worthwhile. As a matter of fact it would not even solve the problem at hand. Even granted the existence of a nonsensuous apprehension and a corresponding set of nonnatural objects to be apprehended, the intuitionist still cannot show that our reason is trustworthy.

Reasoning is an activity of the mind. The awful thought dawns upon us that it may be an arbitrary and capricious exercise of the imagination. What right do we have to trust our reasoning? How can we tell when our reasoning is more than mere fancy? An act of inference is correct when it corresponds to an actual implication relation between the propositions involved; it is mistaken when there actually is no such implication. We can know what relations of implication exist in reality by intuition; we can be directly aware of the independently existing realm of propositions and their relations.

The crux of the matter concerns the exact relations between the act of inferring and the act of intuiting. Since the intuition is supposed to justify the inferring, let us assume that they are distinct. On this interpretation the inferring may be either correct or incorrect. We discover whether any particular inferring is correct by checking it against an intuition of the corresponding propositions. But surely this will not do at all. Checking the inferring against the intuition is itself reasoning. We conclude that the inference is correct on the basis of the intuition. By virtue of what do we trust our checking? If we justify it by appealing to another intuition, an infinite regress obviously arises. The theory is that since our inferring might be mistaken, our confidence in it depends upon an intuition. But how do we know that this intuition justifies our inferring? Drawing any such conclusion would be another act of inference itself requiring justification. It seems clear that on this interpretation intuitionism leads to an infinite regress and must be mistaken.

Perhaps it will be thought that I have misinterpreted intuitionism. It does not claim that the inferring is checked against or justified by the intuition but that it *is* the intuition. The true relation between the act of inferring and the act of intuiting is one of identity. No doubt this interpretation is preferred by some, but I cannot see that it can withstand criticism much better than the other. On this interpretation reasoning is simply direct awareness and nothing more. In direct awareness one cannot be mistaken about what is given. The same incorrigibility which makes the sensuous given so dear to the heart of the empiricist makes the nonsensuous given equally precious to the intuitionist. The immediacy of reasoning guarantees that it cannot be mistaken. The great virtue of this view, of course, is that it rules out all error. But is it such a virtue to prove that reasoning is free from *all possible* error? For one thing, it seems clear that we sometimes are mistaken in our inferences. If inferring is interpreted in such a way that it is made infallible, how can one explain the existence of incorrect reasoning? It will not do to say that mistaken reasoning is not really reasoning, for how can one distinguish real from merely apparent reasoning? If they are difficult to distinguish, one can never trust what he thinks is reason. If they are easy to distinguish, one should never be mistaken at all. It is not only incorrect inferences which this theory cannot explain. The infallibility of inference is guaranteed by giving it the form of incorrigible intuition. Such a justification is, alas, too strong, for its point lies in interpreting reasoning in such a way that the distinction correct-incorrect no longer applies. But this implies that, although our reasoning can never be incorrect, it can never be correct either. In short, the intuitionist has justified reasoning by destroying its cognitive claim, its claim to correctness.

It seems to me, therefore, that the intuitionist cannot justify our trust in reason. On one interpretation reasoning is an inferring based upon intuition. This allows incorrect inferences, but it cannot justify the inferring without an infinite regress. On the other interpretation reasoning is both an inferring and an intuition. This view cannot explain how we ever make mistakes, and it leaves reason with no cognitive claim to be trusted. Since the intuitionist has misunderstood the nature of reason, it is no wonder that he cannot explain our ethical reasoning.

6. *A Misplaced Issue*

One of the crucial questions for any epistemology of ethics is whether ethical judgments can genuinely claim any objective validity? The intuitionists have seen that ethical judgments can make good their claim to objectivity only if it is possible to support them with reasoning. But at this point their mistaken view of reason leads them to misplace the real issue. Reason, they suppose, is intuition and intuition is a kind of seeing. Clearly, seeing is possible only where there is something to be seen; one cannot be directly aware of the nonexistent. It follows that judgments about value and obligation can be rationally justified only if there exists a realm of entities, values and obligations, to be seen with the mind's eye. The basic issue between those who affirm and those who deny the objective validity of moral judgments is the epistemological one of whether there are good reasons for ethical sentences. The intuitionists translate this into the ontological problem of whether or not there exist,

79

or subsist, a special class of nonnatural properties and relations. My fourth main objection to ethical intuitionism is that this is to misplace the issue.

On the view of ethical intuitionism the question worth taking seriously is whether or not there exist a peculiar set of nonnatural characteristics of which we are all aware by a kind of nonsensuous awareness. Since the intuitionists claim that in fact they are aware of such characteristics and the naturalists claim that for their part they are not aware of them, something of a dilemma arises. Either the naturalists have a moral blindness or the intuitionists have moral hallucinations. Neither alternative is very attractive. One would hate to say that the intuitionists are mistaken about what they claim to apprehend directly, for the given is precisely that which can never veil itself. Yet the prospect of saying that the naturalists, who seem perfectly capable of making correct moral judgments, are morally blind is no more seductive.

There is, moreover, a good deal of difficulty over the exact status of these characteristics. They are supposed to be radically different from all natural characteristics, but all the attempts to state the precise nature of this difference have been unsatisfactory. Even more revealing is the supposed relation between these two sets of characteristics. The ethical characteristics seem to depend in some way upon the natural characteristics for their very existence; they are resultant or consequential. I suggest that when one reads carefully what the intuitionists write about this relation of existential dependence he will realize that it is more like a logical relation than an ontological one. The epistemological relation between ground and consequence has been misinterpreted as an ontological relation between constituent and resultant properties.

The intuitionist has confused two distinct issues. One is

whether there are reasons for and against ethical statements. The other is whether there exist a specifically ethical set of nonnatural characteristics. No doubt these two questions are related, but they are not identical. This can be seen by noticing that an affirmative answer to one need not result in an affirmative answer to the other. It would be quite possible to hold that there are reasons for ethical judgments without committing oneself to the existence of these nonnatural characteristics. Ethical naturalists, for example, interpret ethical sentences in such a way that they can be established by empirical evidence. In quite another way, Toulmin and Baier have argued that ethical reasoning can exist without the existence of any nonnatural realm. The converse is also true. One could admit the existence of this nonnatural realm and still deny that there were any reasons for moral judgments. As we have seen, the central ethical questions concern the choice of goals or actions. Let us imagine that someone does see this realm of nonnatural characteristics with his mind's eye. What is the relevance of this realm for his deciding? How does the existence of these peculiar entities constitute a valid reason for choosing in one way rather than another? Turning Moore's remark[1] against the intuitionists, the substance of their teaching amounts to "Do, pray, act so, because the word 'good' is generally used to denote actions of this nature." Granted that a given notion possesses some nonnatural property called "goodness," does this provide any real reason to choose that action? This question remains open.

And it is this remaining question which is the crux of the matter. To decide whether moral statements are objectively valid we must discover whether there are considerations by which their correctness can be rationally determined. Are there valid reasons for and against ethical judgments? This

[1] G. E. Moore, *Principia Ethica* (Cambridge, 1903), p. 12.

is an epistemological question calling for an analysis of moral sentences and their logical properties. The intuitionists translate this question of the evidential relations between judgments into one of the existential dependence of characteristics. In this way a complex of ontological problems arise which are incidental to the real epistemological issue. It would be far easier to raise the evidential question in the first place, since it must be raised eventually by anyone seriously concerned with the grounds for rational choice. The intuitionists never face this real issue because they have misplaced it.

7. Descriptivism

One reason why they have misplaced the issue of objective validity is that they have misinterpreted the meaning of ethical sentences. Ethical intuitionism holds that ethical words refer to certain nonnatural characteristics. To say that something is good, therefore, is to say that it possesses the nonnatural property of goodness, and to say that some action is wrong is to say that it possesses the nonnatural property of wrongness. Ethical sentences turn out on this view to be a special sort of description. What is special about these descriptions is that they predicate a set of specifically ethical characteristics of their subjects. My last main objection to ethical intuitionism is that the meaning of ethical sentences cannot be understood descriptively.

The ethical intuitionist probably takes it for granted that ethical sentences are descriptive because of the general conception of language with which he approaches ethics. To assert anything is, it would seem, to assert a predicate of a subject. Unless one asserts something he can hardly be said to say anything. Thus a linguistic utterance says something only when it describes the object in terms of its properties.

To say nothing is surely to be devoid of meaning. Hence all significant discourse is description and all meaning descriptive. Some such view is, I take it, assumed by the ethical intuitionist. I shall try to explain why I find this view inadequate.

Much of the plausibility of descriptivism comes from thinking of words like "red," "taller," and "soluble." Surely these words stand for properties or relations possessed by various objects, and to assert such a word of an object is to describe it. The array of descriptive adjectives is legion. But the fact that so many words are descriptive should not lead the philosopher to assume that all words are such. To what does "or" correspond? I do not really believe that there is a relation of orness either in my mental hesitations or in the objective realm of propositions. Nor is it any easier to see how "if . . . then" or "entails" could be descriptive. The existence of entities such as propositions to possess such relations is very dubious. Nor does it seem to me when I reflect upon my own reasoning that I decide when such words are to be used by inspecting an objective realm of logical entities. Proper names are another class of words which seem misplaced as descriptive adjectives. The problems which arise when one ascribes connotation to them are well known. Demonstratives like "this" and "that" may refer to that which is described, but they seem to have no descriptive content in themselves. Finally, the difficulties which arise from taking "exists" as a descriptive adjective have been made notorious by the ontological argument. There are many words which cannot be plausibly interpreted as descriptive adjectives.

The descriptivist might admit this but reply that such words are syncategorematic. It is unfair to require that each individual word be descriptive, for it is the sentence as a whole which does the describing. I would agree that the unit of language is the sentence and that it is the sentence as a whole which is meaningful. Can it be claimed, however, that all meaningful sentences are descriptions? The intuitionists themselves have insisted that there is a fundamental and radical difference between the ought and the is. How can they then interpret statements of obligation as descriptions of actions in terms of what their nonnatural characteristics *are?* Leaving indicatives aside, there are questions, imperatives, and exclamations to be considered. These are not meaningless babbling, yet they do not seem to be descriptive. Why must they be? In fact, it is hard to see how they could be plausibly interpreted as asserting a descriptive adjective of a subject.

There is one desperate manner in which the descriptivist can defend his thesis that all meaningful sentences are descriptive. He can distinguish between meaning in the strict sense and meaning in a looser sense. No doubt language has many functions other than description. Quite possibly imperatives, questions, and exclamations are not used to describe the world. But since these nondescriptive sentences assert no proposition and are neither true or false, they are not literally meaningful. One can even make descriptivism analytic by defining "literal meaning" as descriptive. But what is gained by such a stipulation? A theory of meaning must either explain all linguistic functioning which is not sheer babbling or win a Pyrrhic victory. If one reserves the label "meaningful" for his favorite kind of sentence, then he must invent a new label for the rest of language. Any adequate semantics must explain satisfactorily all the language we ordinarily regard as significant or be rejected as incomplete. And, once it is admitted that some language is nondescriptive, it becomes possible to say that ethical language belongs to this nondescriptive part of language. In short, one cannot conclude that ethical sentences must be descriptive on the grounds that all meaningful language is descriptive. For if one uses the word "meaningful" widely enough to cover all language which is not mere babbling, not all meaningful language is descriptive; and if one uses the word "meaningful" in a more restricted sense, then ethical sentences might be located in the large areas of significant language to which the magic word has been denied.

Descriptivism goes deeper than a theory of language, however. The intuitionist might admit the existence of non-descriptive meaning and still maintain his position. Of course there are many meaningful sentences which do not describe anything. Questions, imperatives, and exclamations are obvious illustrations of this fact. They illustrate another important fact as well, that at the point at which language ceases to be descriptive it also loses its claim to objective validity. Questions, imperatives, and exclamations cannot be said to be either true or false. It is not the meaningfulness, but the objective validity of ethical sentences which requires that they be interpreted descriptively.

Here we go beneath a theory of semantics to a theory of objectivity. Our thinking often proves mistaken and must always be suspected of being arbitrary. What test can we have of the correctness of our judgments? Only correspondence with reality. It is the correspondence or lack of it between judgment and reality which constitutes truth or falsity. This seems obviously true of empirical judgments, and even the validity of our inferrings is to be judged by their conformity to the independently existing implication relations. Where the test of correspondence cannot be applied it makes no sense to speak of correctness or incorrectness at all. In this way all objective validity is assimilated to descriptive correspondence, and all rational judgment becomes an attempt to describe the universe as it actually is. It follows that, unless one is willing to admit that ethical judgments have no objective validity, they must be descriptive.

In the case of ethical judgments, however, this will not do. We have seen that ethics is autonomous in the sense that the practical cannot be reduced to the theoretical. This autonomy is lost when the problem of choosing to act becomes the problem of describing the action. What follows from the limitation of the distinction between correct and incorrect to that which describes? Since doing is not describing, action itself is no longer subject to rational crititicism. In effect, the intuitionists deny the very possibility of ethics! Instead of thinking about the choice of the action itself they have thought only about the assertion *about* the action. They have sought to defend the objective validity of the assertion by a theory which would deny any validity to the action. Since choosing to act is not describing the action, the choice can be correct or incorrect only if objective validity is not limited to descriptive correspondence.

It is not enough to be able to describe the action correctly. What are we to say of the incontinent man who admits that an action is wrong but goes ahead and does it? Since he has correctly described his action, he is beyond criticism on any theory which limits rational criticism to descriptive correspondence or the lack of it. Again, what would it mean to describe an action as right or wrong if the action, not just the description of it, were not itself right or wrong?

It is very tempting to conceive of the objective validity of all judgment in terms of descriptive correspondence. What better guarantee could there be of the correctness of our thinking than its conformity with its object? What other guarantee, in fact, could there be that our judgment is more than mere imagination? Morality, however, is concerned with the choice of goals and actions; moral judgment is, at least in part, decisional rather than descriptive. This implies that a genuinely practical reason cannot be interpreted as a concealed form of descriptive judgment. Either moral judgment is not rational and can claim no objective validity, or rational judgment is not limited to the descriptive. Since I agree with the intuitionists in defending the objectivity of moral judgment, I must give up their descriptivism.

The admission that rational judgment need not be descriptive has implications for the analysis of language. Ethical judgments are not descriptions of objects and actions. It is unlikely that our language would be unable to formulate such an important range of human judgments. Moreover, there are many sentences which seem on the face of it to express ethical judgments. Very probably, then, there are some sentences which put our ethical judgments into words. It would follow that, although these ethical sentences can claim objective validity, their meaning is not descriptive. This, I take it, is the real point of the naturalistic fallacy. To hold that ethical sentences are a special kind of description is to deny their ethical status. The best comment was made by Moore himself: "Immensely the commonest type of truth, then, is the one which asserts a relation between two existing things. Ethical truths are immediately felt not to conform to this type, and the naturalistic fallacy arises from the attempt to make out that, in some roundabout way, they do conform to it." [2] This is an excellent analysis of what causes the intuitionist to make the very same mistake with which he charges the naturalist. He is led to believe that, either because of their meaningfulness or their objective validity, ethical sentences must be some peculiar

[2] G. E. Moore, *Principia Ethica*, p. 124.

87

form of description. I have tried to argue that this is not so. It is basically mistaken to hold that the meaning of ethical sentences is descriptive.

8. *Recapitulation*

Ethical intuitionism is the view that ethical sentences ultimately are known by intuition. On this view ethical sentences describe objects and actions in terms of their non-natural characteristics. Thus ethical intuitionism constitutes one answer to the question "What do ethical sentences mean?" On this view ethical sentences have descriptive meaning, and the peculiarities of ethical language reflect its special subject matter.

I have argued that ethical intuitionism is mistaken. It is not shown to be correct simply by the alleged inadequacies of ethical naturalism. There are many features of our ethical knowledge which it cannot explain satisfactorily. Its concept of the nature of reason is fundamentally in error. It misplaces the real problem of the objective validity of ethical sentences. It fails to see that genuinely ethical sentences cannot be simply another form of description. For all these reasons I find ethical intuitionism unacceptable. There is, however, another interpretation which insists on the nondescriptive nature of ethical sentences. Let us see if this emotive theory of ethics is the true answer to our question.

The Emotive Theory of Ethics

During the first two or three decades of this century the two most popular interpretations of ethical language were those which I have just discussed. Ethical naturalism asserted that ethical words refer to empirical characteristics; ethical intuitionism contended that ethical words refer to nonnatural characteristics. In spite of their intense disagreements, both views assumed that ethical sentences must be descriptive in some way. In time epistemological developments revealed the possibility that some sentences have nondescriptive meaning, and a new theory of ethical language emerged.

1. *Principal Doctrines*

The emotive theory of ethics is the view that the meaning of ethical sentences is primarily emotive. This need not imply that ethical sentences have no cognitive meaning at all, but such descriptive meaning must be secondary or only incidental. The truly important and illuminating feature in the interpretation of ethical language is its emotive meaning. Emotive meaning is that property of words or sentences by which they express or evoke feelings, emotions, desires, or volitions. Expressing a feeling differs from describing a feeling in the way that saying "ouch" differs from saying "I am in pain." Thus the significance of ethical sentences is to be understood in terms of their role in expressing the attitudes of the speaker and evoking similar or contrasting emotions in the hearer.

This central thesis of the emotive theory is usually taken to imply several other propositions. First, the distinctive feature of ethical sentences is their normativeness. Certain sentences are classified as ethical precisely because they have a relevance for action which merely factual sentences lack. This relevance is normally interpreted causally; the practical nature of ethical sentences lies in the fact that they are verbal stimuli which cause us to respond by doing or refraining from doing something. While this causal impact upon action could be said to be direct, most emotivists think of its as rather circuitous. Ethical sentences incite or quell action by modifying the attitudes which motivate the actor. The peculiarity of ethical language, then, consists of its capacity to strengthen, weaken, and redirect our attitudes in such a way as to affect our practice.

Second, ethical sentences cannot be understood in terms of descriptive meaning. Some emotivists, like Ayer, claim that genuinely ethical sentences have no descriptive meaning at all. To say that Miss Smith is virtuous may, of course, be to describe her relations, or lack of them, with the opposite sex. In such a case, however, it is a purely factual statement and not an ethical sentence at all. If "Miss Smith is virtuous" is meant to be a value judgment, it describes neither Miss Smith nor the speaker's attitude towards her. What it does do is express, rather than assert, the speaker's attitude. Similarly, to declare an act obligatory is to give absolutely no information about it. Other emotivists, like Stevenson, concede a certain descriptive meaning to ethical sentences. To say "This steak is good" may include describing either my liking for the steak or its likable qualities depending upon whether one takes Stevenson's first or second patterns as his model. Such descriptive content is, however, accompanied by and subordinate to the emotive meaning of the sentence. Moreover, if one wishes to understand the specifically ethical functioning of the sentence, he must examine its emotive rather than its descriptive meaning.

Third, ethical sentences possess no real objective validity. Since ethical sentences are not basically descriptive, they cannot be said to be either true or false. No one ethical statement can be said to be more rationally justified than any alternative, for in the strict sense there are no reasons for or against ethical sentences. To be sure, we do argue about which ethical conclusion to accept. But such ethical "reasoning" is more like persuasion than like logical proof. The considerations which one advances to support his ethical statement may cause his hearer to agree with him; but they are not, in any important sense of "valid," valid grounds for agreement. Since there are no rational grounds to prefer one ethical sentence to another, ethical sentences cannot claim any objective validity.

Fourth, ethical disagreements are disagreements in attitude rather than belief. Because ethical sentences are fundamentally nondescriptive, two people who utter conflicting ethical sentences are not contradicting one another logically. When Jones says "Curried octopus is good" and Smith

"Curried Octopus is most certainly not good," they have not uttered sentences which are logically inconsistent. Yet it would be a mistake to say that Jones and Smith do not disagree at all. The conflict between them lies in their attitudes but not in their beliefs. Two people disagree in attitude when they have opposing attitudes towards the same thing and neither is content to leave the other's attitude unchallenged; two people disagree in belief when they have contradictory beliefs about the same thing and neither is content to leave the other's belief unchallenged. Basically ethical disagreements are of the former sort. Although there may also be disagreement in belief in ethics, it is not central; for it is disagreement in attitude which determines when ethical dispute begins and when it is resolved.

2. *Important Contributions*

These are what I take to be the most important points in the emotive theory of ethics. This theory has made several significant contributions to the epistemology of ethics. The first of these is the realization that ethical sentences are not descriptions. The emotive theory has put the naturalistic fallacy in a new light. The ethical intuitionists felt that there is something wrong in the attempt to analyze ethical sentences into empirical descriptions and claimed that ethical naturalism somehow destroys the characteristically ethical features of ethical language. The only positive suggestion which they could make was that ethical sentences must describe a very special sort of characteristic, one which is radically different in some way from all natural properties. Emotivists have seen that the real trouble with ethical naturalism is not its naturalism but its descriptivism and that in this respect ethical intuitionism is equally at fault. The fundamental source of the naturalistic fallacy is the

92

attempt to interpret ethical sentences descriptively. To have argued that the meaning of ethical language cannot be primarily descriptive is an important service. Right or wrong, the emotivist has raised the question of the meaning of ethical sentences in a new and sharpened way. I happen to think that he is right.

Another contribution of the emotive theory is the recognition that a wider theory of meaning is needed. Traditional theories of ethical language had taken it for granted that all meaningful sentences were descriptions. Since the epistemologist is primarily concerned with descriptive sentences and their logical relations, it is only natural that he should frame his theory of meaning with them in view. Unfortunately a theory formulated to explain only the scientific and logical uses of language can do little to illuminate the other uses which language serves. As long as these other uses were thought to be irrelevant to the proper concerns of the philosopher this did not greatly matter; they could be safely left to the philologist and the psychologist. With the rise of the emotive theory, however, it became apparent that philosophers would have to come to terms with modes of meaning other than the descriptive. In this way our semantical horizons were greatly extended.

Ironically enough emotivism arose as a by-product of the attempt to restrict, rather than to extend, the area of the meaningful. Emotive meaning was to be the limbo into which all philosophically puzzling sentences were to be thrown. The recognition of this limbo, however, made its consideration necessary for any systematically complete philosophy, and the importance of the sinners expelled to this region made a serious investigation of it philosophically interesting. It was no longer enough to say of these expelled sentences that they are not descriptive. What are they? A positive and detailed characterization of all modes of meaning, whether descriptive or not, was seen to be required. In this way the emotivists prepared the way for a new awareness of the variety of the uses of language and the need for a detailed investigation of its many forms. This release from the traditional theories of meaning is of particular importance for ethics, because, as we have seen, the practical character of ethical sentences is lost when they are assimilated to the descriptive.

Still another major contribution of the emotive theory is the introduction into philosophy of a new method of clarifying meanings. The use of this new method of clarification is obviously related to the rejection of the traditional theories of meaning, for those methods of analysis which had proved successful in explaining descriptive language often could not be applied to emotive meaning. Three basic conceptions of what a philosophical definition should be were commonly accepted. Those with metaphysical inclinations, like Moore, thought that one really defined a word only when he analyzed the essence or characteristic for for which it stood into its constituents. Since emotive words do not stand for characteristics at all, this sort of definition is clearly inapplicable to them. More linguistically oriented philosophers thought that one properly defined a word by equating it with another expression which could be substituted for it in all contexts. It turns out, however, that purely emotive words do not seem to have synonyms in exactly the same sense that descriptive adjectives do and that even fairly close emotive equivalents do not analyze the original in the way in which a linguistically complex expression seems to unpack a single descriptive word. When neither of these two techniques for the definition of individual words was useful, philosophers resorted to definitions in use. In effect this meant that any sentence containing some obscure expression was to be translated into another sentence with the same meaning but without the troublesome expression. Since there seems no precise sense in which one part of emotive language is any clearer than another, such translations of emotive sentences solve no philosophical problems.

As a result emotivists gave up the attempt to give strict definitions of emotive expressions; instead they described the meaning of such language. Descriptions of how a given word or phrase is used are, of course, common in dictionaries, but heretofore philosophers had thought that something more was required of any philosophically respectable definition. Now that description was accepted in place of definition, the amount of information which could be brought to bear on a perplexing expression was greatly increased. Not just the analysis of an essence or a synonymous expression, but almost any feature of the situation in which the word is used could be appealed to to explain the word's meaning. The object of this new method of clarification is not to substitute a better vocabulary, but to gain a firmer grasp of the old one. It seems to me that description proves more illuminating than definition when one comes to explain the meaning of ethical sentences.

The fourth contribution of the emotive theory to the epistemology of ethics is the realization that attitudes are central to the analysis of ethical language. The contention that ethical sentences express attitudes rather than factual beliefs has an important measure of truth to it. It seems to me that the emotivists have stressed the emotional aspect of attitudes at the expense of other features which they possess. Also, I doubt whether judgments of obligation express attitudes in any very direct way. Still, to have connected value judgments with attitudes is to have gone a long way in explaining the peculiarities of this segment of ethical language. Not content with saying merely that value sentences were not descriptions, the emotivists have taken the first step towards positive analysis of evaluations.

If the reader can agree with me that the emotive theory of ethics has made the contributions which I have mentioned, he will also agree that this theory marks a turning point in the epistemology of ethics. The real importance of the emotive theory is negative; it asserts boldly that the previously accepted theories of meaning and methods of analysis are inadequate to ethical sentences. Perhaps the emotivists have not refuted the assumptions that ethical sentences are descriptions and that the goal of analysis is to define ethical words, but at least they have questioned these assumptions in a way which cannot be ignored. Thus they have rid the minds of many of certain conceptions which distorted their understanding of ethical language. Positively, the achievements of the emotivists will probably be less lasting. Although they have opened up vast new possibilities for analysis, their actual analyses of ethical words seem to me to be quite mistaken. Let me explain why.

3. *Inconclusive Arguments*

My first objection to the emotive theory of ethics is that it is not established by the usual lines of reasoning. One reason that many people doubtless accept the emotive theory is that it affords a way out of the impasse between naturalism and intuitionism. To these people the open-question argument and perhaps some of the other arguments which the intuitionists employ against the naturalists seem convincing. Yet their epistemological presuppositions and their ontological skepticism make them unwilling to admit that we obtain ethical knowledge by intuition or that there exists a realm of nonnatural characteristics. How can they cling to their empirical epistemology and metaphysical naturalism without admitting that ethical sentences are either complete nonsense or empirical descriptions? When it is realized that there may be some sort of nondescriptive meaning, the way out of the dilemma is obvious. The emotive theory of ethics, then, is accepted as the only alternative to two clearly inadequate interpretations of ethical language.

That the emotive theory is one way out of the dilemma cannot be denied; what should be questioned is that it is the only way out. Even if naturalism and intuitionism are both mistaken, which naturalists and intuitionists can be counted upon to deny, there might well be other alternatives. I agree, for reasons which I have tried to explain, that ethical sentences are not descriptions. But from the fact that ethical sentences have nondescriptive meaning does it follow that they emotive meaning? If "emotive meaning" is defined as all meaning which is not descriptive, then I suppose that it does. Something like this is done by those emotivists who make the absence of truth or falsity in the strict sense their criterion of emotive meaning. However, if the emotivist adopts this purely negative conception of emotive meaning, then he is giving no positive analysis of ethical sentences when he says that they have emotive meaning. Any adequate epistemology of ethics must explain what ethical sentences do mean as well as what they do not mean. If "emotive meaning" is defined positively, as expressing emotions or issuing commands, for example, then it does not follow that ethical sentences have emotive meaning simply because they do not have descriptive meaning. It would follow, if we could assume that language performs just two functions, describing and emoting; but it is becoming increasingly apparent that language has a great many distinct functions. Therefore, one cannot conclude that ethical sentences must have emotive meaning from the inadequacy of naturalism and intuitionism alone.

If the emotive theory of ethics is to be established, there must be some positive evidence that the language of ethics is emotive. Well, how do we decide when a given bit of language is emotive? How, for example, do we discover that the word "maiden" is relatively emotive while "young unmarried woman" has little emotive meaning? Often the word "maiden" is classified as emotive on the grounds that it is rich in imagery, but the tendency to call up images has no essential relation to the usual definitions of emotive meaning in terms of attitudes or feelings. What we need to show is that the word expresses and evokes attitudes, not that it communicates images.

Let us assume, as the emotivists seem to, that attitudes are basically emotional. We might, then, use as our criterion of emotive meaning the presence of emotion in the speaker or hearer of the word. We might detect this emotion by introspecting as we say or hear the word "maiden." Or we might watch for signs of emotion such as blushing, perspiring, random rapid motion of the fingers, and so on. We might even check on the pulse, blood pressure, and glandular activity in the speaker or hearer. Granted that we could show in some such way that speaking or hearing the word "maiden" is always or usually accompanied by emotion in the speaker or hearer, what would that prove? Our first problem would be to show that the emotion did not just happen to accompany the word, that it has a causal connection with the use of the word. It might be that I always blush when I hear the word "maiden" because the person trying to establish the emotive theory of ethics happens to be a voluptuous blonde. Although this raises no insurmountable theoretical difficulties, it is important to show

98

that the use of the word is not merely accompanied by, but connected with, the emotion.

More serious is showing that the connection between word and emotion is *direct*. It might be that the word "maiden" means to me curvaceous blonde and that this descriptive content causes me to blush. The mere presence of emotion does not show that the word has emotive rather than descriptive meaning; it may indicate only that the descriptive meaning has emotional connotations. One might counter that this could not be the case, since "maiden" has the same descriptive meaning as "young unmarried woman" which can be shown by the appropriate tests to be relatively nonemotive. But how can it be shown that the two are exactly synonymous? Quine and White are correct, I think, in suggesting that we have no adequate criterion of precise synonymy. In this case, as in the case of most examples used, it seems plausible to claim that the descriptive connotations of the two expressions differ even if their strictly literal meaning is the same.

Although my exposition has been indirect, my point is simple. What criterion does the emotivist use to determine the presence of primarily emotive meaning? Unless the emotive theory of ethics can suggest some test by which emotive meaning can be recognized, its claim that ethical sentences are emotive can have no direct support. Notice that the test must be such that it can be applied to ethical language. Even if it could be shown that there is some emotive language, this would not prove that ethical language is also emotive. I suggest that the mere fact that certain language is accompanied by emotion is insufficient. The observation that we are usually more emotional when we talk ethics than we talk physics or chemistry, therefore, is no proof of the emotive theory of ethics.

There is another argument for the emotive theory which

has become fairly popular recently. Clearly the meaning of ethical sentences is primarily emotive rather than descriptive; for when two people dispute about some ethical statement, they are disagreeing in attitude rather than in belief. Ethical disagreement, it is claimed, is disagreement in attitude. No doubt this may be accompanied by disagreement in belief, but it need not be. In any event, the disagreement in attitude is more fundamental, for this determines whether the parties dispute the ethical question and when they settle the dispute. If people who disagree about some ethical sentence are disagreeing in attitude rather than in belief then presumably the ethical sentence expresses an attitude rather than a belief.

This argument is a strong one provided its premise is accepted. It assumes that ethical disagreement is disagreement in attitude rather than in belief. What reason do we have to accept this assumption? Some have asserted that it can be supported by the fact that two people sometimes disagree on an ethical question even though they agree on all the facts. I suspect that in point of fact two people never do disagree on an ethical question when they agree on all the facts. But this is a strong claim, and I will not argue it here. Instead let me argue only that the emotivist cannot show that people ever do continue to disagree on an ethical question when they agree on all the facts. What sort of evidence could the emotivist employ?

If this is a factual question, one would expect the emotivist to give empirical evidence for his assertion, unless he wishes to be committed to the synthetic a priori. But how would one ever know by observation that he had found a genuine instance of this situation? Suppose that a trained observer discovers two men earnestly engaged in arguing with one another. For the moment I will concede that he has some way of knowing that they are discussing an ethical question, although it is by no means clear how one identifies specifically ethical discourse. But how would the observer know that these two people agree on all the facts? The observation that neither appealed to any facts would not show this, as one often uses pure rhetoric to save time, or because he is irrational, or because he has given up the attempt to convince the other of the relevant fact (that is, precisely because the disagreement in fact is so sharp it seems irresoluble), or simply because he cannot at the moment think of any more facts to mention. The key phrase is "all the facts." What does it mean to say that the two arguers agree on *all* the facts? Must they agree on every single fact in or about the universe? This is such a strong requirement that it is hard to see how one could ever ascertain that it was fulfilled even in the unlikely event that such complete agreement did exist. Must they agree only on all the relevant facts? But it is hard to see how the emotivist can appeal to this obvious and sensible restriction, for he denies any logical or quasilogical relevance to ethical reasoning. Since the emotivist holds that to someone or other at some time or other any fact at all might be a reason, he is driven back to the first alternative. It does not seem to me, therefore, that it would be possible to establish empirically that two people do disagree on an ethical question even though they agree on all the facts.

One way to avoid the need for any empirical evidence would be to claim that the issue is a logical one. No trained observer could discover by the examination of actual disputes that certain of them, the ethical ones, happen to be disagreements in attitude where there is no disagreement over the facts. Rather it would take a trained thinker reflecting upon the evidence for ethical propositions to discover it. When one stops to think about the possible reasons for and against an ethical statement, he realizes that no amount of factual information would be sufficient to establish it. This argument, this appeal to what would or would not justify an ethical sentence, is not open to the emotivist; for he denies that there is any logic, as opposed to rhetoric, of ethical "reasoning." He can hardly claim that an ethical question may remain logically undecided in the face of all the logically relevant information, for he has excluded such a thing as logical relevance. If he appeals to psychological relevance (that is, convincingness), he certainly cannot assert on a priori grounds alone that all possible psychologically relevant considerations would leave the two disputants at variance. I do not see, therefore, how the emotivist can establish the statement that in fact two people sometimes disagree on an ethical question when they agree on all the facts. It would follow that he cannot appeal to this alleged disagreement as a fact upon which he can build his theory.

It does not seem to me, then, that the arguments usually employed to support the emotive theory of ethics really prove their case. Although this theory does offer one way out of the impasse between naturalism and intuitionism, it is not the only way out. Thus someone could deny that ethical sentences are descriptive without asserting that they have emotive meaning; they might have some other sort of nondescriptive meaning. I have been unable to think of any positive criterion of emotive meaning which the emotivist could apply directly to ethical language to prove his point. Nor can he argue that ethical disagreements must be disagreements in attitude since they can continue when all factual disagreement is resolved, for this may not be so.

Please do not exaggerate my claims. I have not been trying to show that all possible arguments for the emotive theory are without weight and that there is nothing to be said for this position. There are some features of ethical language to which emotivism does greater justice than either naturalism or intuitionism, and to that extent it is preferable to either. One should accept, reject, or modify emotivism by determining how well it explains all the aspects of ethical language. I would not have the theory rejected without a hearing. What I have been trying to show, however, is that one is not forced to adopt the emotive theory of ethics either as the only alternative to naturalism and intuitionism or because it is conclusively established by appeal to obvious facts. Although something can be said for the theory, one may reject it if it proves inadequate.

4. *Oversimplified Semantics*

I suggest that the emotivist's explanation of ethical language is inadequate because it approaches ethical language with an inadequate semantical framework. The emotive theory of ethics seems to assume that all language is either cognitive or emotive; at least cognitive meaning and emotive meaning are the only two kinds which it bothers to distinguish. My second objection to the emotive theory is that its basic categories grossly over-simplify the actual nature of language. The various uses of significant language can hardly be captured or even adequately classified in the simple dichotomy which the emotive theory employs. The analysis which emotivism gives to ethical sentences is relatively uninformative and misleading because it starts with a concept of meaning which is not sufficiently subtle.

This is not surprising when one considers the origins of the theory. Emotivism began as a by-product of a positivism which claimed that all literally meaningful sentences were either analytic or empirically verifiable. Ethical sentences seemed to present an obvious and embarrassing exception.

Since they are neither analytic nor empirically verifiable, they must be without cognitive meaning; since they are not mere babbling, they must have some sort of noncognitive meaning. In this view the basic categories of meaning are simply cognitive and noncognitive. To classify ethical sentences as noncognitive is to characterize them in a purely negative way; it is to say simply that they do not have the same kind of meaning as philosophically acceptable sentences.

The second impetus to the emotive theory came from those semanticists whose chief concern was the improvement of thought by the clarification of its instrument, language. They were not so much concerned with denying the meaningfulness of ethical sentences as with preventing the confusion of radically different questions and the intrusion of irrelevant considerations into scientific thinking. Emotive meaning was distinguished from symbolic meaning to prevent its interference with the serious business of formulating and communicating truths. By now the nonliteral mode of meaning was not simply defined negatively, but it was positively characterized in terms of the emotions. Any serious consideration of emotive meaning was limited pretty much to poetry, however, by the predilections of the semanticists; detailed discussions of ethical sentences were still lacking.

Gradually there arose a desire to investigate the language of ethics for its own sake, and the positive characterization of its kind of meaning became a task of philosophical importance. Moreover, the need for a more general theory of meaning which would account for noncognitive as well as cognitive meaning became apparent. Stevenson has probably done more than any other man to state the emotive theory of ethics in a way which deserves respectful attention for its own sake. In effect, this new emotivism grounded the old semantical dichotomy between cognitive and emotive meaning upon the psychological distinction between belief and attitude. The old dichotomy remained, however, and the variety of forms which language can take was largely ignored.

It must be admitted, I think, that some progress has been made. The positivists did little to explain the nature of ethical sentences by labelling them "noncognitive" and dismissing them from the realm of philosophically respectable language. The semanticists at least made some positive suggestion about ethical language when they labelled it "emotive" and asserted that it expressed emotions. Stevenson went much further when he tried to explain to some extent the nature of the emotions or attitudes expressed in ethical language and to develop a theory of meaning which would explain the relation between the words used and the attitudes expressed. His mistake, I think, was in failing to realize that the cognitive-emotive dichotomy with which he started oversimplified his subject matter.

For one thing, the dichotomy is far too sharp. By concentrating upon this one fundamental distinction the emotivist overemphasizes the cleavage and compartmentalizes the mind. He opposes beliefs and attitudes as radically different elements in our mental life. One wonders, however, whether this radical opposition is true to the human mind. A consideration of the intimate interplay of belief and attitude in deliberation should warn us not to sever them so sharply that they become unrelated. Our mental life should not be broken up into such totally diverse elements.

Moreover, this sharp distinction obscures the nature of justification. If one starts with the distinction between cognitive and emotive, reason surely belongs on the cognitive side of the fence. But the normative aspects of language and thought belong, presumably, on the nether side. Since justification seems to be normative, it must be opposed to cognition and reason. Yet a second thought assures us that they must be inseparably united; justification is rational or it is nothing. The emotivist is willing to deny that ethical "justification" is rational, but will he do the same for the justification of deductive and inductive reasoning? If not, on what grounds does he treat the moral and logical oughts so differently?

Finally, to overemphasize the distinction between cognitive and emotive is to stress certain differences at the expense of important similarities. Value statements are at least as much like descriptions as they are like exclamations and probably more like them than cries of fear or anger. Yet such similarities are overlooked or explained away while evaluation is distinguished sharply from description and lumped with the child's tears. No doubt it is well to notice that ethical sentences differ from descriptive ones, but to single out this difference as crucial can do nothing but conceal their many similarities.

But if the emotivists separate the cognitive and emotive too sharply, they also fail to make the necessary distinctions within each category. Consider first the strictly cognitive mode of meaning. Here one must at least distinguish descriptions of the given from objective sentences which extrapolate beyond the momentary content of experience. One suspects that there are also important differences in meaning between our everyday descriptions of physical objects and the explanatory statements of the theoretical physicist trying to formulate the laws according to which these objects act. Truths by definition, the principles of deduction, and the principles of inductive logic are other types of sentences whose kinds of meaning differ from one another as well as from empirically verifiable statements. To label all these types of sentence as "cognitive" does little either to classify them adequately or to clarify their meaning.

The confusions obscured by the notion of emotive meaning are even worse. One must distinguish at least the following: exclamations, commands, petitions, questions, expressions of wish, promises, metaphor and other figures of speech, ascriptions of responsibility, judgments of obligation, and evaluations. The emotivists lump together many exceedingly diverse kinds of language under each of their catch-all labels. This hardly provides a theory of meaning which will satisfy an epistemologist, nor does it provide one detailed enough to tell us much about the meaning of ethical sentences.

I have suggested that the distinction between cognitive and emotive meaning is too sharp and that it fails to distinguish many quite different kinds of sentence. The most serious difficulty with this dichotomy, however, is that its nature is not at all clear. The emotive theory of ethics rests upon a fundamental distinction, but precisely what is it?

At times we are told that the distinction is that between sentences which can be said to be true or false and those which have no truth value. Now we are not told very much about ethical sentences when we are told that they have no truth value; if the emotive theory of ethics amounts only to this, it obviously gives no adequate characterization of the positive nature of ethical language. Nor is it so obvious that ethical sentences are without truth value; we often speak of them as though they were true or false. The emotivist can counter that he is speaking of truth or falsity in the strict sense. But what is this strict sense? Those who claim that analytic statements are true can hardly appeal to correspondence with the facts, for they claim that analytic truths are factually empty. Those who interpret analytic sentences as rules or recommendations might, however, define truth in terms of factual correspondence. But can they analyze correspondence in such a way that ethical sentences turn out to lack this feature? Since we appeal to admittedly factual statements to support or refute ethical statements, the latter might be said to correspond with the facts in some sense at least. Thus, if the emotivist is using the words "true" and "false" as they are used in ordinary language, it is not clear that their applicability will distinguish the two areas of language he wishes to separate; if he is using the words in some more precise sense, he must explain precisely what that sense is. Until he does, his distinction remains obscure.

At other times the distinction is supposed to be between those sentences which describe and those which express an attitude or emotion. But what exactly is the difference between describing and expressing an attitude? The crucial difficulty is in explaining the difference between a speaker describing his own attitude and one expressing this same attitude. What is the difference, for example, between saying "I disapprove of you" and saying "you are wicked?" An expression might be said to express an attitude when it is a natural sign of the attitude, that is, when the hearer could infer the presence of the attitude in the speaker from the fact that he uttered the expression. In this respect, however, descriptive and emotive language are quite similar, for I can infer that the speaker has an attitude of disapproval from the fact that he describes himself as having it. Moreover, it is not clear how the cognitive relation being-a-sign-of serves to define a specifically noncognitive mode of meaning. One might say that to express an attitude is to communicate it to the hearer. But in some sense at least the description of an attitude conveys it to the hearer. And can a speaker be said to express himself only if the hearer is caused by his utterance to feel exactly the same way? Besides, one would think that Robinson Crusoe should not be denied on logical grounds the inalienable right of self-expression. Finally, to express an attitude might be equated with venting it. The idea seems to be that attitudes build up emotional pressures within one which is released by speaking much as steam is let off by a teakettle. If venting is limited to violent release or the verbal reduction of strong emotional pressures, it would seem to be inappropriate to the use of much ethical language. There are times when we discuss an ethical question with little internal agitation. If venting is allowed to include the deliberate and unemotional use of words, it is not clear how one would draw the line between expressing and describing. In addition, one should point out that the meaning of a sentence seems to have more to do with what is said than the way it is said.

More recently the distinction between cognitive and emotive meaning has been defined in terms of the distinction between belief and attitude. In this way the psychologist is called upon to clarify the semanticist's categories. Those who have read Wittgenstein's *Philosophical Investigations* will wonder whether it is very helpful to try to explain language as putting into words our various mental states, processes, or dispositions. One suspects that this approach to language puts the cart before the horse. Instead of clarifying obscure linguistic differences in terms already acknowledged by the empirical psychologist, it all too often invents various psychological entities to reflect the different types of sentence with which we are all familiar. This explains little unless the exact relation of psychological entity and language is made clear and the precise nature of these entities can be established by some method other than a study of language. Another difficulty with this attempt to clarify the distinction between cognitive and emotive in terms of that between belief and attitudes is that the latter distinction is far from clear. It turns out that the genuinely scientific psychologist has very little light to throw on the difference between attitudes and belief. Finally, this sort of analysis raises the question of the causal relation between belief and attitude. The emotive theory of ethics seems committed to the thesis that at least some emotive meaning is independent of cognitive meaning. This implies that there are some attitudes which are not a function of our beliefs. Whether or not all of our attitudes are causally dependent upon our beliefs seems to be a question which has not been settled by the psychologists themselves. Thus the emotivist's distinction between modes of meaning is made to rest upon a precarious psychological hypothesis.

Although it is a step in the right direction to admit that there can be kinds of meaning other than descriptive, the attempt to interpret all sentences as either cognitive or emotive does not take us very far. Such a dichotomy tends to overemphasize the differences between the cognitive and emotional sides of our life. Under each category one is forced to group indiscriminately several quite different kinds of language. Finally, there has not yet been a clear and precise explanation of exactly what the distinction between cognitive and emotive meaning amounts to. It seems to me that the basic categories in terms of which the emotivist frames his theory are inadequate both to language in general and ethical language in particular.

5. Misleading Models

The emotive theory of ethics rests upon two fundamental theses, one negative and the other positive, about the nature of language. These are that certain meaningful sentences do not have descriptive meaning and that the sort of meaning they do have lies in expressing and evoking emotions.

This theory could hope to be taken seriously only if it could produce some linguistic specimens to illustrate these theses. Perhaps the most obvious examples of nondescriptive sentences are exclamations and commands. These could hardly be claimed to assert any description, for clearly they assert nothing at all. This absence of all assertion is brought home by the fact that truth and falsity seem irrelevant to such utterances. Moreover, exclamations and commands could be interpreted in such a way that they support the positive thesis as well. Almost anyone could see that exclamations are used to express the speaker's emotions, and it seems plausible to say that imperatives express the speaker's wish that a certain act be done. These two types of sentence, then, seem to be the prime examples of emotive meaning.

For these reasons the emotivists seize upon exclamations and commands as the two models of emotive meaning. It is only natural that, when they come to analyze ethical sentences, they try to analyze them in terms of these two models. My third fundamental objection to the emotive theory of ethics is that these two models do more to obscure than to illuminate ethical language. To be sure, they do underline the important insight· that ethical sentences are nondescriptive. Exclamations can, if interpreted as Stevenson does, suggest the sense in which evaluations are pro and con. Moreover, imperatives can help to remind us that judgments of obligation have a direct bearing on action. Beyond this, however, exclamations and imperatives are quite unlike ethical sentences.

To begin with, notice that the two models which the emotivist uses are marked off from the rest of language by their grammatical form. Exclamations and imperatives are sentences which are in moods other than the indicative. Now if ethical sentences are really so much like exclamations and imperatives, why do we formulate them, like descriptions, in the indicative mood? In other areas of language, form seems to follow function. Why do we formulate ethical sentences in a way which conceals their true meaning?

I remain unconvinced by the most common explanations of this fact. It is sometimes suggested that we feel more strongly about ethical matters than about those things at which we exclaim. However, before I use a four-letter word I usually feel pretty strongly. If it is suggested that ethical attitudes are calm passions, I reply that they are not always so very calm. Our avoidance of the imperative mood is often explained as a way of trying to disguise our attempts to impose our will upon the hearer. But why do we need ethical language when there are other ways of expressing a polite command? And how polite can a command get and still be a command? It is not impossible, of course, that exclamations and commands bring out the nature of ethical sentences better than indicatives. But if so, the emotivist must explain convincingly why we choose to express our ethical judgments in an apparently inappropriate grammatical form. In all probability our choice of grammatical form is subconsciously determined by certain features of ethical judgments which makes us reluctant to formulate them in either the exclamatory or the imperative mood. If so, the emotivist's models will tend to distort these aspects of ethical language.

The fact of persistent and pervasive ethical disagreement might seem to support the use of these models. After all, when two people disagree about the truth of a descriptive sentence, there are recognized ways of settling the dispute. Although some such disputes may remain undecided, this is the exception rather than the rule. In ethical disputes quite the contrary is true. It almost never seems possible to decide definitely whether an ethical sentence is true or false. One begins to wonder whether it makes sense even to speak of ethical truth or falsity when there is no method of determining it. But if ethical sentences have no truth value, there is at least one important respect in which they are like exclamations and commands. In this way the fact that ethical disputes cannot be settled seems to imply that the emotivist's models are not out of place.

But actually the fact of persistent ethical disagreement shows that these models are inapplicable. We never argue about the correctness of an exclamation. When an acquaintance cheers at my misfortune, I may tell him that he is thoughtless and unkind, but I never try to convince him that he is mistaken. I may object to an imperative that someone issues at me. I may refuse to obey it. I may even try to convince the speaker that his command was unwise. But I never try to prove that what he said was false. Thus we never do disagree about the correctness or truth of either exclamations or imperatives. If these models are appropriate to ethical language, why do we so frequently and persistently dispute about the truth of ethical sentences? The fact of ethical disagreement argues against, not for, the appropriateness of the emotivist's models.

The emotivist might contend that this is only a superficial appearance. Ayer once claimed that, although we may seem to dispute about ethical questions, closer examination will always show that it is some factual question upon which we disagree.[1] An examination of ethical arguments does not seem to bear this out, and Ayer later modified this claim. Stevenson has suggested that, although we do disagree about ethical questions, these disagreements are very different from disagreements in belief. In ethical disagreements one

[1] A. J. Ayer, Language, *Truth and Logic* (London: Victor Gollancz, 1948), p. 110.

does not present reasons which logically establish the truth of the ethical conclusion; rather one presents "reasons" which psychologically convince the hearer to accept one's attitude.[2] An examination of ethical arguments does not seem to bear this suggestion out either. It is not the case that in ethical discussions we consider anything which happens to convince the hearer as a reason: it is only those considerations which one himself finds convincing which he regards as genuine reasons. Ethical discussions seem to be more like attempts to establish the truth than to persuade one another without regard for truth. If this is all an illusion, the emotivist must explain why we continue to harbor this illusion.

This same "illusion" exists in the sphere of individual deliberation. Since our ethical attitudes are supposed to be logically independent of our beliefs, information would seem to be logically irrelevant to them. Why do we require such careful thought in arriving at a decision which is arbitrary in any case? Some reflection upon the facts might be explained as a technique for resolving one's own conflicts in attitude. Yet the mere making up the mind does not seem to satisfy us. We normally distinguish between the considered judgment of one who is well informed and the hasty judgment of one who is given to snap decisions. Why do we insist upon the importance of having all the facts and weighing them carefully, when these facts are logically irrelevant? On the emotive theory all that matters in deliberation is that the individual reach a fixed attitude. This does not seem to recognize sufficiently the individual's conviction that he might be mistaken. In short, to employ exclamations and imperatives as models of ethical language

[2] C. L. Stevenson, *Ethics and Language* (New Haven: Yale University Press, 1944), p. 168.

is to suggest that no questions of truth or falsity can arise in ethics. Yet an examination of what we actually think and say in ethical disagreement and deliberation indicates that our primary concern is with the truth of our ethical conclusions. One hesitates to admit that this is all an illusion.

Another difficulty is that the emotivists have not noticed that they are in fact using two distinct models. Exclamations and imperatives are used interchangeably as examples of emotive meaning. Both are nondescriptive; both seem to involve the emotions in some way. It is tempting to label them both "emotive" and consider them equivalent. The mere fact that both are nondescriptive, however, indicates no very great similarity; for there are many different kinds of nondescriptive language. And the fact that both involve the emotions proves no real identity unless it can be shown that they involve the same emotions and in the same way. Actually exclamations and imperatives illustrate quite distinct kinds of meaning.

That the distinctness of these two models is not noticed has led to some confusion when they are applied to ethical sentences. A comparison between exclamations and evaluations might well be helpful, for both seem to involve attitudes in some way. But to compare exclamations and judgments of obligation is not so helpful, for exclamations have only a very indirect relevance to action. In this respect imperatives seem more analogous to judgments of obligation. One cannot take imperatives as his model for evaluations, however; for while imperatives are limited to possible actions, evaluations can be made of objects as well as acts. The end result of the identification of exclamation and imperative is the failure to distinguish judgment of value from judgment of obligation. As I shall try to show later, these two kinds of ethical sentence have very different kinds of meaning. This important distinction between value and obligation has been obscured by the way in which the emotivist uses his models.

Even if the emotivist used his models more carefully, they would still be inadequate. Suppose that evaluations are interpreted in terms of exclamations only. To do this suggests that the key to evaluation is the notion of venting or releasing emotion, but this distorts evaluations in two ways. For one thing, this suggests that in evaluation we feel strongly and that we allow the agitation in our soul to escape through our verbal expression. Now at times we are very excited over moral issues, but more often value judgment is as calm and deliberate as any other form of judgment. The real relevance of attitudes for evaluation is not their emotional strength, but their character of being for or against their objects. The model which he chooses tempts the emotivist to neglect this pro-con aspect and to over-emphasize the emotional one. For another thing, the emotivist's model neglects one important feature of evaluation. Expression is a matter of the relation of the language used to that within the speaker which it expresses; venting is a relation between verbal utterance and speaker. But in evaluation the important relation is not so much that between language and speaker as that between language and object. Evaluations are *about* their objects in a more important way than exclamations are about anything. "Damn" may be shouted at a man, but it is not predicated of the man as "evil" might be. Concentration upon the sentence as expressing the speaker's feelings obscures the fact that the crux of evaluation lies in what the sentence says about the object evaluated.

Again, suppose that imperatives are taken as models of judgments of obligation and not evaluations. Still, it does not make sense to now tell someone to do something in the past, but judgments of obligation can be in the past tense without any straining of their meaning. If the two have fundamentally the same sort of meaning, it would be a mystery why only one of them becomes senseless in the past tense. Moreover, imperatives seem peculiarly at home in the second person, but judgments of obligation have no more affinity for one person than any other. One suspects that this difference reflects some distinction of meaning obscured by the model which the emotivist chooses. On the whole, then, the models which the emotivist uses to enlighten ethical language confuse as much as they clarify. The emotive theory of meaning does not supply us with an adequate interpretation of the meaning of ethical sentences.

6. *Objective Validity*

The point at which I find the emotivist interpretation of ethical sentences most objectionable is that at which it denies that ethical sentences can have any objective validity. Ethical sentences seem to be true or false; we commonly speak of them as true or false. Why does the emotivist deny their objectivity? It is because he is convinced that they express attitudes. Since attitudes are personal and nonrational, the sentences which put them into words must be equally nonrational. This assumption that attitudes, because of their very nature, can have no objective validity is a common one. Those who stoutly maintain the objectivity of ethical judgments feel bound to deny that they express attitudes; those who have come to the conclusion that ethical judgments express attitudes feel that they must deny their objectivity. In spite of the fact that this assumption is so common, I wish to challenge it. My fourth major objection to the emotive theory of ethics is that it mistakenly assumes that attitudes are not subject to rational criticism.

(1) It is often pointed out that attitudes have definite psychological causes. We explain his hate for the Germans by the fact that his mother and father were killed in a concentration camp; we realize that her infatuation is the result of sexual attraction. Our attitudes, like physiological reactions, are the product of the organism reacting to its environment.

I would not deny that attitudes have such causes; I only point out that beliefs do also. My knowledge of geography was caused by my teacher and my beliefs about economics were absorbed uncritically from the newspapers. The fact that beliefs have causes, however, does not alter the fact that they are subject to rational criticism. Why should the psychological origin of attitudes destroy their rationality?

(2) We feel love or hate, approval or disapproval; attitudes are to be classed with our feelings. But feelings, such as hunger or pain, are no more true or false than the mere sensation of redness is; where there is no cognitive reference beyond the pure datum, the question of validity cannot arise. Feelings, and thus attitudes, are below the level of objective validity.

Now in one sense attitudes are indeed feelings; they are felt and our awareness of them is immediate. But it does not follow that attitudes are feelings in the sense that pain and the sensation of red are. Attitudes are not self-contained states of consciousness; rather they refer beyond themselves to their objects. Attitudes are felt toward or about something. We cannot, therefore, deny their objectivity on the grounds that they do not refer beyond the momentary given.

(3) The emotivists have taken exclamations as a prime example of emotive meaning. Now "hurrah" seems to be

a way of letting off emotional steam. This was suggested to the emotivists that the attitudes expressed in emotive language are agitations or commotions within the soul. Attitudes may, of course, be emotions; but they need not be. Emotions, in the sense that is relevant here, are agitations of the spirit which are felt intensely. The definitive trait of attitudes is not their emotional intensity, but their character of being for or against their objects. Thus it is a mistake to think of attitudes as essentially mental commotions. An attitude may or may not be emotional.

But even if attitudes were always emotional, this need not destroy their objective validity. Emotions are relatively intense feelings which are apt to be disturbing; they are often so disturbing that they sweep aside our critical faculties. They are blind and impetuous, are not deliberately felt, and may even destroy the capacity to deliberate. For this reason emotions are often branded as irrational, and so many of them are. But this is quite a different thing from being *non*rational, for rational criticism is presupposed in branding the emotion irrational. To hold that emotion is irrational is to grant its objectivity, for only reason can determine what is contrary to reason.

No doubt emotion often interferes with the exercise of reason and may override rational judgment. This is unfortunate but logically irrelevant. The syllogism is not made invalid by the fact that many are too hurried to follow its reasoning; its validity remains to criticize their jumping to a conclusion. In emotion also the validity may remain to brand the impulsive attitude as irrational. Terror, for example, might be unjustified when there is no danger. If emotions may claim objectivity, so might attitudes.

(4) It is a commonly accepted maxim that there is no disputing about tastes. If we can get to the bottom of this saying, we shall realize what tempts people to treat attitudes

119

as beyond rational argument. For one thing, it is often difficult to make the grounds of one's judgment of taste explicit. The taste of a wine is so simple that it defies description; it is just this taste, and its flavor cannot be captured in words. It is the flavor which justifies my liking the wine, but I cannot convey this unique and unanalyzable taste in my words. What, then, can I say to justify my liking this wine? The reason I have for my liking is what I taste when I sip the wine, but I cannot state this reason to others or even to myself. As another example take my dislike of a certain painting. Here the given is no longer too simple to be described. I can, in fact, make many true descriptive judgments about what I see when I look at the painting. Yet these are all abstract and indeterminate in comparison to the rich concreteness of the visual presentation. I cannot catch its sensuous fullness and complex structure in words. Here again it is impossible for me to formulate in language the grounds of my attitude. Yet this does not prove that I have no grounds, that my judgment is beyond reason. One may have reasons which he cannot give; some reasoning starts with premises which escape formulation. This in no way destroys the objective validity of one's judgment, although it makes verbal defense of it impossible. Dispute, which must use language as a medium, becomes useless. But validity remains, for one can still directly confront the experience of sipping the wine or seeing the painting.

Another factor which makes us less willing to dispute over questions of taste is that we are unsure of our own opinions in such matters. When we are unsure of our judgments of taste, we insist upon their correctness less firmly. We are not fully convinced that our judgments of taste are correct. When we turn to others for corroboration, we find that often they are either of the opposite opinion or without any fixed opinion at all. We remember how frequently we have changed our minds in the past about questions of taste. We find it difficult or impossible to find convincing evidence for our judgments. For all these reasons we relax our claim to objectivity, but this does not destroy the genuineness of the claim. The fact that it is hard to know which opinion is right makes dogmatic assertion irrational, but it does not show that no opinion is right. In fact, we can be in doubt over the correctness of any judgment only when the question of correctness remains. Tolerance may well replace dispute when tentative conclusions are all that is possible. But even tentative conclusions are arrived at and criticizable by reason.

Finally, we find by bitter experience that dispute over matters of taste is ineffective. We talk ourselves blue in the face, and still our obstinate friends refuse to agree with us. Since argument proves unable to settle differences of opinion in this area, we stop wasting our efforts in such an idle and ineffective use of words. I would not wish to deny that it is often practically foolish to dispute about questions of taste; what I do deny is that this proves that there is no distinction between right and wrong here. One judgment may remain right even though we cannot reach agreement upon which it is. Agreement is not the basis of our knowledge of which opinion is correct; rather agreement presupposes individual judgment upon the correct opinion. Each person must judge in the light of the evidence. Agreement is the product, not the premise, of such reasoning. Thus the fact that disagreement cannot be resolved does not show that there is no correct or incorrect opinion; on the contrary, disagreement is genuine only when it is a difference of opinion over which of the two judgments is the right one.

We are inclined to say that there is no disputing about questions of taste because in these matters we are often

unable to state the reasons for our judgments, our own uncertainty makes us reduce our claim to correctness, and
discussion proves unable to arrive at agreement. We have
seen that none of these factors proves that the distinction
of correct and incorrect does not apply to judgments of
taste. Neither will analogous considerations prove that
attitudes have no objective validity.

(5) Perhaps the fact that attitudes are genuinely right or
wrong comes out most clearly in our experience of changing
our minds. I decide that I really dislike the profession which
I once thought that I loved, or I come to respect the man
whom I once despised. Such a change is not merely a
transformation, but a reversal. As I grow older I change my
height. Yet my new inches do not disprove my old height
or lead me to conclude that I was mistaken to be so short
before. When one changes one's mind, however, the new
state of mind forces one to condemn the old one. When
one arrives at a new attitude, his old attitude is not merely
replaced, but it is also judged to have been incorrect.

This is not true even of all mental states. Suppose that I
become hungry after a big meal. I would not say that my
hunger was wrong to come upon me so early, nor would its
disappearance upon taking a short nap show that it had been
mistaken. But my changes in attitude are often of exactly this
nature; additional experience may lead me to conclude that
an attitude I once held was mistaken. It is in the experience
of realizing that our past attitudes have sometimes been
mistaken that we recognize the claim to objective validity
which attitudes possess.

(6) It is often claimed that, while the experience to which
I refer is genuine, my interpretation of it is incorrect. When
I decide that I was wrong to love Mary, it is not that I find
my attitude to have been mistaken; rather I find that my
beliefs about her were false. Perhaps I discovered that her

bank account was not as large as she had hinted or that she did not make quite such good pies as her mother had led me to believe. In any case, my attitude was mistaken only in the loose sense that it presupposed mistaken beliefs.

No doubt mistakes in attitudes often are the result of erroneous beliefs. I may have loved Mary because I thought that she was a good cook. In this case the error in my attitude is obviously based upon that in my belief, and my attitude will change as soon as I taste her cooking. There are times, however, when I come to the conclusion that my attitude has been mistaken without discovering any mistaken belief. It is quite possible that I loved Mary without believing that she was a good cook and yet changed my attitude when I first tasted her loathsome pies. Here it is the attitude itself which was mistaken, for no error in belief was present.

It might be objected that the belief must have been at least presupposed by the attitude or the attitude would not have been affected by the quality of Mary's cooking. But in what sense was the belief presupposed? It cannot have been logically presupposed, for to admit this would be to grant my point that attitudes are subject to rational criticism. Perhaps the belief was presupposed in the sense that it was implicit within the attitude; to love Mary includes believing, in a confused way, that she is a good cook.

It seems to me that it is very misleading to talk as though I must have believed in Mary's culinary skill all along. By the ordinary criteria of believing, I need have no such belief. I might not have been conscious of this belief. If asked to justify my attitude, I might not have given this belief as a reason to support it. If asked to describe Mary, I might not have mentioned her abilities as a cook. If asked whether she was a good cook, I might even have answered that I did not know. (To such a question I would be tempted to reply

123

that, after all, I cannot be expected to think of everything. Yet this is precisely what is required by the theory in question.) Finally, I might greet my discovery that her cooking was unspeakably poor with disappointment but without surprise. By what right, then, does one suggest that I *must* have had the belief or my attitude would not have changed? We should reject the theory that attitudes are corrigible only through the beliefs which accompany them. More plausible is the view that attitudes may themselves be right or wrong.

(7) The need to deny validity to attitudes comes partly from an unfortunately narrow concept of validity. We all recognize that statements which are empirically true or false are objectively valid. It is clear that descriptive correspondence provides a criterion of correctness in all such assertions. Moreover, we soon come to realize that the standards of validity extend beyond the boundaries of descriptive truth. An inference may be valid even when it moves from false premises to false conclusion. Also, the standards of validity apply to abstract deductive systems quite independently of any considerations of descriptive truth. Almost everyone would be willing to grant that empirical description and deductive logic possess genuine validity. We feel at home with these and are confident that they can be trusted; in these areas there are generally recognized methods of determining truth or error. Most people agree that we can justifiably believe whatever can be immediately seen to be empirically true or which can be deduced from such premises.

Now there are some who would hold that this is all that we can really know. Experience and deduction are our only two standards of rational belief; whatever goes beyond them can claim no objective validity. This is not enough. Living in this world requires extrapolation beyond the given in a manner which deduction will not justify; it is precisely here that the problem of induction arises. I wish to suggest that inductive extrapolation does give us knowledge; past experience does give us good, although not conclusive, reason to believe that the sun will rise tomorrow. That inductive inference is valid is recognized nonempirically in just the same way that the validity of deduction is perceived. This step of admitting that valid inference extends beyond deduction is the big one; the limits of validity are now open rather than closed.

However, the big step is not the only step. Both deduction and induction are formal in character. The validity of the reasoning is independent of the subject-matter and depends only upon the form of argument used. Thus the correctness of the argument depends solely upon the use of certain logical constants and can be tested by a formulated criterion or schema. It would be convenient if all valid reasoning were formal, but this is not so. Science involves more than extrapolation. It does not rest content with inference from experienced instances to additional instances of the same nature; it also embodies explanatory hypotheses. These integrate the phenomena into systems of thought by reducing the many experienced and predicted facts to certain fundamental categories or models. Explanatory reasoning argues from the facts to be explained to the hypothesis which renders them intelligible. This reasoning is just as valid as deduction and induction and is known to be cogent in the same way. Yet it differs from these other modes of reasoning in being nonformal.

We must be careful not to deny that any sort of argument is genuine reasoning because it does not fit our preconceptions of what reasoning should be. Some would limit valid reasoning to deduction. Others would admit induction as well but would limit rational inference to arguments

THE LANGUAGE OF ETHICS

which can be formalized. It seems to me that neither limitation can be maintained. The fact that attitudes cannot be deduced from descriptions of the given or that there is no formal mode of reasoning which will justify them, therefore, does not prove that they are without objective validity. Once we have realized how various are the forms which reasoning takes, we can accept the idea that attitudes might be rationally grounded also.

(8) That this is the case is supported by the fact that we distinguish between rational and irrational attitudes in everyday speech. Attitudes are frequently thought to be appropriate or inappropriate, suitable or unsuitable. Respect is suitable to an upright man, but is most inappropriate towards a scoundrel. It is sensible to like pleasure but quite irrational to desire pain. Since we ordinarily recognize the possibility of rational criticism of our attitudes, we at least assume that they have objectivity.

(9) The last and crucial argument to show that attitudes are rational is that there are reasons for and against them. Their correctness or incorrectness is shown by the fact that there are considerations relevant to their rational justification. That Mary is a poor cook is a reason for not loving her. That John enjoys hurting animals is a good reason for disapproving of him. The rationality of attitudes is shown by the existence of considerations by which they may be rationally criticized.

To call this an argument is, perhaps, a bit misleading. I can hardly claim to *prove* the validity of attitudes; I can only appeal to the reader's own sense of their objectivity. I contend that there are grounds which support or weaken attitudes. Whether or not my claim is correct can be determined only be each individual's reason. It is to the reason of each reader that I appeal. In rational matters that is all one can do; fortunately it is all one need do. When I reflect upon the considerations which might be said to be relevant to this or that attitude, it seems to me that they are genuine reasons. All those whose reflections indicate the same thing must agree with me that attitudes have a genuine claim to objective validity. To recognize this is to give up the assumption which the emotivists accept as so obvious that it requires little support and which I have been arguing against at such length.

7. Recapitulation

The question to which I have been trying to find a satisfactory answer is "What do ethical sentences mean?" Both ethical naturalism and ethical intuitionism assumed that in one way or another their meaning must be descriptive. But challenging this preconception the emotive theory of ethics marks a sharp break with past theories of language. It underlines the need for a wider concept of meaning and new methods of semantical analysis. In these ways it prepares the way for a deeper understanding of the language of ethics.

At the same time, the emotive theory of ethics does not itself give us this fuller understanding of ethical language. The more obvious lines of reasoning, at least, do not compel one to interpret ethical sentences emotively. The basic dichotomy of cognitive vs. emotive meaning is too simple to tell us very much about ethical language. The models which the emotive theory uses obscure more than they clarify. And one cannot assume that ethical sentences have no objective validity simply because they express attitudes. In short, the emotive theory of ethics does not give us an adequate interpretation of the meaning of ethical sentences. Can we find some other approach which will do greater justice to the complexity of ordinary language?

— V —

The Ordinary-Language

Approach

So far we have considered three answers to the question "What do ethical sentences mean?" Ethical naturalism holds that ethical sentences are essentially empirical descriptions. Ethical intuitionism maintains that they are descriptions of a nonnatural subject matter. The emotive theory of ethics contends that, although they may have some slight descriptive content, their primary meaning is emotive. Where do philosophers such as Hampshire, Hart, Urmson, MacDonald, Toulmin, Hare, Nowell-Smith, and Baier belong in this classification? It would be unfair to put them into any of these categories, for they all insist that all three of these answers are inadequate.

Nor would it be quite accurate to say that these philosophers present one more answer to our central question. Although each has something to say in answer to our question, they do not agree on what kind of meaning ethical sentences do possess. Hampshire seems to locate the characteristically ethical use of language in its quasi-imperative force. Hart argues that the language of ascription is not unlike certain legal terminology. Urmson points out that value words are similar to grading words in certain respects. MacDonald uses the language of ceremonials and rituals as her model of ethical language. For Toulmin ethical sentences mold our attitudes and actions into a social harmony. Hare locates the central use of ethical sentences in their prescriptiveness. Nowell-Smith hints at several uses of ethical sentences, although he relates them all to the context of choice. Baier claims that ethical sentences declare which action is supported by the best reasons. Clearly there is no party line here. Although these various interpretations of ethical sentences are not always incompatible with one another, they can hardly be said to represent a single theory of the nature of ethical language.

At the same time, it would be a mistake to regard these various positions as entirely unrelated. Although their answers to our central question differ, their approach is the same. They do not agree on what kind of meaning ethical sentences have, but they do agree on how the problem of ethical language should be attacked. Perhaps it would not be unfair to label this way of attacking the analysis of ethical sentences the ordinary-language approach to ethics. In this chapter I shall be concerned both with the presuppositions which lie behind the approach and with its current results.

1. *Principal Presuppositions*

Since those who employ this approach usually do not explain the principles which underlie their practice, I shall take some pains to make them explicit. Probably the defining presupposition is the thesis that ethical sentences have a meaning all their own. In fact, this approach might well borrow the motto of *Principia Ethica:* "Everything is what it is, and not another thing." For Moore this implies that the property of goodness cannot be reduced to any other property. The ordinary-language approach might construe the same motto as condemning any attempt to reduce ethical sentences to any other kind of sentence. The meaning of ethical sentences is the ethical use of language, and not another use of language.

As exemplified in the writings of those who practice the ordinary-language approach, this presupposition is essentially negative. It does not tell us what the ethical use of language is. We have seen that those who accept this approach do not agree on any single theory about the nature of ethical sentences. They do agree, however, that ethical sentences are neither empirical descriptions, nor nonempirical descriptions, nor emotive utterances. The real point of the principle, then, lies in rejecting ethical naturalism, ethical intuitionism, and the emotive theory of ethics.

Associated with this defining presupposition are several others. One of these is that the meaning of a word is its use in the language. This concept of meaning, which originated with Wittgenstein, seems to be taken for granted by all the practitioners of the ordinary-language approach. The meaning of this slogan, to judge by its use, is twofold.

130

Words have many uses, and each use involves many aspects. The ordinary-language approach to language is doubly pluralistic.

There are many distinct kinds of meaning. It is a mistake to try to reduce all language to one favorite model, such as the combination of names or empirical prediction. Words can be used for very different purposes: to record information, to cause action, to create delightful sounds, to release emotions, to fill awkward gaps in the conversation, to make promises, and so forth. Even the scientist does not use observation reports, mathematical principles, and scientific theories in the same way. These various uses are radically diverse and need not have anything in common. Moreover, the multiplicity of the uses of language is essential to its nature as an instrument in the many activities of living.

To complicate matters further, any single use of a word involves a wide variety of factors. The study of meaning cannot limit itself to the mental pictures which are assumed to accompany our use of words. Nor can it think of words exclusively as names of properties. Nor can it assume that all words are signs of objects. One cannot even take it for granted that the method of verification is the only relevant feature of a sentence. All of these theories oversimplify the meaning words possess. Actually the meaning of a word includes every feature of the way in which the word is used. The tone of voice, facial expression, or accompanying gesture may be just as important for understanding language as anything else. To grasp the use of a word we must know everything about the situation in which the word is used and how the word functions in that situation. Clearly a great many things enter into the meaning of a word.

It is this general presupposition that the meaning of any

word is its use in the language which obviously suggests the ordinary language approach to ethics. If words have many different uses, it is likely that ethical words have their own special use. Thus the view that ethical sentences have a meaning all their own is derived from a general conception of the nature of language. It follows that to treat ethical language as a peculiar sort of description or emotive utterance is just a special case of the more general attempt to reduce all words to one preconceived pattern.

A second presupposition associated with the ordinary-language approach is that the only effective way to analyze the meaning of a word or sentence is to describe its use in detail. If everything involved in the use of a word is included in its meaning, clearly all these things must be contained in any analysis of the word's meaning. We come to understand what a word means by noticing how it is used and then setting down what we have noticed in an orderly fashion. We would notice what kinds of situation the word is used in, what facial expressions and gestures accompany its use, how the hearers react to it, the grammar of the sentences in which it appears, how (or whether) the speaker justifies his use of the word, what other expressions are taken as synonymous, and so so. Obviously any such analysis would be exceedingly detailed and concrete.

In this respect, among others, the analyses required by the ordinary language approach differ from ordinary definitions. To be sure, most dictionary definitions are very brief descriptions of the way in which a word is actually used. As descriptions of use they are similar to the suggested analyses, but it is in their lack of detail that they fall short. As a result, although they provide helpful hints to someone who does not know the language, they are not much help in clarifying the use of a word to someone who is already familiar with it. The philosopher does not need help in learning his language so much as in understanding more fully the language he has learned long ago.

Philosophical definitions were traditionally conceived of as analyses of the essence of the class named by the definiendum. But if we reject the notion that all words are names, this type of definition has a restricted applicability at best. This method would seem particularly unpromising in ethics, for the peculiarities of ethical words strongly suggest that they are not merely class names. Moreover, this type of definition is rather too Platonic for those who have taken Wittgenstein seriously. Even a word which does refer to a class need not stand for some essence shared by all members of that class; the word may stand for a family resemblance instead.

More recently, philosophical definitions have been interpreted as stating an equivalence of meaning between two linguistic expressions. The word to be defined is simply equated with some clearer expression which could be substituted for it without loss of meaning. This technique can be helpful in clarifying certain words; an obscure expression can sometimes be replaced by a more intelligible one. In every such case, however, the original expression is analyzed into another expression of the same kind; for if the definiens had a different linguistic use, it would not be synonymous with the definiendum. This method, therefore, cannot be used to clarify the meaning of an entire class of words of a given kind, for it always requires that one understand at least some words in the class. In particular, it throws no light on the ways in which one *kind* of word differs from another, and it is here that philosophical problems arise. It would appear that none of the standard types of definition are much help for philosophical purposes.

I have been assuming that the purpose of a definition

is to explain what we normally mean by some word. It might be contended, however, that the real purpose of a philosophical definition, as opposed to a dictionary definition, is not to report linguistic usage. There would be no point in a definition which faithfully reproduced all the vagueness and ambiguity of ordinary language. The true virtue of any method of definition is to give a new and clearer meaning to the word defined. In effect, philosophical definitions substitute a new and more precise language for our inadequate everyday language.

The proposal that we can best attain clarity by constructing a more ideal language is rejected by the proponents of the ordinary-language approach. In fact, it is from their insistence that philosophy should not attempt to replace our ordinary language with a more perfect substitute that my label for this group is derived. It is not that they see anything wrong with precise language. Such technical language is helpful, and even indispensable, for certain purposes. What is the purpose of this ideal philosophical language? Presumably to help us solve our philosophical problems. But since philosophical problems arise out of our everyday use of language, any technical philosophical jargon will prove useless. If it cannot serve the purposes for which we use our ordinary language, it will be no true substitute for it. We will have to continue to use our everyday language for the purposes of everyday living, and the old philosophical problems will continue to arise. If this new language does fulfill our everyday needs, it will be forced to reproduce in new forms the logically distressing features of our everyday language; for the nature of a linguistic expression reflects its use. Besides, how will we construct this ideal language? The techniques of definition presuppose the existence of a language, and what other language can we start with but our everyday one? Therefore, we cannot hope to dispense with ordinary language as a whole. The real problem is not to replace ordinary language with a clearer one, but to become clearer about our language as it is. The only effective way to do this is through detailed descriptions of the ways in which words are actually used.

A third presupposition associated with the ordinary-language approach is that ethical sentences have a logic all their own. This might seem to be simply a corollary of the definitive thesis of this approach. Positivists, pragmatists, and other analysts have taught us to recognize that meaning and verification are intimately connected. If ethical sentences have a meaning all their own, it would seem to follow necessarily that they have a logic all their own as well. At times this transition does seem to be taken as so obvious that it needs no justification.

It would be quite possible, however, to make exactly the opposite inference. If ethical sentences have a meaning all their own, they cannot be either empirical descriptions or analytic propositions. Thus they cannot be established either by empirical verification or by logical analysis. Since these are the only two ways of rationally justifying statements, they cannot have any claim to objective validity. In short, the discovery that ethical language has certain peculiarities which set it off from the language of empirical science and mathematics might be taken to imply that there can be no logic of ethical sentences. Stevenson, for example, has argued that specifically ethical "reasoning" is not strictly logical at all.

This is precisely the conclusion which the ordinary language approach denies. The fact that ethical sentences have a meaning all their own does indeed imply that they cannot be verified in the same way that scientific sentences can. It need not imply, however, that they are beyond all rational criticism. Even in the case of exclamations and imperatives, which no one would dream of considering true or false, there is a distinction between the correct and the incorrect use of language. To shout "hurrah" when one breaks his leg is not only odd but, to borrow an expression used in a related context, linguistically odd. Similarly there is a real difference between the legitimate and illegitimate use of an ethical sentence. There are certain criteria which objectively determine when a given ethical expression can be correctly used. One of the criteria for the use of ethical sentences is that the speaker can justify his utterance. It is possible to give reasons for and against ethical statements. This process of justification is quite different from, but no less objective than, the special logics of deductive and inductive argument. In this sense ethical language has a logic all its own.

These seem to me to be the most important presuppositions of the ordinary language approach to ethics. The definitive thesis is that ethical sentences have a meaning all their own. Associated with this insistence upon the autonomy of ethical language are certain other assertions. The meaning of a word is its use in the language. The only philosophically effective way to analyze the meaning of a word is to describe its use in detail. Finally, ethical sentences have a logic all their own. Together these presuppositions constitute a theoretical framework which determines the way in which the problem of the meaning of ethical sentences is to be attacked.

The importance of these presuppositions seem to lie in the recommendations which they suggest. Do not try to reduce ethical language to nonethical language. Do not have too narrow a concept of what meaning is. Do not hope to achieve clarity by definition or translation. Do not assume that there are no objective standards for the justification of nonscientific statements. Like the ten commandments, these injunctions seem to be predominantly negative, but perhaps we can see one positive suggestion in this approach. If you wish to resolve your philosophical problems about the nature of ethical language, describe the way these sentences are actually used. The ordinary-language approach to ethics consists of following these recommendations.

My own approach to the problem of the meaning of ethical language is along similar lines. My objections to the ordinary-language movement are not so much to its approach as to the philosophical position by which this approach is justified. If properly understood, these recommendations constitute excellent advice to anyone investigating the meaning of ethical sentences. It does not seem to me, however, that they have generally been understood correctly. This is probably because of a certain lack of clarity in the presuppositions that lie behind the ordinary language approach. When this approach is put into practice, therefore, the inadequacy of its presuppositions is reflected in the unsatisfactory nature of its results. I shall try to explain why I object to these presuppositions and where they lead one astray.

2. The Ethical Use of Language

Let us begin with the central presupposition of the ordinary-language approach, the principle that ethical sentences have a meaning all their own. At times this seems to be interpreted as asserting that the meaning of ethical sentences is the ethical use of language and not another use of language. On this interpretation the principle is almost tautological. Of course the ethical use of language must not be confused with any nonethical use of language.

This is simply a special case of the logical principle that P and non-P, in this case "ethical" and "nonethical," are logical contradictories. It is obviously a mistake to try to reduce ethical sentences to some kind of nonethical sentence.

Those who practice the ordinary language approach agree that ethical naturalism, ethical intuitionism, and the emotive theory of ethics all make this obvious mistake. But are these theories so obviously mistaken? The ethical naturalist stoutly maintains that ethical sentences do in fact provide empirical descriptions. The ethical intuitionist contends that ethical sentences predicate certain nonnatural characteristics of objects or acts. The emotivist argues that the characteristically ethical use of language is to evince and evoke emotions. Before these suggested analyses can be ruled out, it must be shown in detail that these uses of language are in fact nonethical. To assume without proof that these theories reduce ethical language to nonethical language is to beg the question of which uses of language are genuinely ethical.

The ordinary-language approach is, then, faced with a mildly embarrassing dilemma. If its central presupposition is interpreted as asserting only that ethical language is not nonethical language, then it is obviously tautological and requires no defense. The rejection of existing theories of ethical language cannot, however, be justified solely by appealing to such a tautology. To the degree that the principle is obvious it is also empty. If the principle is interpreted to imply that ethical sentences do not have descriptive or emotive meaning, then it becomes strong enough to rule out ethical naturalism, ethical intuitionism, and the emotive theory of ethics. At this point, however, it is no longer tautologous. It requires a good deal of analysis and argument to show exactly which uses of language are ethical and which are not. While the more responsible practitioners of the ordinary-language approach have attempted to show in detail why ethical sentences cannot be empirical descriptions, nonempirical descriptions, or emotive utterances, others seem to consider this too obvious to call for any reasoned justification. The principle that ethical sentences have a meaning all their own is an excellent motto, but it is no substitute for philosophical argument. As long as the precise meaning of this principle remains unclear, it will remain an invitation to dogmatism.

Clearly one should not confuse the ethical use of words with any nonethical use of language. In this sense, at least, ethical words do have a meaning all their own. But does this imply that all ethical words have the same kind of meaning? To speak of *the* ethical use of words strongly suggests that there is one and only one linguistic function which ethical words can properly fulfill. I believe that in fact ethical words have several distinct uses, although they may be related by some sort of family resemblance. This possibility that the language of ethics performs several functions is, in fact, strongly suggested by the linguistic pluralism which the ordinary-language approach accepts. Although there is nothing in the ordinary-language approach which requires that all ethical sentences have the same kind of meaning, some of its representatives, such as Toulmin and Hare, seem to assume that there is only one use of language which is truly ethical. We must be careful not to overemphasize the "a" when we assert that ethical sentences have a meaning all their own.

We must also be careful about stressing "all their own." Obviously it would be a mistake to reduce the ethical use of language to any nonethical use; but it would also be a mistake to assume too quickly that a given use is nonethical. The claim that ethical sentences cannot be empirical descriptions, nonnatural descriptions, or emotive utterances must be defended in detail. The problem is complicated by the fact that there may be several ethical uses of language and that there certainly are many nonethical uses of language. Can we be sure that none of these many uses of language is ever shared by any species of ethical sentence and some species of nonethical sentence? Perhaps ethical sentences do not *all* have a meaning *all* their own.

In short, if the presupposition that ethical sentences have a meaning all their own is to have any point, it must draw some distinction between the ethical use or uses and the nonethical uses of language. How can the ordinary language approach enable us to distinguish ethical from nonethical uses of language? The easy way, of course, would be to propose a stipulative definition for "ethical use of language." But this would hardly settle anything, for the naturalist, intuitionist, and emotivist could each propose his own definition.

Another way would be to appeal to our language sense. Since we already know ordinary language, we must know the difference between ethical words and nonethical words. Certainly. We know very well when to use words like "good," "wrong," and "ought" and when not to use them. But this is not the problem. Knowing how to use words is not at all the same as knowing what we are doing when we use them. The problem is to establish a theory about the nature of ethical language. Apparently our language sense is not much help here, for naturalists, intuitionists, and emotivists continue to disagree. Their language sense does not tell them that they are all mistaken.

If our familiarity with ordinary language will not enable us to agree about the essence of ethical language, perhaps it will help us to recognize some examples of it. By avoiding borderline instances we might be able to agree that a few sample sentences were fairly typical of ethical language. It would be convenient if we could also collect a representative group of sentences which were admittedly nonethical. This would give us some ordinary language to approach in the approved manner. We could describe in detail exactly how each of these sentences is used, and possibly we could draw some conclusions about the nature of the distinction between ethical and nonethical language. Personally, I would endorse such a program wholeheartedly. This appears to me to be an excellent way to approach the problem of the nature of ethical language.

Unfortunately, this program does not seem to have been carried out by the representatives of the ordinary-language approach. As a rule, the exponents of this approach fall into one of two groups. Some of them, like Hart and Urmson, restrict themselves to pointing out similarities between the use of one or a few ethical words and some other set of words. This limited analysis is certainly legitimate and may be illuminating, but it does not help us to draw the distinction between ethical and nonethical language in general. Others, like Toulmin and Hare, seem to approach the language of ethics with a fixed conception of its essence. Although Toulmin's entire argument in *Reason in Ethics* hinges on the assumption that the real function of ethical language is to harmonize the attitudes and actions of individuals in such a way as to make society possible, he does not, as far as I have been able to find, give any justification for this crucial assertion. Hare announces on the first page of *The Language of Morals* that "the function of moral principles is to guide conduct." Although he does present reasons to show that if ethical sentences are to guide conduct they must be similar to

141

imperatives in being prescriptive, he presents no reasons in support of his claim that they do in fact guide conduct.

Probably Nowell-Smith comes closer than anyone else to combining the virtues of both groups. He attempts to describe the various uses of ethical sentences in such a way as to clarify differences of meaning, and at the same time he tries to show their relations in the total fabric of ethical language. Still, he does not actually carry out the program I outlined above. In his *Ethics*, at least, he does not derive his descriptions of the various uses of ethical language from a detailed examination of particular sentences in their concrete situations of use. Moreover, he is so much aware of the variety of ethical language that he never does give any clear statement of what makes it specifically ethical. Finally, he seems to assume without proof that in some unexplained way all ethical sentences function within the context of choice.

As far as I have been able to discover, none of the representatives of the ordinary-language approach succeeds in explaining exactly what the ethical use of language is or how it differs from the various nonethical uses of language. Until this is done their insistence that ethical sentences have a meaning all their own remains somewhat empty.

3. *Meaning as Use*

Let us turn from the definitive thesis of the ordinary-language approach to those presuppositions associated with it. The first of these is that the meaning of a word is its use in the language. This principle has been widely used as a sort of slogan to warn us against the muddles in the accepted theories of meaning. Not every word, it is pointed out, is the name of some object; in fact, genuine names are relatively uncommon in our total vocabulary. One explains very little by assuming that the language we utter is accompanied by a series of mental pictures. There are many kinds of sentence where it is not very helpful to ask for the method of verification.

I agree that we need a concept of meaning which is wider than those repudiated by this slogan. My objection is that the slogan does little to replace these rejected theories with a more adequate conception of the nature of meaning. Certainly there is little to be gained by speaking of meanings as some sort of obscure entity hidden in the mind or in Plato's heaven. But I cannot see that it is much of an improvement to talk of the use of a word. What sort of an entity is a use, anyway? Perhaps I am being unfair in pushing the grammar of their slogan so far. To be sure, the representatives of the ordinary-language approach talk and write about uses (or jobs or functions) of words, but this is only a manner of speaking. They do not wish to imply that uses are entities of any sort. They insist that we must not think of a word and its use, but only of the word as used. Fine! Now please explain exactly what it is for a word to be used, what a person does with a word when he uses it. Unless this can be done, and so far it has not, the assertion that the meaning of a word is its use offers no positive insight into the nature of meaning.

But surely the slogan that the meaning of a word is its use must have some positive content. Well, let's see. It does claim that if we want to understand the meaning of some sentence we must not limit our attention to the method of verification or our mental pictures. But what else must we consider? We must take everything about the use of the sentence into consideration. Until we know what a use really is, however, we are hardly in a position to know what is included in it. Is everything about the way the word is spoken and every feature of the speech situation relevant to the meaning of the word? Then we should have to include the timbre of the speaker's voice, the regional accent of the speaker, the color of his tie, the color of the hearer's hair, and the exact time of day or night. Until we have some criterion for deciding precisely what is contained in the use of a word, we are not noticeably helped by being admonished to consider everything included in that use. The tone of voice or facial expression, for example, may be important to the meaning of what is said. This is particularly true of exclamations. It is not so clear that they are important to the meaning of some statement like "the chair is green." When should these be included in the meaning of what is said?

Another implication of the slogan that the meaning of a word is its use in the language is that language has many different uses. The very same words, it is said, can have several distinct uses on different, or even the same, occasion. To talk of the many distinct uses of language, however, has little point unless we are told how to distinguish between different uses. Unfortunately, it is far from clear what makes two uses two instead of one. To take one of the simpler examples, under what conditions may we say that two sentences have different uses? Not simply when they are uttered by different speakers or at different times or in voices of a different pitch. What criterion would enable us to decide whether "Hurrah" and "I am overjoyed" have the same or different uses? Hardly the mere fact that they seem to be saying different things, because two descriptive sentences can have the same use without being synonymous. As the disagreement over proposed definitions of ethical words clearly reveals, there is little agreement over either synonymy of meaning or difference of use. How, then, can we distinguish the different uses of language? Unless the ordinary-language approach can offer some criterion of the distinctness of uses, there is little to be gained by insisting that language has many uses instead of just one use.

One of the things which should be required of any adequate concept of meaning is that it be able to distinguish between meaningful and meaningless words and sentences. It should at least enable us to understand the difference between significant language and meaningless sounds. Will the slogan that the meaning of a word is its use in the language do this? Presumably any sound or shape which has a use in any language would be meaningful. This would seem to imply that no sound would be meaningless, for the mere fact that the sound is made would show that it has some use. Or is using a sound more than merely uttering it? Until it is explained clearly what it is to use a word, one is not in a position to deny significance to any utterance at all. The view we are considering does, of course, require that the word have a use *in the language*. It might be possible to declare certain sounds meaningless on the grounds that they are not properly linguistic. But what is a language? If one defines language as meaningful sounds or shapes, we are right back where we started. We have learned nothing about what distinguishes language from what is not language, the meaningful from what is not meaningful.

It seems to me that the principle that the meaning of a word is its use in the language has only limited usefulness. In one respect the import of this presupposition is quite clear. It is obviously a repudiation of the previously accepted theories of meaning. It reminds us, helpfully I think, that sentences are not just combinations of names, verbalized mental pictures, or verifiable predictions. On the other hand, it does not offer any new theory of meaning to replace

145

these inadequate ones. It presents no positive concept of meaning clear enough to be very helpful. In fairness to those who espouse the ordinary language approach it must be admitted that many of them do not pretend that this slogan is a theory of meaning. Wittgenstein, from whom they borrowed their slogan, explicitly disclaimed any intention of defining the essence of language or of meaning. I cannot refrain from adding, however, that if this is not meant to be a theory of meaning it should not be used as such. Somehow the insight that the meaning of a word is its use in the language is supposed to be the key to understanding the nature of language and to resolving problems of meaning. Aside from its negative implications, however, I doubt whether this concept is precise enough to be very helpful.

4. *A Method of Clarification*

Perhaps we can best discover how helpful this conception of language is by examining the practical advice suggested by it. The best way to analyze the meaning of a word or sentence is to describe its use in detail. This is the second presupposition associated with the ordinary-language approach to ethics. Here is some definite advice about the most effective method of clarifying the meaning of any philosophically troublesome expression. As I have already suggested, the proponents of the ordinary-language approach seldom do give detailed and concrete descriptions of the use of ethical sentences. The fact that they often do not use the method they advocate raises the question of its true usefulness.

We are advised to describe the use of any word or sentence whose meaning puzzles us. How de we discover the use of a word? Clearly the ordinary-language approach objects strongly to simple introspection. It would be a great mistake to think of the meaning of a word as some mental picture or mental act of intending which accompanies our use of the word and of which we are immediately aware. We are not, therefore, to look into our minds and discover our meanings by direct inspection.

We might, of course, observe someone else using the word. We can see and hear the person using the word. We can see or hear the word he is using. It is not obvious to me that we can see or hear the use itself. Suppose we hear someone say "ouch," see his contorted face, and feel the warm sticky blood oozing from his cut finger. How are we supposed to decide what he is doing with the word? He might be describing his pain, or expressing his feelings, or calling for help, or simply releasing air from his lungs. It does not seem to me that we can tell how he is using the word simply by looking and listening. More likely we guess what he means by imaginatively putting ourselves in his place. We ask ourselves what we would mean by this word said in the same way in the same situation.

If this is so, the ordinary-language approach does not really avoid an appeal to our own awareness of what we mean. Detailed explanations of the nature of our sense of meaning and careful justifications of its use are surprisingly absent from the writings of those who practice the ordinary-language approach. They seem to assume that somehow or other our familiarity with ordinary language will tell us how its various words and sentences are used. As I have pointed out before, there are two senses in which one might know how a word is used. He might be able to use the word correctly and correctly interpret others when they use the word, or he might be able to characterize the use of the word correctly. We certainly do know how the words in our everyday vocabulary are used in the first sense; we can speak, write, and interpret them easily and without misunderstanding. In the second sense, however, we do not seem to know how our words are used. The very fact that we seem unable to agree on whether the naturalist, intuitionist, emotivist, or none of these has correctly characterized ethical language shows clearly that appealing to our awareness of what we mean settles little. How can we derive reliable knowledge *that* a word's use is such and such from merely knowing *how* to use the word? Until this question is answered, one does not know how to go about discovering the use of any puzzling word.

But suppose that we did discover the use of a word. How could we describe it? First of all, we must decide what is to be included in our description of the use. Must our description refer to the hesitation in the speaker's voice, the color of his hair, and the boredom on the face of the listener? At this point the vagueness of the concept of use results in a corresponding vagueness in the advice to describe the use. Moreover, it seems doubtful whether we have, or even could have, a vocabulary adequate to the task. It would be very difficult to describe the exact tone of voice, the precise lift of the head, and the peculiar expression on the face as the word was spoken. Even a skilled novelist or poet can only hint at such things. The suggestion that we give a complete detailed description of the use of a word in concrete terms seems impractical. I can understand why the advocates of the ordinary-language approach have not practiced what they preach.

What would such a complete and detailed description of the use of a word be like if it were attainable? Since each use of the word includes many different aspects, this description would be very complicated. And since the same word may have several different uses, we would want descriptions of a good many different instances of its use. Would such a description really enable us to understand the meaning of the word? I suspect that this mass of detail would overwhelm us instead. Such a complicated description would be confusing rather than clarifying. To grasp something we must perceive the pattern in it. It seems to me that those who advocate the ordinary-language approach have overemphasized the importance of detail. In reaching understanding the theoretical framework is just as important as the concrete details. It would be advisable to develop general concepts of the main kinds of meaning and their relations. Then we could describe the uses of particular words in terms of this semantical theory.

The ordinary-language approach to ethics suggests that we can resolve our problems about ethical language by describing how ethical sentences are actually used. This advice does not appear to me as practical as one would wish. It is not at all clear how one discovers how a sentence is used. There seems no reliable way to decide which characterization of the use of the sentence is correct. We would not know what features must be included in our description of the use, nor do we have the language to describe these features accurately. If we had a correct description of use as detailed and concrete as this approach requires, we would be confused by its complexity. It is not so much that I think the advice offered me by the ordinary-language approach is mistaken in principle as that I find it so vague that I cannot tell how to go about following it.

5. *The Logic of Ethics*

The final presupposition associated with the ordinary-language approach, that ethical sentences have a logic all their own, seems equally open to objection. This principle does, I believe, express a real insight. The fact that ethical sentences do not have the same kind of meaning as scientific sentences does not necessarily imply that they have no objective validity; it may still be possible to find genuine reasons for and against them. To speak of the logic of ethical reasoning, however, seems to be misleading. The word "logic" calls to mind a body of principles by which the correctness of certain arguments can be tested. To speak of the logic of ethics, then, suggests that it is possible to formulate a set of criteria by which to judge the cogency of ethical arguments. Is there such a logic of ethical reasoning?

Almost everyone would agree that there are at least two kinds of logic, deductive and inductive. In both of these generally accepted examples of logic there are certain principles which serve as standards of correct argument. In both cases, moreover, these logical principles are formal. That is to say that the correctness of any deductive or inductive argument depends upon its form and not upon its matter. The matter of an argument is its subject matter, that which it is about. Arguments may have man and mortality, dogs and fleas, prices and wages, or proteins and cells as their subject matter. All such content, however, is irrelevant to their logical correctness. The cogency of any argument hinges exclusively upon its logical structure. For this reason it is possible to frame criteria which will apply to any argument on any subject. There are no separate deductive or inductive logics for chemistry, politics, or even ethics.

In the "logic of ethics," as the very name implies, the correctness of any argument does depend upon its subject matter. Whether or not the statement that an act would produce happiness is a good reason for the statement that it ought to be done depends upon the relation between happiness and obligation. The logical relation of the assertion that this movie was boring to the conclusion that it was a bad movie similarly depends upon the ethical relation of boringness to disvalue. Clearly the cogency of such arguments does depend upon their ethical content. For this reason there can be no formal criteria of relevance in ethical arguments as there are in deductive and inductive arguments.

But why could there not be material criteria of relevance here? Such principles would provide a material rather than a formal logic. No doubt one could frame certain material principles of correct argument in ethics. The fact that someone promised to do an act is a good, although not conclusive, reason why he ought to do it. The statement that something is pleasant is evidence for the statement that it is intrinsically good. However, it would be misleading to call such a set of material criteria of relevance a logic, for such principles of ethical reasoning would not be related to ethical arguments in the same way that the principles of formal logic are related to deductive and inductive arguments.

For one thing, formal logic is independent of the subject to which it is applied; its principles do not presuppose the truth of any specific conclusions in physics, biology, ethics, or agriculture. Therefore, people who disagree about a given subject can still use the same deductive and inductive logic. This means that they have common standards of reasoning by which to try to settle their dispute. This would not hold true, however, of material logic. To say that the fact that someone promised to do an act is a good reason why he ought to do it is, unless the argument is enthymematic, to presuppose a deontological theory of obligation. To accept the principle that the statement that something is pleasant is evidence for the statement that it is intrinsically good is to assume the intrinsic value of pleasure. Thus the principles of ethical reasoning presuppose the truth of a system of ethics. Clearly such ethical reasoning

151

cannot be used to settle the fundamental issues in ethics, for they assume that we already agree on the nature of value and obligation.

One might still hope, however, that they could be used to decide specific disagreements in ethics. Perhaps ethical reasoning does require that we already agree on the fundamental issues, but once we have reached agreement on these we would have criteria of relevance to use in criticizing particular ethical arguments. Faced with a difficult choice, for example, a man might think of several plausible reasons for and against telling the truth. His father trusts him, the habit of truthfulness is useful to society, it would be embarrassing to be found out. On the other hand, he would not want his father to know the worst, the doctor has said that he must not be worried, he promised the nurse that he would not disturb his father. A set of material principles of ethical reasoning might allow the perplexed man to exclude certain considerations as irrelevant and assure him that the others were in fact good reasons.

However, an argument does more than present a list of premises, it draws a conclusion from them. Precisely at this crucial point the "logic" of ethics becomes useless. These material principles say nothing about whether or not a given conclusion follows from a given set of premises, except in the uninteresting case where the evidence is all on one side and there is no need of any logic in the first place. Although the "logic of ethics" may tell us which are good reasons, it says nothing about which arguments are good arguments. This is because it gives us no way to weigh the relevant considerations against one another. Therefore, the reasoner must think each argument through on its own terms. Since there can be no general principles of correctness in ethical reasoning, there is no logic of ethics in any ordinary sense.

THE ORDINARY-LANGUAGE APPROACH

Let us, then, drop the notion of a "logic" of ethics and speak simply of ethical reasoning. This leaves intact the important contention of the ordinary-language approach that there is a kind of reasoning in ethics which is neither deductive nor inductive. I would agree that genuine reasoning extends beyond the boundaries of formal logic. I cannot agree, however, with the way in which the ordinary-language approach explains this wider conception of reasoning. At times these writers simply assert that there are good reasons in ethics; at other times they present a list of the main types of good reasons. In addition to their dogmatism, such bare assertions do little to explain what makes these good reasons in the epistemological sense rather than simply persuasive considerations.

When the practitioners of the ordinary-language approach do attempt to show that certain considerations are actually good reasons, they usually appeal to some definition of "ethics" or "reasons." One cannot deny that these are good reasons in ethics, for this is what we mean by "good reasons" in "ethics." The very fact that we give these reasons when asked to defend our ethical statements and that we acknowledge their relevance when presented by others shows that these are good reasons in the ordinary sense of the term.

For one thing, I am not always convinced that the reasons suggested in the writings of the ordinary-language group are in fact those which my friends do give when challenged, and I am quite sure that they are not always the ones I admit as relevant. But suppose that they are what are called "good reasons" in ordinary language. Then it would indeed be meaningless for me to deny that they are good ethical reasons in the ordinary sense of the term, but I might meaningfully assert that they are not so much like what we call "good reasons" in deductive and inductive logic as our ordinary language would suggest. I might even contend that although they are generally counted as evidence they ought not to be. It does not seem to me that the fact of justification is settled by the general opinion about what constitutes justification.

On the whole it appears to me that the assertion that ethics has a logic all its own clothes a genuine insight in very obscure language. The conclusions which I have pointed out are admirably illustrated by the writings of the main persons representing the ordinary-language approach. When Toulmin seems to be presenting the logic of ethical reasoning he is really presenting his own ethical system. In the guise of an impartial logician he is really pleading for a limited deontological theory of obligation qualified by a negative utilitarianism on the social level.[1] On the other hand, when Hare proposes his logic of prescriptives, he is actually carrying out the traditional role of the formal logician. As a result his logic becomes useless when we reach the real problem of ethical reasoning, the justification of one's basic ethical principles.[2] Together these two writers illustrate my contention that one cannot have a set of principles which is both relevant to the problems of ethical justification and strictly logical. Nowell-Smith avoids this dilemma by refusing to give any specific principles of correct ethical reasoning. Instead he relies upon our sense of linguistic oddness in each particular case.[3] This would seem to have all the drawbacks of any version of intuitionism. There is not much gained by giving our immediate aware-

[1] S. E. Toulmin, *The Place of Reason in Ethics* (Cambridge: Cambridge University Press, 1950), chs. X, XI.
[2] R. M. Hare, *Language of Morals* (Oxford: Clarenden Press, 1952), chs. II, IV.
[3] P. H. Nowell-Smith, *Ethics* (Oxford: Basil Blackwell, 1957), pp. 72, 74.

ness of relevance a new name unless one can explain more clearly what linguistic oddness is and just why it has any bearing on the problem of justification.

6. *Strengths and Weaknesses*

By now the reader may begin to suspect that I do not entirely accept the ordinary-language approach to ethics. It seems to me that the presuppositions which lie behind this approach are very unclear. Although they are not entirely false, they do not provide an adequate theoretical framework for a successful attack on the problem of the nature of moral judgment. This conceptual confusion is reflected in the unsatisfactory nature of the results which are obtained when the main representatives of this approach try to put it into practice.

The ordinary-language approach has produced many different views about the nature of ethical language. Each representative of the approach seems to have his own answer to the question "What do ethical sentences mean?" Although these various answers provide a wealth of various hints, no one of them constitutes a complete, or even adequate, answer. I have already suggested some of my objections to the more important of these interpretations of ethical sentences. Let me now make a few general observations. Many of the practitioners of the ordinary-language approach seem to assume that ethical sentences all have basically the same use. It seems to me that their own presuppositions suggest, and reflection confirms the fact, that ethical sentences have several distinct kinds of meaning. Those who do resist the temptation to oversimplify ethical language make the opposite mistake of failing to explain sufficiently the relations between the various uses of ethical sentences. What is needed is a theory which is both systematic and sensitive to the various meanings of ethical sentences. I do not think that the ordinary-language approach has yet given us such a theory.

It would, however, be a mistake to think that I reject the ordinary-language approach entirely. It does contain certain basic insights which I would like to borrow. First, it is quite right to insist on the autonomy of ethical language. Ethical sentences are not just disguised empirical descriptions. Both the intuitionists and the emotivists realized that there was a difference, but neither was able to explain it properly because of their restricted theories of meaning. I fear that the proponents of the ordinary-language approach have not done much better in their positive analyses of the nature of ethical language. They have performed an important service, however, in forcefully restating the contention that ethical language has important differences from other kinds of language.

The ordinary-language approach is also right to defend the objectivity of ethical judgment. The mere fact that ethical sentences have a different kind of meaning from scientific sentences does not imply that they lose all objective validity. Even though they cannot be verified scientifically, it may be possible to find evidence to establish them in some other way. The ordinary-language approach has put its finger on the precise issue here. Are there or are there not good reasons for and against ethical judgments? Quite correctly, I believe, they claim that there are.

A third important insight is the recognition that we need a wider concept of meaning. It is a mistake to believe that all meaningful sentences are really descriptions. Nor is it enough to add a second category of emotive meaning. When one thinks in terms of the descriptive-emotive dichotomy, the term "emotive meaning" becomes a wastebasket into which all nondescriptive sentences are thrown despite their obvious and important differences. Actually there are many distinct kinds of meaning, and to avoid misunderstanding these must be carefully distinguished.

Finally, the ordinary-language approach, as the name suggests, sees the need of a new approach to the problem of clarifying language. Philosophic understanding is not to be reached by the definitions of the key words. Correspondingly, philosophical analysis of troublesome sentences cannot take the form of translation into less obscure sentences. Both of these attempts to replace one expression with another either change the subject or reintroduce the old problem. The proper method of analysis is simply to describe the use of the unclear expression. If one will admit that some general classification of the main kinds of meaning is as important to these descriptions of use as their concrete detail, I can accept this suggestion gratefully.

The real value of the ordinary-language approach to ethics, it seems to me, is in clearing the way for a new attack on the problem of the meaning of ethical sentences. Like the emotive theory of ethics, it has challenged the truth of generally accepted assumptions which have restricted our vision of ethical language. It contends that any theory which overlooks the distinguishing features of ethical language must be rejected, that one must not assume that the nondescriptive nature of ethical language excludes all objective validity, that the generally accepted theories of meaning are too narrow to do justice to the meaning of ethical sentences, and that the generally practiced methods of achieving clarity will not help very much in understanding the nature of these sentences. Together these criticisms of previous approaches to ethical language sweep away preconceptions which unduly limit one's possible analysis.

157

In addition, the ordinary-language approach suggests the method of description as the best way to reach an understanding of ethical sentences.

Because I recognize the importance of these suggestions, I have not been trying to refute the ordinary-language approach to ethics. Rather I have been attempting to purify this approach by rescuing its genuine insights from the philosophical inadequacies of its presuppositions. In the present chapter I have done this as best I can.

The task before me is now clear. First I must try to distinguish and characterize the main kinds of meaning relevant to ethical sentences. I will not attempt to give a complete classification and analysis of all the uses of language, but only those of special importance for the language of ethics. Next, I must try to describe sample words and sentences which are typical of our ethical language in terms of these kinds of meaning. This should serve both as a test of the adequacy of my characterization of the kinds of meaning and as a clarification of a small part of our ethical vocabulary. Finally, I must try to derive some conclusions about the nature of ethical language from the sample which I have analyzed. It is high time to begin this formidable undertaking.

— VI —

Descriptive Meaning

Many theories of meaning attempt to conceive of all meaningful language in terms of description. Although I shall try to avoid this mistake, I find it convenient to begin my characterization of some basic kinds of meaning with a consideration of descriptive sentences. For one thing, these sentences are obviously an important kind of language, even if not the only kind. For another, they have already been studied more carefully than any other sort of sentence.

One does not have to look far to find some typical examples of descriptive sentences:

That is an elephant.
The book was on the table a minute ago.
Philosophers are not happy unless they are disputing.
Sugar is soluble.

How can we characterize the kind of meaning that these and similar sentences possess? Traditionally such sentences have been said to assert a predicate of a subject. We might well start with this accepted formula.

Every descriptive sentence has a subject. That is to say that it singles out some object or objects from the rest of reality as its subject matter. I call this selection of that which the description is about "indication." This something is then said to be of a certain sort or have a specified character. This specification of the kind of entity I call "quasi-comparison."

Indication and quasi-comparison are obviously related to the two sorts of analysis which are often recognized. In partitive analysis a spatio-temporal whole is mentally broken down into smaller units which stand in external relations to each other and which together make it up; in abstractive analysis the various properties or characteristics of any object, each of which might be shared with any number of other objects, are discriminated. For example, one might dismember a chair into four legs, a seat, and a back in his imagination; or he might notice separately the brownness, hardness, uncomfortableness, and sturdiness of the chair.

In description, however, we go beyond this twofold analysis. We rejoin in our judgment that which we have isolated in our conception; a synthesis is required for description to occur. The property isolated in abstractive analysis is asserted to inhere in the part isolated by partitive analysis. We say, for example, that the seat is hard or that the seat is not hard. I call this synthesis in judgment the "assertion-denial" dimension of description.

To my mind, the three fundamental features of any descriptive sentence are indication, quasi-comparison, and assertion-denial. Every description asserts or denies one or more descriptive predicates of one or more parts of reality.

The meaning of a description, then, consists in telling what something is like. Now I must explain each of these factors more carefully.

1. *Indication*

Indication is the reference to some object or objects described by the sentence. Every description is *about* something, and indication is this aboutness. Demonstratives like "this," "that," "now," "I," and "it" are ways of referring to subjects of conversation or items to be talked about. In some ways these words are like so many pointed fingers. They point out the object which the speaker has in mind and direct the hearer's attention to it. When the object is present, these words may cause the hearer actually to glance at or listen to the object; when the object is not immediately perceptible, they cause the hearer to think of it.

But indication involves more than directing the attention toward the subject matter of the sentence; it also involves limiting the relevance and the liability of the sentence. Thus "this book is red" tells one about the color of the book, but it says nothing about the color of the table or my fountain pen. Since the sentence claims to supply information about only a limited part of the world, it has a correspondingly limited corrigibility. One does not refute a description of the book as red by showing that the lamp is a brilliant green, nor could one establish it by pointing out how red the sunset is. That aspect of a sentence which makes it a description of this and not that is its indicative meaning.

I have suggested that indication is reference to some part of the universe, and typically this is so. But there are two qualifications which are necessary if my suggestion is not to be misleading. For one thing, a sentence may be about several parts of the universe, not just one part of it. Thus

161

"John is taller than Mary" indicates two people, while "all men are mortal" indicates as many people as there are. A descriptive sentence may be of or about one or more entities. For another thing, the subject of a description is not always part of the universe; it may, of course, be the universe itself. This is the limiting case of indication just as the whole is the limit of a series of increasingly exhaustive parts. Normally indication is selective; it is a singling out of one or more items from the totality of things. The limiting case of selecting, however, is selecting the totality of things itself.

Indication is that feature of a descriptive sentence by which it is about one or more objects. This aboutness seems to involve two related aspects. Indication reveals which object the speaker is concerned with and directs the hearer's attention to this same object. Also it shows which objects the sentence claims to inform us about and restricts the ways in which the sentence can be confirmed or disconfirmed.

2. *Quasi-comparison*

The second basic feature of a descriptive sentence is what I call quasi-comparison. To describe anything is to tell what it is like, to put it in a class of similar things. To say "it is a dog," for example, is to suggest that the indicated object is similar on the whole to the class of dogs and relatively dissimilar to cats, frogs, tables, and mountains. To describe something is to give it a place in the scheme of descriptive predicates, each of which denotes a class of similar entities.

Why I call this "quasi-comparison" can be best explained by an example. Saying "this is white" is much like saying "this is similar to freshly laundered sheets, the paper I am typing on, fleecy clouds, and snow." It is not just like saying

162

all this, however, for one does not actually mention the sheets, paper, clouds, and snow. In comparison, strictly speaking, one indicates all the objects which are being compared. One says "this paper is white as snow" or "this typewriter is as temperamental as an actress." On the other hand, to say simply "this paper is white" is not to indicate what it is as white as. No comparison is actually made. Yet surely *something like* a comparison is involved in applying any descriptive predicate. In calling anything "white" one is assigning it to the class of white things, and this class is defined by a similarity of color. Since describing something seems almost, but not quite, like comparing it to similar things, I call this feature of description "quasi-comparison."

Quasi-comparison can be of couples, triples, and so on as well as of single objects. To say "the book is on the table" is to quasi-compare the couple consisting of the book and the table with other pairs of objects which are similarly arranged in space. To say "John gave the book to Jane" is to quasi-compare the triplet of John, the book, and Jane with other threesomes in which the first member is similarly generous towards the third. Genuine comparison, thus, turns out to be the quasi-comparison of groups of objects. To say "John is taller than Jane" compares John and Jane with respect to height; this amounts to quasi-comparing this couple with other couples in which the first member is taller than the second. Comparisons are a special case of descriptive judgments, but all descriptions involve quasi-comparison.

To quasi-compare, then, is to specify what class the object belongs in; it is to say what kind or sort of thing it is. We have grasped the meaning of a descriptive adjective only when we know to what class of things it refers. This need not imply that we can list all members of the class, but that we be able to give examples when asked to and be able to decide of any given entity whether or not it belongs.

Our ability to quasi-compare presupposes our past acquaintance with entities which are both similar and dissimilar. These past experiences are not now in our minds as particular memories in the way that my memory of yesterday's sunset is there; yet somehow to see or conceive anything as being of this or that sort is to recognize its likeness to a class of formerly experienced objects. While it is not necessary to speculate about the psychological mechanism of this process, we do wish to be clear about its epistemological character. To know what kind of thing something is is to grasp the degree and respect of similarity required for anything to qualify as a member of the defined class. Putting this quasi-comparison into words is telling what any such member is like, not in the sense of actually indicating those things which are like it, but by expressing a meaning which could be finally explained only be offering examples of such things.

It seems to me that we use descriptive adjectives as a way of marking the similarities and dissimilarities among things and that our use of descriptive language presupposes our ability to grasp these similarities and dissimilarities. I do not pretend to explain either the nature of similarity or our awareness of it by the term "quasi-comparison." I hope only by this term to remind my reader and myself of certain features of our descriptive judgments and to break away from ways of speaking which have become treacherous through their traditional associations. In particular, I wish to avoid the suggestion that similarity involves sharing some universal entity and that our awareness of similarity consists of grasping this universal. It is better, I think, to take similarity and our awareness of it as ultimate.

Perhaps it will clarify my notion of quasi-comparison if I try to explain some of the reasons which led me to it.

Why should I believe that describing something is, in a rather special way, telling what it is like? In the first place, there is the language we use when explaining what it is to describe. If I want my wife to describe an interesting friend she has just met, I might well ask her to tell me "what she is like." If a student asks me whether I have found his fountain pen, I would probably ask him what "sort" or "kind" of pen it was that he lost. These ways of expressing ourselves suggest that a description somehow involves comparing the object described to a variety of other objects.

This suggestion is borne out by a consideration of the way in which we explain what we mean by a descriptive term. Suppose that I did not understand what my wife meant by calling her new friend "exuberant." She could name those of our mutual friends who seemed markedly exuberant and contrast them with those who seemed to lack this quality. Although my wife might have defined "exuberant" in terms of other descriptive adjectives, we can teach a child his basic vocabulary only by presenting examples which are similar in the respect intended and then contrasting them with dissimilar instances. The child and I have not learned our lessons until we can "see what the examples have in common." It would seem that understanding descriptive words involves recognizing similarities and dissimilarities.

I do not wish to take literally, however, the suggestion that the similarity between things lies in a something which they have in common. While I do think that we must recognize sorts or kinds of things, I do not wish to postulate the existence of universals to explain how kinds of things can be and be thought. To be sure, I am unable to explain just what similarity is and what kind of mental process is involved in thinking of similars. But does it really explain anything to go beyond these to a realm of universals? The belief in universals does little to explain how things can be similar, unless one can do better than Plato in clarifying the way in which things participate in these universals. Nor can I accept the view that to see the similarity of two things is to be directly aware of an entity they have in common, for I do not find that I am directly aware of universals. What is more, these universals are no more comprehensible than the mysteries they are supposed to explain. Our conception of thinghood seems thoroughly particularistic; to speak of a universal individual is to confuse one's categories. Certainly it is not to clarify a perplexing situation. It seems better to accept similarity and our awareness of it as ultimate facts.

Do these things which we can clearly see to be similar share any single essential feature? Consider the dogness supposedly possessed by all dogs. It is easy to say that there must be some one thing which makes all dogs dogs. But if all dogs are similar to one another, why must they have something in common? The more one reflects upon the many dogs he is acquainted with the more he doubts whether they do have anything in common. Size, shape, color of hair, disposition, and so on all seem to vary from dog to dog. When these are discarded as unessential, what is left? Perhaps this search for the essence of being a dog is like peeling an onion to find the hidden kernel within. Perhaps we classify dogs together because of a whole set of similarities which coalesce to form a gestalt likeness or family resemblance. What, to take another example, do red and green and blue have in common by virtue of which they are all colors? What, indeed, do a dozen shades of red have in common? When we reflect upon the various examples of any class specified by one of our descriptive predicates, it seems that the very real similarity hides no universal essence.

How do we form our descriptive concepts? Plato's theory of innate ideas and Locke's theory of abstraction are two traditional answers. Both seem to assume that seeing the similarity in things involves seeing what they have in common. According to Plato we classify experienced objects in terms of our innate concepts of the eternal ideas. This theory does little to explain how we grasp similarity; it simply asserts that we do it without appeal to experience. If one accepts Plato's assumption that we acquired these concepts in a previous life, one still does not know how we acquired them; if one rejects the doctrine of recollection, one knows no more about the nature of our concepts. Locke's theory at least tries to explain what is involved in understanding our descriptive concepts. I learned what the word "red" means by abstracting the concept of redness from past experience. Perhaps I looked at my favorite book and noticed its redness. Noticing the redness of the book, according to Locke, involves less than noticing the whole book. One concentrates his attention on the color of the book and pays no attention to the shape, size, texture, and other characteristics of the book. This is not as easy as it sounds. When I get out my big red book and stare steadily at its color, I find that I cannot ignore the shape, size, texture, and so forth. What is the exact phenomenological difference between attending to the color of the book and attending to the shape of the book? I can find none. This leads me to two conclusions. First, abstraction or selective noticing does not lie in the nature of what is given to attention but in the act of attending. I am seeing the entire book, but I am seeing it *as red*. Second, apprehending an object as of a certain kind involves more, not less, than seeing the object in its concrete fullness. Seeing the book as red, for example, does not involve seeing the color of the book without seeing its shape; rather it involves recognizing the similarity of this book to other colored objects which I have seen in the past.

Those who have read the last two paragraphs will not be surprised to learn that I formulated my conception of quasi-comparison upon reading Wittgenstein's so-called *Blue and Brown Books*. With the term "quasi-comparison" I wish to emphasize certain aspects of descriptive sentences. Every description tells what its object is like. Telling what something is like is placing it in a class of similar things without explicitly mentioning what these other things are. Thus descriptive predicates mark the similarities and dissimilarities among things, and our use of these predicates involves our ability to recognize and conceive of these similarities and dissimilarities. This does not imply, however, that we are aware of a universal entity shared by these similar things, for there are no such essences to be named by our descriptive words.

3. *Assertion-Denial*

Every descriptive sentence contains both indication and quasi-comparison, but it also includes more. Not every combination of indication and quasi-comparison is a description, for "red now large" and "the man next door" contain both yet are not sentences. A descriptive sentence asserts the quasi-comparison of the indicated object. "The book is red" is a complete sentence, while "the red book" is not. Of course, not all descriptive sentences are in the affirmative; in some the quasi-comparison is denied of the indicated object. Every description, however, falls somewhere along this assertion-denial dimension. This is the third basic feature of descriptive meaning.

I call this the "dimension" of assertion-denial, because

there seems to be a whole range of possible stands one can take in describing. One can assert the quasi-comparison of the indicated object. When one asserts the description he claims that the quasi-comparison correctly applies to the identified object. One can deny the description; that is, he can claim that the quasi-comparison does not correctly apply to the indicated object. One can entertain the description; in this case he considers the object in terms of the quasi-comparison without making any claim one way or another. One can hypothesize a description; then he puts forward the claim tentatively for purposes of further investigation. One can question a description; he invites others to suggest which claim he should make. One can pretend a description; in this case he makes believe that he is claiming but realizes that no actual truth or falsity is involved. No doubt there are other stands one may take in describing. Certainly a great deal more should be said about each. The point I have been trying to make, however, is that there are various ways ranging from assertion to denial in which indication and quasi-comparison can be combined in a description. Since these all seem to be alternate forms of the claim to correctness, I think of them as falling along a single dimension.

I am suggesting that what unites indication and quasi-comparison in a descriptive sentence is some form of claim. The difference between "the red book" and "the book is red" is that the latter asserts a claim which the former does not make. Asserting a description seems to include saying the sentence to oneself or others, being convinced by it, trying to convince others of it, giving reasons for it, trying to answer those who deny it, and so on. I will have much more to say about claiming when I discuss critical meaning. For the moment let me simply repeat that the assertion-denial dimension consists of the variety of claims one can make toward the applicability of some predicate of an indicated object.

Whichever form of claim one may make, there seem to be several ways to make it. Thus one can assert a description hesitantly, insistently, dogmatically, reasonably, and so on. Or one can question a description eagerly, superficially, persistently. One can assume a description tentatively, tenaciously, uncritically. I am not sure how important such distinctions are for epistemological purposes, but they provide interesting parallels to certain distinctions in the use of imperatives.

I have tried to distinguish and characterize briefly three basic features of descriptive meaning. Every descriptive sentence singles out some object or objects to be about. It tells what its object is like. It makes some sort of claim ranging from assertion to denial about the appropriateness of the quasi-comparision to the indicated object. Indication, quasi-comparison, and assertion-denial together constitute the meaning of a descriptive sentence.

4. *Logical Structure*

So far I have considered only quite simple descriptive sentences. "This is red" could be a model for almost everything I have said. In this particular example each word seems to specialize in performing one function. "This" indicates, "red" quasi-compares, and "is" asserts. One must be careful, however, about being misled by taking the verbal formulation too seriously. "This" indicates only with the help of a pointed finger, a nod of the head, or a situation in which it is obvious which object is being talked about. The word order and tone of voice are as much a part of asserting as the verb used. Moreover, one must not think of descriptive meaning as a mosaic made up of pieces as a sentence is a sequence of words. Indication, quasi-comparison, and assertion are not three separate and distinct kinds of meaning which must be put together to yield descriptive meaning. Rather they are three aspects of a single describing. The same description could have been verbalized in the one word "red" spoken with a nod of the head. It is the logical, and not the verbal, simplicity or complexity which concerns me now.

I should like to point out a few of the factors in the logical structure of descriptions by discussing a few more complicated examples. In "this is red" the distinction of indication and quasi-comparison seems fairly clear cut. In "this book is red" matters become more complicated. Both "book" and "red" are descriptive predicates whose meaning is to be understood in terms of quasi-comparison, but they function very differently in the sentence. Imagine that I am in a friend's house discussing philosophy. To illustrate some point about sense-data I pick up an object from the table and say "this book is red." My friend may inform me that it is not really a book but a cleverly carved cigarette box. What will I respond? I might modify my sentence to "this box is red." But I might, and probably would, say "well anyway, it is red." I brush aside his information that the object is a box instead of a book as unimportant, because I had not intended to claim that it was a book. While I had meant to assert "red" of the object, I had not meant to assert "book" of it. The word "book" was used simply to help indicate which object I was talking about. Thus quasi-comparison can be used as an auxiliary to indication. It can serve merely to single out what the sentence is about without asserting anything of it. In "the large white house is haunted" it is likely that the descriptive phrase "the large white house" is more like a pointed finger than a label.

Usually any descriptive content in the subject of a sentence is an unasserted aid to indication, but this is not always the case. I might say "that juvenile is delinquent" meaning to assert both that the creature in front of me is delinquent and that it is a juvenile.

Another factor which complicates matters is multiple indication. In "this girl and that boy are siblings" two objects are indicated. In this case "girl" and "boy" are both used as aids in indication, but they serve to direct attention to different objects. "Siblings" is asserted of both subjects. The compound nature of the grammatical subject reveals the complex nature of the indication involved.

In "John is taller than Jane" there are also two objects indicated. In this case, however, proper names are used instead of descriptive predicates. In this example the sense of the relation is an additional factor in the structure of the description. It would not be at all the same thing to say "Jane is taller than John" as John's hurt feelings would attest.

Another factor which helps to determine the structure of a description is the relation of modification. Consider the sentence "it is a large fly." Here two descriptive predicates are applied to the inoffensive object. Yet the sentence is not synonymous with "it is large and it is a fly." It may be large for a fly, but it is small compared to most things. When several adjectives are combined into a single description, they are usually not simply added to one another. Rather one is primary and the others modify it. In this case, of course, "large" modifies "fly" and the combination is asserted of the insect at hand.

Where does the grammatical dichotomy of subject and predicate fit into the picture? It seems to me that this dichotomy really covers a variety of different distinctions. To some extent it coincides with the distinction between indication and quasi-comparison, for the subject of a sentence usually indicates what will be quasi-compared in the predicate. But, as logicians have long complained, the grammatical predicate contains both quasi-comparison and assertion-denial without distinguishing the two. Moreover, as I have pointed out, quasi-comparison may often be included in the grammatical subject as an aid in indication. The converse is also possible, indicative elements may fall within the grammatical predicate. "I am taller than you" is one example. Another function of grammatical subject and predicate is to distinguish between that which is taken for granted and that which is added as news. In "the man we just saw as a famous violinist" it is assumed that we just saw a man. No one would bother to utter a sentence to record this obvious fact. What is interesting enough to call for linguistic expression is that he is a well-known violinist; this is the information that the speaker intended to convey. A related function of the subject-predicate structure is to place the emphasis where it is most needed. "New York is south of Boston" and "Boston is north of New York" contain exactly the same information. The former, however, brings to the fore that aspect of the situation of particular interest to one in Boston wondering which way he should drive to get to New York, while the latter emphasizes that feature most informative to the New Yorker who wants to know in what direction he should look for cultural leadership. The grammatical distinction between subject and predicate is a very useful, but confusing, one. It performs many functions in the sentence, only some of which are logical.

The traditional formula which we used as a clue to the nature of descriptive meaning was that a descriptive sentence asserts a predicate of a subject. This hint did suggest correctly the three basic features in descriptive meaning—indication, quasi-comparison, and assertion-denial. A sentence such as "this is red" might serve as a simple model of description. Descriptive sentences are usually more complicated than this, however. While some quasi-comparisons are asserted of the subject, others serve only to help indicate that subject. A description may involve multiple indication; it may be about several objects. When the quasi-comparison involves the relation between entities, the sense of that relation must be borne in mind. Several quasi-comparisons may be combined into a single characterization. While sometimes these quasi-comparisons are simply added to one another, more often one is more basic and the others modify it. I do not pretend to have given a complete analysis of the logical structure of description. I have merely commented upon those aspects of logical structure which seem particularly important for my purpose.

5. *Types of Generality*

Descriptions, as we are all aware, may be more or less general. Since this notion of generality is not entirely clear, I shall try to make a few distinctions which seem to me to be helpful. I suggest that there are four very different types of generality: universality, indeterminateness, abstractness, and applicability.

The universality of a descriptive sentence is a function of the range of its indication. A description may refer to, or be about, a larger or smaller selection of objects. It may refer to this book, some apples, a few men, or all swans. Such differences in the extent of the objects indicated by a sentence has led logicians to distinguish between universal and particular categorical propositions. Modifying this terminology slightly, we can say that a description is universal to the extent that it is about a larger set of objects and particular to the extent that it indicates a smaller collection of objects.

The other three types of generality which I wish to distinguish all have to do with quasi-comparison. Some quasi-comparisons are mutually exclusive and yet have similar objects. Logicians express this by saying that some determinate predicates fall under a single determinable. "Color," for example, is a determinable which includes under it the more determinate predicates "red," "blue," "yellow," and so forth. And "red" is a determinable relative to the more determinate predicates "crimson," scarlet," and so on. Sounds, tastes, feels, and other kinds of qualities are less neat, but equally interesting, examples of this relation of determinable to determinate. Let us say that a descriptive predicate is determinate to the extent that it restricts the degree of similarity required for membership in its denotation and stands opposed to incompatible alternatives; it is indeterminate to the degree that it allows room for dissimilar entities to fall under it.

Quite a different form of generality is abstractness. Any particular object falls under many different determinables. A pencil, for example, has a felt texture, weight, size, shape, color, and hardness. Let us say that a description is abstract to the extent that it specifies the nature of its object along a smaller number of determinables and concrete to the degree that it characterizes the object in many respects. Thus "heavy red pencil" is more concrete than "heavy pencil." Similarly "deep crimson" is more abstract, although less indeterminate, than "red square."

The final form which generality takes in description is applicability. There are two senses in which the application of a descriptive predicate to an object may be incorrect; the application may be false or it may be meaningless. Thus it is quite meaningful, yet incorrect, to predicate "red" of the paper upon which I am writing. It is not even meaningful, however, to say that virtue is red. This is not because virtue has some other color, but because adjectives of color have no significant relevance for virtue at all. As logicians since Aristotle have been fond of pointing out, a man may be blind, but a stone can be only nonseeing. To call a stone blind would not be to say something false, but to fail to describe at all. Let us say that a descriptive predicate has greater applicability to the extent that it may be significantly predicated of a larger range of entities and that it fails of this form of generality just insofar as its meaningful application is limited.

There are, then, four distinct ways in which a descriptive sentence may be more or less general. It is universal to the degree that it is about a larger number of objects. It is indeterminate to the degree that its asserted quasi-comparison allows for a greater degree of dissimilarity. It is abstract to the degree that it characterizes its object along a smaller number of determinables. It is of greater applicability to the degree that its asserted quasi-comparison can be meaningfully predicated of a variety of objects. Obviously a description may be quite general in some of these ways and far from general in others.

6. *Semantical Presuppositions*

Before I leave the subject of descriptive sentences, I must say a word or two about the limits of meaningful description. Suppose that a friend, having just returned from a trip to Europe where he saw everything of importance, remarks casually but seriously "The king of France is bald." What am I to make of this statement? It certainly seems meaningful. Every word in it is quite meaningful, and it has been constructed according to all the rules of good grammar. But since there is no king of France, and has not been one for some time, I cannot figure out what my friend is talking about. What could he mean? Does he really mean anything at all?

Russell suggests that the sentence is meaningful but false. He interprets the sentence "the king of France is bald" to imply "there exists a king of France." Since this existential implication is false, the sentence which implies it must also be false.[1] Strawson prefers to say that the sentence is meaningless, or at least pointless, rather than false. He admits that it does imply the existence of a king of France in a "very special and odd" sense of imply. He denies, however, that this is logical implication.[2] Rather than saying that my friend has described falsely, we should say that he has failed to describe at all. I am inclined to side with Strawson on this matter.

What Russell has done is to extend the treatment which modern logic gives to particular categorical propositions to sentences containing singular descriptions. Perhaps I can explain my attitude toward this gambit by discussing the square of opposition. The introduction of the null class into modern logic raised serious problems about the traditional square of opposition, for the square assumes that all the terms in a categorical proposition have denotation. What becomes of the square if there are no S's? To say "Some S are P" or "Some S are not P" seems clearly to imply that there are some S's. It is customary, therefore, to assign existential import to particular propositions. This means that all particular propositions are false in the event that there are no S's. Now, if universal propositions are also assigned existential import, they also become false and the valuable relation of contradictoriness is lost. For this reason it is usually denied that either "All S are P" or "No S are P" implies the existence of S's. Although this standard interpre-

---

[1] B. Russell, "On Denoting," *Mind*, 14:490 (October 1905).
[2] P. F. Strawson, "On Referring," *Mind*, 59:330–331 (July 1950).

tation salvages the diagonals of the square of opposition, it destroys all four sides.

What are we to say about this interpretation of the meaning of categorical propositions? From the standpoint of formal logic it seems quite helpful. It makes possible a logic of greater range and elegance than traditional logic. If the logician is proposing a new language more precise than ordinary language to be used in formulating and criticizing arguments, I cannot object. If the logician pretends to be explaining what ordinary language really means, however, I do object. In one sense, to be sure, this interpretation of categorical propositions does not do violence to our everyday meanings; it does not violate any fixed conventions about the truth value of categorical propositions. It does not interpret as true any proposition we would ordinarily regard as false, or vice versa. The reason for this is clear; it has simply extended the assignment of truth values to sentences not covered by existing conventions. In so doing it has, it seems to me, modified ordinary language. We do not usually regard categorical propositions about nonexistent objects as either true or false. This strongly suggests that in ordinary language such propositions are meaningless. To assign truth value to them is to give them a meaning which they did not have before. Hence, while I do not object to the modern interpretation of categorical propositions as a proposal for a new and logically convenient language, I do not think that it reflects accurately what we mean when we use similar sentences in ordinary language.

Parallel observations can be made about Russell's interpretation of sentences containing singular descriptions. If Russell wishes to use singular descriptions in such a way that they logically imply the existence of the objects they indicate, I do not object. Russell's language might be a real improvement over everyday English for many purposes; it is not, however, standard English. Ordinarily we do not logically imply the existence of anything when we use a singular description. This is shown by the fact that we hesitate to consider sentences containing singular descriptions false even though we unhesitatingly admit that they do not refer to any existing entity. In fact, it is precisely because his language modifies those conventions of ordinary language which create this uncertainty that Russell prefers his new language. He cannot claim, therefore, that he is explaining what we ordinarily mean when we use a singular description. At the same time, there is something in our ordinary meaning which suggests that Russell is not entirely on the wrong track.

The use of a singular description does not *logically* imply the existence of the object indicated, but in *some* sense or other it does seem to imply this. We are back to Strawson's remark that descriptions imply existence in a "very special and odd" sense of imply. Unfortunately, he does not explain this odd sense of implication. Nowell-Smith, however, has developed a generalized notion of implication, called "contextual implication," which might be of help. He suggests that a statement *p* contextually implies a statement *q* if anyone who knew the normal conventions of the language would be entitled to infer *q* from *p* in the context in which they occur.[3] It might be in this sense that "the king of France is bald" implies "there is a king of France." If my friend is reporting his trip with a straight face, I might be entitled to infer the latter from the former in this context. My inference would be mistaken, of course, but it need not be unjustified.

While I see nothing objectionable in saying that "the king of France is bald" implies "there is a king of France" in this sense, I do not think that this solves our problem. Just

[3] P. H. Nowell-Smith, *Ethics* (Oxford: Basil Blackwell, 1957), p. 72.

because contextual implication differs from logical implication, transposition seems inapplicable to it. Thus from the fact that p contextually implies q and that q is false, we cannot justifiably infer anything about the truth of p. For this reason the notion of contextual implication does not help us to decide whether "the king of France is bald" is meaningful because false or simply meaningless. In short, contextual implication is not the odd sense of implication that Strawson is looking for. This is, of course, no criticism of Nowell-Smith, for he introduced the notion for quite a different purpose.

Our problem remains. In what sense does the use of a singular description imply the existence of the object it purports to indicate? Or, to return to another suggestive example, in what sense does the traditional square of opposition presuppose the existence of S's? If we make the assertion of the existence of S's part of the meaning of a categorical proposition, either as asserted in or as logically implied by the proposition, we are forced to adopt some version of the modern interpretation of categorical propositions. Since this modern interpretation does not accurately reflect what we mean when we use such sentences in ordinary language, we must find some other way to explain the sense in which these sentences presuppose the existence of the objects they purport to indicate. I propose a conception derived from that of logical presupposition to help us here.

To say that p logically presupposes q is to say that p is true only if q is true. Now what concerns us at the moment is not so much the relation between the *truth* of p and the truth of q as the relation between the *meaningfulness* of p and the truth or falsity of q. Therefore let us introduce the notion of semantical presupposition as a parallel to that of logical presupposition. To say that p semantically presupposes q is to say that p is meaningful only if q is true. My suggestion is that every descriptive sentence presupposes certain things in the sense that if these are not so the sentence turns out to be meaningless. It is not so much that a description which violates the semantical presuppositions of description is false or incorrect as that it is pointless. Therefore no speaker who knew that these presuppositions were violated would bother to utter the sentence and no hearer in a similar position would see any point in the utterance.

What are the semantical presuppositions of any descriptive sentence? One of them seems to be that the object or objects which it purports to indicate actually exist. One does not meaningfully assert or deny a description of non-existent entities. One can, of course, pretend or assume descriptions without presupposing the existence of the things described. Hypothetical deductive systems or fairy stories illustrate this well. Thus the semantical presuppositions for asserting or denying a description are not the same as those for pretending or assuming one.

A second semantical presupposition of description, whether asserted or not, is that the quasi-comparison claimed to apply to the subject be conceivable. It is meaningless to describe anything, real or imaginary, as a round square, for it is impossible to understand what a round square could be. Similarly it is meaningless to speak of a red sound, if one wishes to suggest that the noise is literally red. One can, to be sure, speak of a soft color, but some sort of figure of speech seems involved here. Certain combinations of quasi-comparisons are ruled out as meaningless on the grounds that they cannot be conceived together. "Sky blue pink" is one common example which is often used in everyday discourse as a model of meaninglessness.

A third semantical presupposition of asserting or denying a description seems to be that there be some possible evidence for or against the description. It does not seem to make sense to assert or deny that something is of a specified kind unless it is at least possible to produce reasons for or against the statement. What this probably amounts to is that the claim to correctness becomes empty in the absence of any relevant considerations to support or weaken it. It is not necessary that one actually have reasons or even that he be in a position to obtain them, but at least it must not be impossible for anyone to ever produce any reason to accept or reject the description.

7. *Summary*

My characterization of descriptive meaning can be summarized very briefly. There are three basic features of any descriptive sentence—indication, quasi-comparison, and assertion-denial. Every description refers to one or more objects. It tells what these objects are like. And it makes some sort of a claim about the appropriateness of the quasi-comparison to the objects indicated. The internal structure of a description may be complicated by such factors as multiple indication, the use of quasi-comparison in indication, the sense of relational quasi-comparison, and the fact that one quasi-comparison may be modified by another. There are four senses in which a description can be more or less general—universality, indeterminateness, abstractness, and applicability. Finally, every descriptive sentence which is asserted or denied seems to semantically presuppose that the object or objects it purports to indicate actually exist, that the quasi-comparison it predicates is conceivable, and that it would be possible to discover some reason to accept or reject the claim which it makes.

— VII —

Emotive Meaning

After an analysis of descriptive meaning one naturally expects some discussion of emotive meaning. This is probably because so many semanticists have gone so far as to suggest that the only two kinds of meaning are descriptive and emotive. The temptation to approach language with the descriptive-emotive dichotomy is most unfortunate, for it causes one to overlook precisely those distinctions needed to undertand ethical sentences. This semantical oversimplification is an expression of a preoccupation with scientific language together with an excessively narrow interpretation of science. As a result empirical predictions are taken as the model for all meaningful language, and the attempt is made to show that all cognitively significant sentences are variations on this pattern. However, the awkward fact that many sentences which have some sort of meaning in our language are not disguised descriptions cannot be ignored. One must admit that there is noncognitive meaning as well as cognitive meaning. But what kind of meaning could this be? One obvious answer is that these sentences express emotions or feelings instead of cognitions or thoughts. Appearances are saved by conceding emotive meaning to all language which fails to meet the criterion of being literally meaningful.

The main difficulty with this approach to emotive meaning is that the term "emotive meaning" becomes a waste-basket term. Under this general rubric are lumped together all sorts of nondescriptive language. The label "emotive" does not mark any positive feature which these various sentences share, but it serves only to stress their negative feature of not being predictions of experience. There are many kinds of nondescriptive language: promises and petitions, poems and novels, exclamations and imperatives, and the language of ritual and rite, to mention the more celebrated examples. When these are lumped together the important differences between them are ignored. The fish are never separated from the fowl, however, for those who use this label are not primarily interested in any study of emotive language for its own sake. Their real interest is in purifying cognitive language of all irrelevant and disturbing emotion. Emotive meaning is something to be avoided and otherwise ignored. Under such circumstances the term "emotive" is more of a warning and a reproach than an enlightening characterization.

Fortunately there are those who realize the need for distinguishing emotive language more carefully from the other kinds of sentence and for characterizing its meaning in illuminating terms. Stevenson has probably given us the most complete and penetrating analysis of the nature of emotive meaning. As a result it is no longer possible to doubt that emotive sentences are an important part of our language. Somehow or other we must come to terms with them and characterize their meaning adequately.

1. *Selecting a Model*

There are three kinds of sentence which are stock examples of emotive meaning. One obvious type of emotive sentence is those in the exclamatory mood. To murmur "alas" does not seem quite the same as describing one's feelings of despondency. "Ouch" does not appear to have the same kind of meaning as "I am in pain." Sentences such as "damn you" have a function in our language quite different from descriptive sentences. Let us call the kind of meaning which such sentences have "emotive meaning." Exclamations, then, will serve as a model of emotive sentences.

Are there any other striking examples of emotive sentences? Imperatives are usually presented as a second illustration of emotive language. It seems to me, however, that this is using the one term "emotive" to cover two quite different kinds of meaning. No doubt there are some imperatives which do function like exclamations. If I say "go to hell," I am saying "damn you" in other words. Certain imperatives, like "drop dead," do seem to have emotive meaning. But these are unusual imperatives with a meaning quite unlike ordinary imperative sentences. Normally imperatives are used to tell someone to do something rather than to express one's feelings toward him. "Open the window," for example, instructs the person to whom it is addressed to do an action of the window-opening kind.

One might, I suppose, try to assimilate all imperatives to those which express our feelings by suggesting that to tell someone to do something is really to express one's desire that the person told do the action specified. Thus to command "open the window" is simply another way of exclaiming "oh how I wish that the window were opened by you." Now it is probably true that no speaker would command someone to open the window unless he in fact desired that the person commanded open the window. However, I wonder whether the point of uttering the imperative lies in expressing this wish. It seems more plausible to hold that the primary intention in commanding someone to do something is in getting him to do it. That there is a real difference between exclaiming and commanding can be seen as soon as one tries to put them both into the past tense. One can easily express a wish that someone had done something which he did not in fact do. It makes sense to say "oh how I wish that you had opened that window an hour ago." It seems quite meaningless, on the other hand, to say "opened the window an hour ago." The fact that the imperative mood has no past tense suggests that it is a mistake to interpret most imperatives in terms of emotive meaning. I shall, therefore, reserve my comments on the garden variety of imperative until I discuss directive meaning.

There is a third example of emotive meaning which is often appealed to in recent discussions; this is the sentence containing emotionally charged language. Words such as "maiden," "garret," and "home" seem richer in meaning than their descriptive equivalents such as "young unmarried woman," "attic," and "house." Part of this richness consists of connotations which are purely or primarily descriptive. It seems likely, however, that these words also have emotional connotations which add to their meaning. Moreover, the fact that we borrow some of them, particularly the four-letter words, for frequent use in exclamatory sentences would suggest that their meaning might be partly emotive. We must, therefore, bear emotionally laden language in mind when framing any theory of emotive sentences.

At the same time, I would prefer not to use sentences containing emotionally charged words as my primary model of emotive meaning, for their descriptive meaning complicates analysis. It is not easy to know what part of their meaning is descriptive and what part emotive or how these two are related. In particular I should like to avoid the vexed question of whether or not emotive meaning is causally independent of descriptive meaning. Do the words cause a belief which in turn causes an emotional response or do the words cause the emotion directly? As long as psychologists do not seem to agree on the answer, I will not pretend to settle this question. Since I will not identify the emotive meaning of an utterance with the emotion it happens to cause in the hearer, the precise mechanism by which this causation operates need not detain me. It is easier to avoid such complications by taking exclamations as the model of emotive sentences. Since exclamations seem clearly to have some kind of meaning quite different from descriptions and somehow involving the emotions, it seems safe enough to label this "emotive meaning." When we have discovered exactly what kind of meaning it is that we have labeled, it will be time to decide whether emotionally charged sentences have the same kind of meaning.

2. *Evincing and Evoking*

How, then, are we to characterize the kind of meaning which exclamations possess? One accepted formula is that exclamations evince and evoke emotion. Words evince emotion when they reflect the feelings of the speaker; words evoke emotion when they call forth some emotional response in the hearer. It is not clear to me why evincing emotion and evoking emotion should be considered two aspects of the same thing, emotive meaning. Surely the use of words to release pent-up feelings is one thing, and the use of words to create a feeling is another. There is not even any need for them to go together. My cry of jubilation at the racetrack leaves the bystander who bet on another horse strangely unmoved. The announcer reading his emotionally charged copy may not even like the product he causes his listeners to desire so ardently. Even when evincing and evoking do go together, the emotions may be quite different. The "poor dear" which evinces the wealthy matron's pity may evoke only scorn or resentment in the beggar. Evincing and evoking are distinguishable and separable. Why should we include them both in a single mode of meaning?

Let us, therefore, consider each separately. Is it correct to say that exclamations evince emotion? No doubt exclamations do evince emotions in a variety of ways. But which of these various senses of the word "evince" helps to explain the meaning of exclamations?

To evince an emotion may be (1) to release pent-up feelings. On this interpretation exclamations reduce the emotional pressure inside us by a kind of linguistic catharsis. It does seem as though exclamations are often used for letting off steam in this way. Yet there seems to be more to the use of emotive language than purging the speaker. I may shout "damn you" to make you feel uncomfortable as well as to make myself feel more comfortable. Also it seems to me that we sometimes use exclamations to express emotions which are not very strong. In such cases releasing the emotional pressure is not central. I might say "oh no" playfully when I see my wife's new hat. This need not imply that I have any strong feelings of sarcasm. Still, as long as one does not overemphasize the explosiveness of the feelings expressed, emotional release does seem to be part of the meaning of exclamations.

To evince an emotion may be (2) to be accompanied by

emotion. The mere fact that the speaker happens to feel some emotion at the same time he utters the exclamation, however, might be quite accidental. If a person bet against his college football team, he may be both sorry and glad when it wins. His "darn it" may mean the former but hardly the latter. The meaning of an emotive sentence is not just any emotion in the mind of the speaker.

To evince an emotion may be (3) to be a sign of an emotion. Certainly the hearer can infer the presence of emotion in the speaker from the exclamation which comes out of his mouth much as he can infer the presence of fire in a building from the smoke which comes out of its windows. But one suspects that this fact throws little light on the meaning of the exclamation. To point out that an exclamation means (is a natural sign of) the speaker's emotion to the hearer is not to explain what the speaker means (intends to say) by the exclamation.

To evince an emotion may be (4) to be caused by an emotion. An exclamation means an emotion in the sense that the emotion caused the speaker to utter the exclamation. Thus "ouch" means pain, for the noise I made was caused by the pain I felt. On this interpretation, however, the word "ouch" would no longer mean pain, or at least not have emotive meaning, when uttered by a person who was not in pain. Consider the person who says "ouch" to mislead his hearers. It is precisely because the word retains its original emotive meaning even though the speaker does not happen to feel the emotion involved that he can pretend to be in pain by using emotive language. The sense in which the word means the emotion is not, therefore, as simple as being caused by it.

To evince an emotion may be (5) to tend to be caused by an emotion. Emotive meaning is a dispositional property of certain words to be uttered because of the emotion the speaker feels. This view can explain how a person can pretend to be in pain by uttering emotive language. Although "ouch" was not caused by any pain this speaker felt on this occasion, it still tends to be caused by feelings of pain. It seems to me that this analysis of evincing is correct as far as it goes. My objection with it is that it does not go far enough to explain what kind of dispositional property emotive meaning is. "I am in pain" also tends to be caused by the pain the speaker feels. Since emotive and descriptive meaning are different, presumably "ouch" and "I am in pain" tend to be caused in different ways. What is the difference? One might say that the former is caused directly by the pain while the latter is caused indirectly through the belief about the pain. In order to explain why I find this gambit unconvincing I must take another example. A speaker might describe his feelings towards a book by saying "I am enjoying the book." He might evince his enjoyment by exclaiming "fine book." If one says that the exclamation is caused directly by the enjoyment while the description is directly caused by the belief about the enjoyment, what does one do with the claim that "the book is enjoyable." I do not believe that one is describing the book when he calls it "enjoyable." Neither do I think it correct to say that "the book is enjoyable" has emotive meaning, for it makes a claim to correctness which exclamations lack. No doubt exclamations do tend to be caused by the emotions which the speaker feels, but one must explain more fully just how they tend to be caused before he has adequately characterized emotive meaning.

To my mind none of the generally accepted concepts of evincing adequately characterizes the meaning of exclamations. For this reason I will drop the word "evince" with its misleading associations. At the same time I cannot ignore the fact at which the persistent talk of evincing points; the meaning of exclamations is somehow tied up with the emotions which the speaker does or tends to feel. I shall say that emotive language "expresses" the emotions of the speaker. This change in terminology will be of little help, however, unless I can explain exactly what it is for a sentence to express an emotion. In what sense does an exclamation put an emotion into words? Since I do not know the precise nature of the causal relation between emotion and utterance, I cannot explain the relation of expressing in terms of the psychological mechanism involved. I must content myself with trying to point out the epistemological aspects of the expressive use of language.

Before I turn to my own account of expressing, however, let me examine the other side of the evincing-evoking polarity. Does it help to explain the meaning of exclamations to say that they evoke emotions? Once more this depends upon how one conceives the explanatory notion. To evoke an emotion might be (1) to cause the hearer to feel that emotion. But we cannot say that an exclamation means any emotion it may happen to cause in the mind of the hearer, for he may misunderstand the emotive language and feel joy when he should feel sadness. Surely it makes sense to say that I might misunderstand exclamations in Russian or Swahili; yet this would be impossible if their meaning was identical with the feelings I actually had when I heard them.

Moreover, an exclamation may suggest many emotions without actually meaning them. "Egghead" may actually cause me to favor the man at whom it was uttered, but the emotive meaning of the word seems to be negative. The situation here is analogous to that in the case of descriptive language. We must distinguish between what a sentence means and what it suggests. "Jones is poor" may suggest to me that he is thin and hungry, but it hardly means this.

The word "coed" may suggest a vision attractive enough to be homecoming queen, but it means only a girl attending a coeducational college. Nor is this distinction between what a word means and what it suggests limited to descriptive meaning. The word "alas" means grief, although it may suggest pity. One cannot identify the meaning of an emotive word with the emotions which it happens to cause in the hearer. It may cause the hearer to feel emotions which were not meant either because he misunderstands the language or because of its suggestiveness.

One can meet these objections by holding that to evoke an emotion is (2) to tend to cause it in the hearer. Thus the fact that I feel sad when I hear a Russian cheer does not affect the meaning of his exclamation, for it still tends to cause happy feelings in most people. Again, the fact that an exclamation suggests some emotion to me does not make this a part of its meaning unless it tends to cause the same emotion in most people. However, it does not seem to me that this quite does the trick. The mere fact that a word suggests something to most people does not make that suggestion part of the strict meaning of that word. "Jones is an athlete," to borrow Grice's example, may well suggest that Jones is tall to most people; yet tallness is not part of the strict meaning of "athlete." Again, "coed" probably calls up visions of loveliness to most Americans, but the word still is correctly applied to the most unattractive girl on any college campus in the country. Why should the situation be different in the case of emotive meaning? The exclamation "alas" continues to mean grief, although we can hope that it suggests pity in the minds of most hearers.

Another difficulty is with the exact sense in which the hearer is supposed to feel the emotions caused by the utterance. "Hurrah," one presumes, is supposed to cause most hearers to feel joy. Must the hearer feel actual joy to understand what the speaker said? Does the exclamation "ouch" cause most hearers to feel pain? Compare emotive language with descriptive language. It might be said that a descriptive sentence tends to cause a certain belief in the mind of the hearer, and no doubt most hearers do believe what they are told. I doubt, however, that this is what is involved in communication. I can understand Muskrat Joe when he describes his adventures in the great northwoods even though I know that he is the grandest liar on earth. Understanding the descriptions he utters does not require that I believe them myself, but only that I entertain his beliefs. Similarly understanding emotive language does not require that the hearer actually feel as the speaker does, but only that he understand how the speaker feels. If exclamations communicate emotions this need not imply that they tend to cause the hearer to actually feel the same emotions as the speaker. The hearer can entertain the emotion without actually having it. Understanding language seems to be more complicated than simply being caused to have the same state of mind as the speaker; one understands a speaker, rather, when he realizes what the speaker was trying to do with the words. To understand emotive language would seem to be coming to realize what emotion the speaker was trying to express by his words. Thus expression is central to emotive meaning, and the effects of the language on the hearer are derivative. Therefore it does not seem to me that the evocative aspect of emotive meaning is primary.

3. *Emotive Meaning vs. Emotive Force*

At the same time there is an important lesson to be learned by this discussion. One must distinguish between what a sentence means and what it suggests in the case of emotive meaning no less than in description. Therefore, I propose that we distinguish the emotive meaning of a word or sentence from its emotive force. The emotive meaning of a word or sentence is determined by the emotion or emotions which it expresses, the emotive force is a function of those emotions suggested by, but not expressed by, the word or sentence.

What, really, is the difference? The emotive meaning of a sentence is determined by the emotion the speaker should use it to express; the emotive force of the sentence is determined by the emotions which it happens to cause in the hearer. Thus part of the difference lies in who feels the emotion. In the case of emotive meaning it is the speaker who feels, or pretends to feel, the emotion. In the case of emotive force it is the hearer who feels the emotions involved. In addition, there is a difference in the nature of the connection between the utterance and the emotion involved. In emotive meaning the emotion is related to the utterance semantically; it is the emotion which the sentence should be used to express according to the rules of the language. In emotive force the emotion is related to the utterance causally; it is the emotion which is in fact caused by the use of the sentence.

To speak of the rules of a living language is something of a figure of speech. There are, of course, grammar books; but when the rules they state deviate too far from everyday usage, it is the rules, and not the usage, that are declared mistaken. There is no explicitly formulated set of rules that determine how ordinary language should be spoken. Can we put the matter less metaphorically? If the rules of ordinary language are mere descriptions of actual usage, perhaps meaning can be defined, as Stevenson has attempted to do, as a disposition of certain words to be used in certain ways. I do not object to this attempt on principle. No doubt meaning involves some sort of complex causal disposition. At the same time I do not feel that Stevenson has said enough about the exact kind of causal disposition involved in meaning in general or about the differences between the causal dispositions involved in the various kinds of meaning. Since I am not able to give a more accurate and explicit description of the exact causal mechanisms involved in the various uses of language, I prefer to hide my uncertainty about the ultimate nature of meaning by speaking glibly of the rules of language.

This is only a figure of speech. However, in whatever sense there really is a distinction between the correct and the incorrect use of a word, this metaphor reflects a genuine feature of language. It seems to me that such a distinction does exist for emotive language. It is correct to express joy by "hurrah" or "whoopee" but incorrect to express it by "alas" or "woe is me." If the New Englander feels flattered when a Southerner calls him a "Yankee," he has not understood the language of the South. Emotive language can be used correctly or misused, understood correctly or misunderstood, just like any other meaningful language. This fact that emotive meaning is covered by the rules of the language is one justification for calling it a mode of meaning.

Now is probably the best time to reconsider the nature of emotionally charged language. Words like "maiden," "garret," and "home" seem to be emotionally laden as well as descriptively significant. Much of their emotional load is composed of emotional suggestions which are not strictly part of the meaning of these words. However, it seems quite likely that we sometimes use these words to express our emotions as well. Emotively charged language certainly has emotive force and probably has emotive meaning. Nevertheless, it will be helpful to refrain from confusing the two.

I seem to have rejected most of the usual characterizations of emotive meaning as inadequate. Can I do any better? What can I say about the meaning of emotive sentences? All emotive sentences have the two characteristics of emotionality and expressiveness. They may or may not possess the additional characteristics of indication and partiality. Let us consider these one by one.

4. *Emotionality*

Every emotive sentence puts some emotion into words. In this sense the meaning of the sentence might be said to be emotional and the sentence to have emotionality. One of the problems in coming to understand the meaning of emotive sentences, then, is reaching an understanding about the nature of emotion. What is an emotion? I do not intend to rescue the term "emotion" from the convenient vagueness and ambiguity it possesses in everyday speech. I use the word widely to cover all of our feelings. But notice that there are two senses of "feeling." A feeling may be anything which we feel, any state of consciousness of which we are directly aware. In this sense feelings include all of our sensations. However, sensations, even the internal sensations such as kinesthetic ones, are not emotions. In the sense in which we are interested here, a feeling is the way we feel about something. It is our noncognitive reactions insofar as they emerge into consciousness that are our emotions. Thus pain and hunger, which seem to involve our reactions to our bodily condition, probably are emotions, but the feelings of warmth or cold probably are not. More clearly, admiration and anger are emotions, but the sensation of redness is not.

When emotions are conceived this widely they include all states of feeling, agitations, moods, and desires. States of feeling tend to be relatively small bits of our inner experience such as pains, a glow of pride, a shock of surprise, or a twinge of guilt. Agitations like anxiety, irritation, embarrassment, or amazement tend to be commotions in the mind violent enough to disturb our powers of intelligent response and confuse the rest of experience. Moods, such as sadness, gaiety, determination, loneliness, or depression, are not bits of experience as much as feeling tones which pervade all of our experience at a given time and may persist for a length of time. Finally, desires such as longing for company, love of money, the wish for fame, or an aversion to spinach may be included insofar as they are felt impulses. The variations between these kinds of emotion are many. What they share is the character of being conscious responses of a noncognitive kind.

One feature of emotion which has a direct bearing on the nature of emotive language is its intensity. The difference between "darn" and "damn," for example, reflects the difference in the intensity of the emotion put into words. It is convenient to speak of emotive language as more or less strong. The strength or weakness of an emotive sentence is a function of the intensity of the emotion it formulates. The intensity to which I refer here is simply the felt intensity of the emotion. This intensity in feeling-quality must be distinguished from other kinds of emotional intensity. The intensity of an agitation depends partly upon the degree to which it distracts us from the rest of our experience and disrupts our powers of reasoning and acting. The intensity of a mood depends partly upon the degree to which it retains its grip on us over a period of time and resists our efforts to change it. The intensity of a desire depends largely upon the degree to which it wins out over other desires and controls our behavior. But these other kinds of intensity do not seem to be reflected in emotive language. The strength of an emotive sentence seems to depend only upon the intensity with which the emotion is felt.

Every emotive sentence, then, possesses emotionality; that is, it puts some emotion into words. An emotion is some feeling of noncognitive response. The same thing could probably be put by saying that our emotions are the conative-affective side of our mental life. Differences in the felt intensity of our emotions is reflected in variations in the strength of our emotive utterances.

5. Expressiveness

"Alas" means grief, but not in the way that "grief" means it. I call the very special way in which emotive language means emotions "expressiveness." Every emotive sentence expresses some emotion; it puts the emotion into words. But in what way is the emotion put into the words? Not the way in which eggs are put into a basket or even the way in which words are put into a sentence. Precisely what is it for a sentence to express an emotion?

It is easier to tell what expressiveness is not than what it is. To express an emotion is not to describe it. The sentence "I am annoyed" describes the annoyance of the speaker. It quasi-compares the speaker's state of mind with other psychological states and claims that it is correctly characterized as of the annoyance kind. The sentence "damn you" expresses the annoyance of the speaker. It does not classify the speaker's state of mind, nor, a fortiori does it claim to be a correct quasi-comparison. That expressing an emotion is not just another way of describing it can be seen from the fact that while it is quite easy for one person to describe the feelings of another, it is quite impossible for one person to express another's feelings. Clearly, to express an emotion is not to describe it.

Less clearly, to express an emotion is not to assert it. "You are annoying" might be said to assert the emotion. Like emotive language it seems to put the emotion itself into words rather than formulating a descriptive judgment about the emotion. Unlike emotive language, it claims that the emotion put into words is appropriate to the indicated object. To say "lions are terrifying" is neither to describe lions as terror-causing animals nor to express one's fear of them. It is to claim that terror is the reasonable way to feel about lions. That such claiming is distinct from describing I will try to show when I discuss critical meaning. That it is distinct from expressing can be readily seen from the fact that rational justification seems uncalled for in the case of exclamations. My friend might disagree if I said "you are annoying" to him. If I said "damn you" to him, he could hardly disagree with my sentence, although he might well resent it.

To express an emotion is neither to describe it nor to assert it. What positive characterization can we give of expressiveness? Perhaps we can find some clues in the ways in which we talk about expressing emotions. For example, we say that an artist expressed his feelings on canvas or that the bereaved widow denied expression to her sorrow. In such cases, to express seems to be to produce something or to do something which externalizes the inner feeling. Emotions are expressed in words in much the same way that they can be expressed in pigments or in tears. The canvas somehow reflects and captures the artist's joy, and the crying releases the sorrow the widow has restrained so long.

What is one doing when he expresses his emotions? What is the point of verbalizing our feelings? First, it seems to be a releasing or letting-out of the emotion. Just as walking up and down may help to relieve one's anxiety so saying "damn you" may help to reduce one's anger. It is a doing something, in this case doing something linguistic, which makes one feel better. Second, it seems to be an ordering or gaining control of the emotion. In putting an emotion into words one at least begins to come to terms with it. In verbalizing his emotion the speaker realizes better how he feels and begins to organize his feelings. To formulate an emotion is to give it form, and to do this is to master it in some degree. But expressing emotion involves the hearer as well as the speaker, as in the case of the friends who call to express their sympathy to the widow. Third, expressing an emotion is displaying it for the audience to perceive. When I bump into someone I say "sorry" to show him how I feel. Often one puts his own emotions into words so that others may be aware of them. The husband who murmurs "my darling" may well be trying to show his wife how much he cares for her.

Thus, to express an emotion seems to be to put it into words in such a way as to relieve the speaker's feelings, to organize them, and to display them. Expressing an emotion is not the same as describing it or asserting it. Such expressiveness is a feature of all emotive language.

6. *Indication*

Whether or not indication is common to all emotive sentences I am not sure. Most emotions seem to be directed to some degree. One is annoyed with somebody, delighted at something, surprised by something, or longing for somebody. To the extent that an emotion is directed at something the sentence in which it is verbalized will have indicative meaning. "Darn those Democrats," "what an attractive necktie," "a rattlesnake under my bed, by golly," and "how I wish that Jane were here"—all these emotive utterances plainly indicate one or more objects at which the expressed emotion is directed. As the emotion expressed becomes stronger we tend to drop the indicative words from the sentence, but the situation in which the words are uttered usually reveals some indicated object. Even a good strong oath such as "damn" is usually hurled at something or somebody. Most emotive sentences seem to possess indicative meaning.

In a few cases, however, it is hard to say whether there is any indicated object. A girl who has been jilted may respond by being angry with her beau, all eligible males, people in general, or the world at large. In each case she might express herself by saying "that damn John," "fellows are no darn good," "nuts to people," or just plain "phooey." In the first three sentences the indicated objects are obvious, but it is not clear whether the last sentence indicates any object at which the emotion is directed. In this case one might be tempted to say that "phooey" indicates everything in the world. Yet consider the case of a person who is suffering from diffuse anxiety feelings. It does not seem as though his feeling of general anxiety is directed at everything. Is he really worried about the pencil he is chewing or the Hottentots about whom he may never have heard? One is inclined to say that his anxiety is directed at no object or objects. If so, any language in which he expressed this feeling would not indicate anything. Thus, although most emotive sentences seem to have indicative meaning, there may be some which do not.

7. Partiality

Another feature which most emotive sentences have is partiality. By partiality I mean the characteristic of being pro or con. Love and hate, desire and aversion, admiration and contempt are all examples of the way in which emotions may be for or against their objects. Sentences which express pro emotions are usually said to have positive emotive meaning, while sentences which express con emotions are said to have negative emotive meaning. Certainly this distinction between positive and negative meaning is an important one for understanding the nature of such language.

Moreover, it is often assumed that all emotive meaning is either positive or negative in this sense. To be neither pro nor con is thought to be without emotive meaning. But consider the "good gracious" uttered by the matron who finds a fly in her tea or the "oops" uttered by the maid who almost dropped the crumpets on the floor. These seem to express emotions which are neither for nor against their objects in the usual sense. One can, of course, define "emotion" so that only those feelings which are pro or con are genuine emotions. But this seems to obscure unnecessarily the basic similarity between the way in which "darn" expresses our anger and "golly" our surprise. Therefore, I prefer to classify all sentences which express our feelings as emotive. If one accepts my classification, then some emotive sentences are neither positive nor negative. Most of them, however, do possess the characteristic of partiality.

8. *Comparison with Description*

It would seem that the meaning of emotive sentences can be characterized in terms of four main features—emotionality, expressiveness, indication, and partiality. It might be helpful to see to what extent descriptive and emotive sentences share the same characteristics.

Every description contains an indicative element. Although there may be no words which indicate what the sentence is about, every descriptive sentence is about something or other. Emotive sentences may or may not be indicative. In some cases the emotion expressed is clearly directed at some object or objects. Then the language which expresses the emotion will indicate, either explicitly or implicitly, what the object of the emotion is. To the extent that the emotion expressed is undirected its linguistic expression will obviously lack any indicative meaning.

Since the point of describing an object is to tell what it is like, quasi-comparison is probably the central feature of descriptive meaning. Every descriptive sentence specifies what kind of thing its object is. But emotive sentences do not do this. "That damn John" does not place John in a class of similar things; its use is not to specify what kind of a person John is. Rather it says how the speaker feels; it expresses the exclaimer's emotions towards John. What takes the place of quasi-comparison as the central feature of emotive meaning is emotionality.

The third feature of descriptive meaning is the assertion-denial dimension. Every descriptive sentence takes a stand on the claim that the quasi-comparison specified is appropriate to the indicated object. An emotive sentence, on the other hand, makes no such claim to correctness. To express an emotion is to put it into words without claiming rational justification for it. This is why it seems pointless to wonder whether an exclamation is really true or false while that query seems always in order in the case of a description.

There seems to be no fourth feature of description to correspond with the partiality which some emotive meaning possesses. Descriptive sentences are never for or against their objects in the sense that emotive sentences may be. If to call something a "senseless extravagance" seems derogatory, that is because these words have emotive meaning, or perhaps emotive force, as well as descriptive significance.

Emotive meaning turns out to be quite different from descriptive meaning. Emotive sentences are used to express emotions rather than to assert quasi-comparisons. While they may share the indicative aspect of descriptions, they need not do so. These differences in meaning are partly reflected in differences in the grammatical structure of the two kinds of sentence. Descriptions are almost always formulated in the subject-predicate manner. It would be possible, of course, to construct a descriptive sentence without this form. One could describe a house by saying "red" as he pointed or nodded at it. In the case of emotive sentences the subject-predicate structure is much less frequent. One may say "you are a fool" or "he is a bungling bureaucrat." Here the grammatical subject indicates the object towards which the emotion is directed. However the indication may find itself expressed grammatically as an object instead of a subject. "Damn you" or "nuts to women" would be examples. At others times there seems to be no expressed subject or object at all. "Damn" or "good gracious" or "alas" show this. Thus, while there seems to be one grammatical syntax which is particularly appropriate to descriptive sentences, any number of grammatical constructions serve in the formulation of emotive sentences.

While we are comparing describing and emoting, we should notice some interesting parallels with the less central features of descriptive language. A descriptive sentence is ambiguous when, according to the rules of the language, it could be used to formulate more than one description. Similarly an emotive sentence is ambiguous when it could be correctly used to formulate more than one emotion. "You brute" has one meaning when hurled at a bully and quite another when murmured by an adoring maiden to her manly lover. Again, "good gracious" can express genuine surprise or only the sarcasm of mock amazement.

The parallels do not end there. Just as descriptive language can be vague, so can emotive language. A description is vague to the extent that it is impossible to determine whether or not it applies to real or imaginable objects. This vagueness is a reflection of the indefiniteness of the rules of language which permit borderline cases to exist. The greater the number, or perhaps percentage, of borderline cases the vaguer the word. In such cases one cannot be quite sure which is the correct word to use. In emotive language, too, there can be borderline cases where there is doubt about which expression is correct. Is it correct to express rather slight annoyance with a "damn"? Emotive language is vague to the degree that it is impossible to determine whether or not it correctly expresses a given emotion.

Finally, emotive sentences can have different degrees of universality. An emotive utterance can indicate a greater or smaller number of objects, just as a description can be about various numbers of objects. "Darn you," "nuts to women," "I hate everybody," and "everything is rotten" are increasingly universal. If there are emotive sentences which do not indicate, of course, they are neither more nor less universal.

9. *Summary*

In spite of these parallels, however, emotive sentences retain their distinct kind of meaning. Every emotive sentence gains its meaning from the emotion which it puts into words. The strength of the emotive language will reflect the felt intensity of the emotion. The sentence means the emotion in the special sense that it expresses it. To express an emotion is neither to tell what it is like nor to claim that it is rationally justifiable. Rather, it is to verbalize the emotion in such a way as to relieve the speaker, to structure the emotion, and to display it to the hearer. Most emotive sentences seem to indicate one or more objects at which the emotion they express is directed, but perhaps some have no indicative meaning. It is likely that some emotive sentences are neither for nor against anything, although many have positive or negative emotive meaning. This is the best I can do to characterize the kind of meaning which emotive language possesses. Whether or not this kind of meaning is important to ethical language we shall see later.

— VIII —

Evaluative Meaning

It is not hard to believe that emotive meaning is fundamentally different from descriptive meaning, for "alas" seems to say something obviously different from "I am grieved." This might, of course, be an illusion; but prima facie, at least, emotive sentences are not descriptions. In the case of evaluative sentences, however, the appearances seem rather to be on the other side. To say "that man is evil" sounds very much like saying "that man is tall." The grammatical and epistemological smilarities are great enough to lead one to wonder whether evaluations are not just a special kind of description. Before we can decide to what extent evaluative meaning is similar to descriptive meaning we must discover what the main features of evaluative sentences are.

THE LANGUAGE OF ETHICS

1. *Indication*

As in description, one feature of evaluation is indication. Evaluation selects the object or objects to be evaluated from the many objects which make up the universe; it points out some limited portion of reality as the subject of conversation. Every evaluative sentence is about one or more objects and does not refer to anything else in the world. It is intended to be relevant to the indicated object and responsible to it alone.

2. *Partiality*

The second feature of evaluative sentences is one which we did not find in descriptive sentences, although we touched briefly on it when discussing emotive utterances. The central feature of evaluation is partiality. To be partial, as I am using the term, is to be pro or con. Like all fundamental notions there is not much one can say to explain it. Partiality is not a property of substantial things or our experiences of them; rather it is the kind of response to these givens. It it not an object to which the mind addresses itself, but a characteristic of the orientation a mind takes towards the objects with which it is confronted. This pervasive and familiar orientation of being for or against something is best explained by examples. Love and hate, admiration and contempt, desire and aversion, approval and disapproval, liking and disliking are all partial. To be partial is to be concerned or interested. If interestedness is taken in its broadest sense, as defined by Perry,[1] it is exactly what I mean by partiality. However we must be careful not to surreptitiously narrow our concept of interest, as Perry does, until desires or appetitive drives are the only forms of

[1] R. B. Perry, *General Theory of Value* (New York: Longmans, Green, 1926), p. 115.

interest. For this reason I prefer to speak of instances of being pro and con as attitudes.

For terminological convenience it is desirable to use the term to cover cases where the concern is neutral as well as those where it is positive or negative. This unites each polarity (love vs. hate, desire vs. aversion) into a continuous dimension through a neutral middle zone. This median is not an absence of concern as much as a point at which concern finds nothing to choose either way. Thus we see that partiality is all forms of indifference and its opposites. It is the characteristic of being for or against something in any degree.

To evaluate anything is to place it on a scale ranging from good through indifferent to bad. In some sense, therefore, all evaluation is comparative. To call something "bad" is to rank it relatively low on the pro-con scale. To call something "good" is to say that it is better than those things which are bad or indifferent. It is this fact which has led some to contend that "better" is the basic value word and that "good" and "bad" should be defined in terms of it. I shall not examine the various ways in which this might be done, since I am not particularly interested in defining one value word in terms of another. Rather I hope to characterize the kind of meaning which all value words possess.

There is also another sense in which comparison is implicit in most value judgments. Suppose that someone says that *Pickwick Papers* is a good book. Now there are many respects in which this is an excellent book; it has interesting characters, a robust humor, and a discerning insight into human nature. On the other hand there are certain respects in which the book is not so good; the characters are only slightly sketched and the plot is diffuse. To say that *Pickwick Papers* is a good book is to weigh the good points against the bad ones and to assert that the book is good on the whole. Every value judgment is comparative in that it involves comparing the pros and cons and reaching an over-all estimate of worth.

There is a special class of value judgments which is comparative in an additional sense. To say that *Pickwick Papers* is a better book than *Martin Chuzzlewit* does more than weigh the pros' and con's of each book separately; it compares the over-all estimates of value against one another. A judgment of comparative value asserts that one object is to be preferred to another, that one thing is worthy of more favor than the other.

I have suggested that there can be many pros and cons toward the very same object. Jane may be virtuous and admirable, but not likeable or interesting. This brings out the fact that there are many ways of being pro or con, that there are many different kinds of attitude. Corresponding to these differences in attitude are the various value predicates. Words like "intrinsically good," "good as a means," "beautiful," "skillful," and "admirable" formulate quite distinct forms of partiality.

There is one kind of value predicate which calls for special mention. What does it mean to call something "morally good" as opposed to just plain "good"? The word "good" can be correctly used to formulate any kind of over-all favor, but the term "morally good" can be used only to put specifically moral approval into words. To understand what sets judgments of moral value apart from other value judgments, then, we must understand what distinguishes the attitude of moral approval from other forms of partiality.

There seem to be three things which distinguish one attitude from another—the kind of object it takes, the kind of action it leads to, and the kind of reason which would count for or against it. For example, contrast sexual love and admiration. Love normally requires an object of the opposite sex and somewhere near the same age as the lover, but no outstanding skill or attribute seems necessary. Admiration can be addressed to a person of either sex and of any age provided that he has some striking ability or characteristic. Sexual love leads to physical contact, kissing, caressing, and sexual intercourse. Admiration tends to result in applause, emulation, and even reward. Finally, love can be defended or challenged by almost any characteristic of the person loved, but admiration can be supported only by naming some outstanding feature of merit which the admired object possesses.

If what I have just said is correct we should be able to characterize moral approval in terms of the kind of object it takes, the kind of action it leads to, and the kind of reason which counts for or against it. Only a human being or his actions can be morally approved or disapproved. Such approval or disapproval tends to result in praise or blame, rewards or punishments, and emulation or its opposite. Finally, only personality traits, habits, or actual actions are relevant to the rational justification of moral approval or disapproval. Sentences of moral evaluation are a separate class of evaluation because they are pro or con in this special way.

3. *Assertion-Denial*

The third feature of evaluation is the familiar one of assertion or denial. In evaluating, one claims that the attitude of favor or disfavor taken is appropriate to the object indicated. Every evaluative sentence claims that it fits its object and can be judged correct or incorrect in the light of its nature. This claim may be asserted, questioned, entertained, hypothesized, doubted, pretended, or denied. Thus we see that the assertion-denial dimension is involved in evaluative meaning.

It might be thought that I have ascribed to evaluative sentences two incompatible features. Evaluations cannot both be pro and con and make a claim to correctness. Partiality is readily acknowledged in emotive sentences that make no claim to rational justifiability, and assertion-denial is a recognized feature of descriptive sentences. As the vast difference between emoting and describing shows, however, they could hardly be joined in a single judgment of value.

One way to defend this objection would be to appeal to the nature of attitudes. If evaluative judgments are really pro or con they must be attitudes. Since there is no way to justify attitudes rationally, they cannot be said to be either correct or incorrect. Therefore, attitudes cannot be asserted or denied in the same sense that descriptive judgments can be. In my discussion of the emotive theory of ethics I explained at some length why I do not find this reasoning compelling. It cannot be taken for granted that attitudes have no claim to objective validity; in fact, the evidence seems to show that they can be correct or incorrect.

Another way to defend this objection would be to appeal to the nature of correspondence. Descriptive judgments can claim to fit reality because they mirror reality in some way. But, since evaluative judgments do not tell what any real object is like, the nature of that object can hardly be said to fit or fail to fit the judgment. This argument seems to me to rest on an oversimplified conception of descriptive correspondence. A descriptive judgment is thought of as some sort of replica of reality. Its correspondence with the facts is then judged by comparing it with reality as a shoe is compared with a foot or a picture with a person. But surely the idea of a large thing is not large and the word "red" is not red. Correspondence is not resemblance, and our measure of truth is not comparison in the usual sense. Once we have discarded this too simple notion of correspondence, it becomes an open question whether or not value judgments can be said to correspond with their objects.

I think that a value judgment may correspond to its object. A judgment corresponds to its object when the apprehension of the indicated object is a good reason for asserting the judgment. The orange, or its taste, is sweet and good. One may bite into the orange and find a seed, but he finds neither the sweetness nor the goodness. To recognize the sweetness of the orange one must quasi-compare it with other foods; to recognize the goodness of the orange one must favor or disfavor its taste. Both descriptive judgment and evaluative judgment go beyond the mere tasting. At the same time, both are justified in terms of what one does taste when he eats the orange. The inference by which one passes from the content of experience to such fundamental judgments is neither deductive nor inductive, but it is rational and genuinely justificatory. Is that noise loud? Is it disagreeable? To hear the noise is to know the correct answer to the second question as well as to the first. Value judgments can make good their claim to objective validity just as descriptive judgments can. In spite of the differences between evaluations and descriptions, we were right in suggesting that they both fall upon the assertion-denial dimension.

I am prepared to claim, therefore, that the three main features of evaluative meaning are indication, partiality, and assertion-denial. Every evaluative sentence is about one or more objects. It directs one's attention to the object and its claim is limited to it. Every evaluative sentence is pro or con; it is for or against its object in some degree including the zero degree. Finally, every evaluative sentence takes some sort of stand on the claim that the attitude which it formulates is the correct one. It claims that the partiality which it puts into words is appropriate to the indicated object.

4. *The Relevance of Attitudes*

I have suggested that the central feature of value judgments is partiality. It is customary in recent writings to use the word "attitude" to refer to any mental state, act, or disposition which is for or against its object. My interpretation amounts, then, to the suggestion that the meaning of value sentences can be clarified by thinking of them as putting attitudes into words. However, I do not believe that evaluation is illuminated by dwelling upon the affective or emotional aspects of attitudes. Neither felt intensity nor internal commotion is to the point; evaluations are never pure feelings and need not be agitations. That aspect of attitudes which does throw light upon evaluative meaning is their partiality, their character of being pro or con. Since all value judgments are for or against their objects, it can be said that all value judgments are, or formulate, attitudes.

Probably the converse cannot be said. There seem to be some attitudes which are not, or would not be expressible as, value judgments. To detest is hardly the same as judging detestable, to desire not quite the same as thinking desirable. In one case we have a psychological state *of* the subject with reference *to* an object, in the other a judgment *by* a subject *of* an object. One is a mental event in the life of an individual person, an existent which claims no objective validity; the other is an appraisal which claims to do justice to its object and to have a meaning and validity independent of the particular appraiser.

Provided these reservations are kept in mind, however,

it does seem to me that the peculiarities of evaluative sentences are best understood by interpreting them as putting certain of our attitudes into words. The emotivists have made much of the importance of attitudes for evaluation, but they have not succeeded in explaining that relevance satisfactorily. What reasons are there for thinking that attitudes do have a genuine relevance for understanding value judgments?

(1) Probably much of the attractiveness of the analysis of value judgments in terms of attitudes comes historically from the fact that it provides one way out of the impasse between ethical naturalism and ethical intuitionism. To many it seemed that the intuitionists had made a strong case against the view that ethical sentences describe their objects in terms of empirical characteristics. To most of these same people the postulation of a realm of nonnatural characteristics was a metaphysical extravagance. Here was a way of interpreting evaluations consistent with an empirical epistemology which did not reduce them to empirical descriptions. Incidentally, it helped to substantiate the suspicion that the intuitionists had themselves committed something like the naturalistic fallacy.

(2) Phenomenological reflection seems to bear out the intimate relation of attitude and value. While it is quite natural to think of goodness as a quality shared by all good things and to which the word "good" refers, a close inspection of the variety of objects which we call good will give one pause. Can we really say that such radically different things as people and pictures, acts and experiences, houses and horses all have something in common by virtue of which we apply the same word to them? For my part I do not find any single characteristic common to all such cases. Even when consideration is limited to examples of intrinsic goodness, I do not believe that reflection upon my experi-

ences of these objects lights upon any common quality of goodness. It does seem to me, however, that in all cases I do find some favorable attitude. It does not seem to be true, for example, that all good experiences are pleasant, but it can be said of them all that I like them. Whenever I judge anything good, I find some favorable attitude towards the object. It seems quite likely, then, that attitudes are at the heart of evaluation.

(3) There are certain logical peculiarities of value terms which set them off from descriptive adjectives but which could be explained if they were taken as formulating our attitudes. It is a familiar fact that certain determinable characteristics take on more determinate forms. The determinate characteristics are similar to one another and yet mutually exclusive. Redness and blueness, for example, are both colors, and nothing can be both red and blue. The varieties of goodness would seem to form a group of similar characteristics analogous to the varieties of color, if they are characteristics at all. However, they are not related as determinate forms of a determinable goodness, for they are not mutually exclusive. This sets goodness off from similarity ranges of descriptive attributes and suggests that both the unity and diversity of value are derived from that of our attitudes.

Another logical peculiarity of value terms lies in the fact that the distinction of intrinsic and instrumental applies to them. In calling some things good we mean that they possess value on account of their own natures; in other cases we mean only that they contribute to the existence of other things which are good for their own sakes. With rare exceptions, we are not tempted to use descriptive terms in this way. We call both the paintbrush and the picture good, but we would hardly call a paintbrush abstract or impressionistic. This distinction between intrinsic and instrumental is applicable to values but not to natural properties. We could account for this on the theory that evaluations involve attitudes, for we favor both those things which we like for their own sakes and those things which contribute to the existence of such things.

A third peculiarity of value terms lies in the range of their meaningful application. In the case of descriptive predicates differences in application may be conclusive evidence that two people are using the term with different meanings. Thus if you consistently applied the word "table" to little four-legged animals which bark but never to articles of furniture which support objects at a convenient height, this would show me that what you mean by the word differs from what I mean by it. On the other hand it is never possible to tell from a difference in application alone that two people mean different things by their value terms. If you consistently applied the word "good" to all sorts of things which I consider evil and nauseous, I would not know whether you were using the word with the meaning I usually express with the word "bad" or whether your valuations just differed radically from mine. A total difference in the application of value terms might reflect complete disagreement over evaluations, but total disagreement over the correct application of a descriptive adjective must reveal a difference in meaning.

(4) The language we use in expressing our value judgments strongly suggests that attitudes are at the heart of evaluations. We say that something is "admirable," inspiring," "praiseworthy," "delightful," "shocking," "lovely," "disgusting," "fascinating," and so on. The very words we use remind us that in some sense what we are saying depends upon our attitudes. This language of evaluation invites the analysis of value sentences in terms of the attitudes they come so close to naming.

(5) Close observation of the people who use evaluative language would seem to bear out this suggestion. We are usually somewhat disgusted by what we judge to be disgusting, and we generally like the people whom we take to be likeable. At the very least attitudes and corresponding evaluation accompany one another. This might, of course, be a remarkable coincidence, but it would make more sense if we suppose that attitude and evaluation are either the same thing or the same in kind. Notice how reluctant anyone is to predicate "good" of that which he dislikes or call "evil" that of which he approves. The use of value terms seems grounded in one's attitudes in some way.

There are two situations where the close relation between our value language and our attitudes becomes particularly obvious. One is where we are speaking to a small child. Notice the smiles with which one intones "good" for the child's benefit or the grimaces and frowns which accompany "bad." The other situation in which attitudes seem to predominate is in disagreement over value judgments. The salient fact in value disagreement is that one party is for something and the other is against it; one favors what the other disfavors. The argument begins when this divergence becomes apparent and ceases when it is resolved. The logical relevance of these attitudes to moral issues may be disputed, but their actual occurrence in value discussions cannot be denied. The fact that evaluative language and attitudes occur together can best be explained by assuming that they are not unrelated.

(6) Finally, there is the fact that evaluations seem to be pro and con in a way which is not dissimilar to that in which certain attitudes are for or against their objects. It is to be observed that certain attitudes can be arranged in pairs—love and hate, admiration and contempt, liking and disliking, approval and disapproval. This cleavage can be

brought out by saying that some attitudes are for and some against their objects. Similarly, evaluations are for and against their objects. The opposition of good and bad, virtuous and vicious seems not unlike that between pairs of attitudes. The sense in which evaluations are pro and con would, therefore, be clarified by analyzing them in terms of those attitudes which bring out the nature of this opposition.

My conclusion is that value sentences should be interpreted as putting attitudes into words. The central feature of evaluative meaning is its partiality, and this pro-con dimension of consciousness is typical of our attitudes. Evaluative sentences do not, however, express our attitudes in the same sense that emotive language expresses our emotions. Rather an evaluative sentence claims that the partiality which it formulates is appropriate to the object it indicates. It might be said that such sentences assert or deny our attitudes.

5. Comparison with Other Kinds of Meaning

Evaluative meaning is quite distinct from descriptive meaning, although the two kinds of sentence do share certain features. To mention one, both are indicative in nature. Every descriptive sentence selects some object or objects from the universe to quasi-compare. Similarly, every evaluative sentence is about some object or objects and does not refer to anything else in the world.

Also, both evaluation and description fall upon the assertion-denial dimension. In every descriptive sentence some sort of stand is taken on the claim that the quasi-comparison specified is appropriate to the object indicated. Similarly the partiality formulated in an evaluative sentence can be asserted, denied, questioned, hypothesized, pretended, or entertained. Every evaluative sentence takes some sort of a stand on the claim to objective validity. There are those who contend that evaluations possess no objective validity at all. I will not pretend to settle that question here. What I do claim, and I hope that those who reflect upon the meaning of evaluative sentences will agree with me, is that evaluations normally *make* such a claim. Although this does not prove that this claim can be substantiated, it does seem to be prima facie evidence that the claim is not entirely empty.

It is in their central feature that description and evaluation differ. To describe is to tell what something is like. Thus quasi-comparison is the heart of any descriptive sentence. The core of evaluation, on the other hand, is partiality. Every evaluation sentence is for or against its object in a way that descriptive sentences never are. To evaluate is not to classify an object but to favor or disfavor it. To evaluate is not to place the object in a classificatory scheme according to similarity, but to place it upon a scale of good, indifferent, or bad. Thus, to evaluate an object is to compare it with others, but not in the sense in which to compare is to specify similarities and dissimilarities. The difference can be brought out by contrasting the two dichotomies of like-dislike with like-unlike. It is this positive or negative feature of partiality which sets evaluative sentences apart from descriptive ones.

The relation between evaluative meaning and emotive meaning is somewhat more complicated. There are two features common to all evaluative sentences which may or may not be possessed by emotive ones. Every evaluation indicates one or more objects about which it is partial. While most emotive sentences indicate the object or objects toward which the emotion expressed is directed, it seems quite possible that some emotive utterances have no indicative meaning. Likewise many emotive utterances share the feature of partiality with evaluative sentences. But, while all evaluations must be pro or con to some degree, it seems that there are some emotive sentences which are neither for nor against their objects.

What is essential to all emotive sentences is their emotionality. It does not seem necessary, however, that the attitudes which evaluative sentences put into words be emotions. Many of our value judgments seem entirely unemotional. Since we often do feel strongly about questions of values, it is probable that many value sentences do express emotion, but this emotionality seems irrelevant to their nature *as evaluations*. Thus, while sentences with evaluative meaning may also have emotive meaning, their emotionality does not seem part of their evaluative meaning.

Probably the most significant difference between evaluative and emotive sentences is that while evaluations claim objectivity emotive utterances make no such claim. Evaluative sentences fall upon the assertion-denial dimension. Each takes some stand on the appropriateness of the partiality formulated to the object indicated. Emotive sentences, on the other hand, make no claim which might be challenged or defended with reasoning. While evaluative sentences assert or deny the attitude they put into words, emotive utterances put emotions into words without making any claim that they can be rationally justified.

Evaluative meaning, then, is quite distinct from both descriptive meaning and emotive meaning. At the same time, some of the distinctions which I made in the case of descriptive sentences can be applied, with the appropriate modifications, to evaluative sentences. Since evaluations share with descriptions the feature of indication, universality applies equally to them. One might say that this boy is good, that some men are evil, or that all women are beautiful. Clearly a smaller or larger aggregate of objects can be selected to be evaluated. Thus evaluative sentences can range from particular to very universal.

Applicability is another form of generality which is as much a feature of evaluation as of description. The breadth of applicability is the range of objects of which a given term may be meaningfully predicated. Attempts to apply certain evaluative predicates to certain classes of objects are not simply false, but literally senseless. Anything may be good, but only something which could conceivably be contemplated as an esthetic object could be judged to be beautiful or ugly; all sorts of things are bad, but only a moral agent can be evil. Evaluations vary in the extent of their applicability.

With indeterminateness the situation becomes more complicated. A determinable is a generic trait that takes on a number of more specific forms that are bound together by similarity yet are mutually exclusive. A descriptive adjective is indeterminate to the extent that it specifies a broader similarity range and allows for more incompatible subranges to fall within it. Thus "color" is indeterminate in comparison to "red" or "yellow." Now the relation of "color" to "red," "yellow," "blue," and so on is very similar to that of "good" to "desirable," "loveable," "admirable," and so on. One can profitably say that "good" is relatively indeterminate and that "admirable" or "desirable" is relatively determinate.

This parallel between descriptive and evaluative predicates is not, however, complete. The similarity ranges which define the logical relations lie in the objects in the one case and in the attitudes toward the objects in the other. The result is that while the more determinate descriptions under a more indeterminate one are mutually exclusive, this need not be the case in evaluation. Although no object can be both red and yellow, there is nothing to keep a person from

222

being both loveable and admirable. Nevertheless, it will be convenient to speak of evaluative adjectives as being more or less indeterminate. Only we must be careful to remember that this relation is not identical in all respects with the analogous one in description.

In their abstractness or concreteness also evaluations are analogous to, but not the same as, descriptions. A description is concrete to the extent that it specifies its object on many determinables; it is abstract to the extent that it treats of the object in only a few respects. Since evaluative predicates do not quasi-compare, they do not specify an object in any respect at all. Yet there is an analogous distinction which can be drawn here. We might say that "good" is more concrete than "morally good," for the former applies to a man by virtue of all aspects of his being while the latter applies to him only insofar as he is a moral agent. Let us say that an evaluative predicate is concrete to the extent that many aspects of the object are relevant to its predication. Or, perhaps more exactly, we can say that an evaluative predicate is abstract or concrete to the extent that the description of any object to which it might be applied in all respects relevant to its application is abstract or concrete.

Now in an important sense evaluative predicates are relatively concrete and most descriptive predicates are relatively abstract. For example, only the color of an object is relevant for the application of "red" to it, and only the taste determines whether an object is sweet or not. But there are many aspects of the object which determine the predication of "good" to it. Consider the wealth of information necessary to decide whether Mary is a good wife or this picture is more beautiful than that. It is partly because of this relative concreteness that value judgments are capable of less conclusive verification and subject to more constant revision than descriptions. One must grasp the object or act to be evaluated in almost its full particularity. In some ways the sort of insight required for value judgment is displayed better in the novel or drama than in mathematics or science. We must not imagine, however, that evaluation is fully concrete. Some information about the object would be irrelevant to its evaluation, not all its aspects are to the point. Moreover, descriptive judgment is often very concrete. Consider what is implied by saying that a certain painting is in the Monet style. On the whole, however, one may say that evaluation is more concrete than description.

6. *Semantical Presuppositions*

What are the semantical presuppositions of evaluation? Since evaluative sentences share some of the features of descriptive sentences, it is not surprising that some of the conditions of their meaningfulness are the same also. To assert or deny an evaluative sentence semantically presupposes that the object or objects which that sentence purports to indicate actually exist. However, one can pretend an evaluation, as in a story or poem, even though the evaluated object is unreal. Another semantical presupposition which evaluations share with descriptions is justifiability. It is meaningless to utter an evaluative sentence unless there is some conceivable evidence which could count for or against it. One need not actually possess, or even be in a position to obtain, that evidence at the moment of utterance. Still, it makes no sense to say that something is good or bad unless one can specify some possible information which would tend to support or weaken the formulated attitude.

Evaluative sentences also possess certain semantical presuppositions of their own. Every evaluative sentence is for or against its object to some degree. As the familiar pairs of attitudes illustrate, there are a variety of ways in which one may be pro or con. Love and hate, admiration and contempt, approval and disapproval, liking and disliking—these are so many different forms of partiality. As I have already suggested, each kind of attitude normally takes a certain kind of object. It does not seem to make sense to assert an attitude toward an object that is not of the sort toward which that attitude or its opposite could be appropriate. Thus one of the semantical presuppositions of any evaluative sentence is that the object indicated is of the kind toward which that form of partiality asserted or denied might normally be addressed. It is meaningless, for example, to predicate moral goodness or wickedness of a tree or a table. Similarly judgments of esthetic value are significant only when made of objects which are or could be esthetically contemplated.

A special case of this restriction upon meaningful evaluation reveals itself in the case of judgments of comparative value. Which is better, a virtuous woman or a beautiful symphony? A new car or a skillful actor? As these questions stand they cannot be answered. Comparative evaluation is possible only within the same form of partiality. In spite of the genuine similarity which attitudes share by being partial, we cannot compare the objects of two different attitudes. It makes no sense to ask whether wealth is more desirable than virtue is admirable. One can only ask which is more worthy of effort or which one should desire more to attain. All sentences that state explicit comparative evaluations semantically presuppose that the objects being compared are the objects of the same form of partiality. Judgments of betterness are possible only where it is the same kind of goodness which is in question.

Several times I have suggested that to evaluate is to place some object or objects upon a scale of better or worse. It now appears that it would be well to replace this concept of a single scale of value with one of several scales. Instead of the model of a single line upon which all objects could be placed, we might use a set of parallel lines. Their identity of direction shows that they share the trait of partiality, that they are all ways of being pro or con. The plurality of lines shows that direct comparison is possible only within the objects of a single attitude, that comparative evaluation is sometimes meaningless.

These seem to be the main semantical presuppositions of evaluation. An evaluative sentence can be meaningfully asserted or denied only when the object it purports to indicate actually exists. Evaluation is meaningful only if it is possible to cite some possible evidence which would count for or against it. A determinate value predicate can be significantly asserted or denied only of an object which is of the same genus as those toward which the kind of attitude it formulates would normally be directed. Finally, meaningful comparative evaluation requires that the objects be compared with regard to the same form of partiality.

7. *Summary*

The main features of evaluative meaning are now evident. Every evaluative sentence indicates one or more objects. It is only these objects about which it intends to say anything and in terms of which it is corrigible. Moreover, evaluations are partial; they are for or against their objects. This pro and con dimension, or set of dimensions, is the core of evaluation. Finally, evaluations fall upon the assertion-denial dimension. Every evaluative sentence takes some stand on the appropriateness of the partiality formulated to the object indicated. The sentence may be asserted, denied, questioned, pretended, or hypothesized. It is in these

226

three features of indication, partiality, and assertion-denial that the meaning of such sentences lies.

We have seen that evaluation is as distinct from description as partiality is from quasi-comparison. Since they share the assertion-denial dimension, however, this distinctness should not mislead us into identifying evaluative sentences with emotive utterances. There is no need to save the respectability of evaluative sentences by showing that they are a disguised form of description and as little need to deny their objectivity by admitting that they can have only emotive meaning. A sheep dog is neither a sheep in wolf's clothing nor a wolf in sheep's clothing. It is a sheep dog. It may not yield much wool, but neither will it kill and eat the sheep. What it will do is to tend the sheep very adequately, and that is what it is meant to do.

Directive Meaning

The imperative mood of speech has long been recognized by grammarians as being distinct from either the indicative or the exclamatory mood. Sentences like "open the window" do not seem to make assertions or express feelings as much as to call for action. Since it is equally possible to call for action by using a sentence in some other mood, I prefer not to label this kind of meaning with the grammatical term "imperative." Instead I shall speak of "directive" meaning. Any sentence which directs action or tells someone to do something may be said to have directive meaning.

There are many kinds of directive sentences. Polite requests, insistent demands, military orders, advice, recipes, instructions, exhortations, some moral codes, the laws of the land, and the rules by which we play games are so many examples of this kind of meaning. In one way or another all of them enjoin action. Since ethical sentences also seem to call for action in some way, it would be well to discover whether they are practical in the same sense that directives are. To do this we must try to characterize the kind of meaning which directive sentences have.

1. *Indication*

The first feature of directive sentences is our old friend indication. The directive "shut the door, John" is not fulfilled if Mary shuts the door, if the wind blows the door shut, or if John shuts the window. The sentence is about or refers to John and the door in a way in which it points to nothing else. This restriction of reference, this drawing attention, is indication.

Every directive sentence refers to one or more agents. The person or persons who are called upon to act must be indicated. Often, however, it is not the words but a nod of the head, a pointed glance, or simply the situation in which the words are uttered which indicates who the agent is expected to be. Grammarians recognize this fact by considering the word "you" as the unexpressed subject of every imperative which has no explicit subject. In addition to the agent, the directive may indicate one or more patients. These are objects other than the agent which are involved in the action. In "cut the cheese with this knife, John" John is the agent, and the cheese and the knife are the patients.

The indicative element in directive sentences also contains a time reference. One could say "open the door within the next few minutes, John." More likely, one would simply say "open the door, John." Here there is an implicit time reference. It will not do for John to open the door next week. The objects indicated are John and the door of the next few minutes.

2. *Quasi-Comparison*

There is, of course, more to directive meaning than indication. It is not enough to point out that John is to be the agent and the door the patient. John could do many things to the door. He could open it, shut it, knock on it, walk through it, take it off its hinges, or even break it down. Which action is he directed to do?

Some characterization is needed to supplement indication. John and the door are told to be related in the shutting fashion. Here quasi-comparison is used to specify what sort or kind of action is called for. Unless some sort of characterization were included, the directive would be empty. There would, for example, be no point in saying "do what this sentence tells you to do." Unless the *what* of a directive is specified, no specific directions are given. For this reason almost every directive sentence contains some descriptive predicates.

This is not always the case, however; "be good" and "don't do wrong" are directives which include evaluative and critical predicates respectively. If these have any content, it is because they assume that the hearer knows what kinds of action are good or wrong. Such entirely nondescriptive directives are understandably rare. Therefore I shall speak in the rest of my discussion as though all directives had some descriptive content. While this is not quite correct, it will greatly simplify my exposition. My remarks can be readily extended to cover directive sentences with no quasi-comparative factor if the reader so desires.

3. *Prescription-Prohibition*

The first two features of directive sentences are indication and quasi-comparison. However, the third is not, as in the case of descriptive sentences, assertion-denial. The quasi-comparison is neither asserted nor denied of the objects indicated. The directive sentence is not made correct by the fact that it is carried out into action, nor is it shown to be mistaken by the fact of disobedience. Moreover, there is no part of a directive which could be made true or false by any conceivable state of affairs. The action called for is conceived, not as something existing which is to be correctly described, but as a possibility which might or might not be brought into being. Thus the descriptive content of a directive sentence is held in suspension as it were. The action it might claim to describe is envisaged, but the claim to describe is not actually made. There is no claim that the quasi-comparison is or is not appropriate to the object indicated.

Instead of describing an existing action, directive sentences are a way of bringing action into existence. They tell someone to do or not to do something. I express this by saying that directive sentences fall on the prescription-prohibition dimension. To prescribe an action is to call for or require it. To prohibit an action is to call for someone to refrain from doing it. To permit an action is either to withdraw a previous prohibition or to assure in advance that no prohibition is forthcoming. In addition to actually issuing directives one may pretend them, as in stories, or entertain them, as in conceiving them. It is this prescription-prohibition dimension which seems to be the central feature of directive meaning.

In order to bring out the nature of this dimension I will attempt to clarify what is involved in prescribing. A directive sentence prescribes in that it tells someone to do an action of the specified sort. But what is it to tell someone to do something? The most obvious answer is that it is to command him to do it. But this will not do. There are other ways of calling upon someone to act. Requests, recipes, advice, and exhortations all tell someone to do something, although none are strictly commands. Commanding is only one form of prescribing. Moreover, what is it to command? It is not very helpful to be told that prescribing is commanding unless the nature of commanding is explained in detail.

As a rule, telling someone to do something causes him to do it. Perhaps to prescribe an action is to cause the hearer to do it. The point of a directive would lie in the effects it causes in the person to whom it was addressed. Just as a person uses a whip to get a horse to run faster, so he says "shut the door" to produce the desired activity. But directive meaning cannot be equated this simply with inciting. A descriptive or evaluative sentence may cause the hearer to respond; yet their meaning is distinct from that of directives. Nor do all directives prove effective inciters, as those of us who are fond of giving advice are so well aware. There is a vast difference between telling someone to do something and getting him to do it, for a directive sentence may be misunderstood or disobeyed. I may not be able to comprehend what the model airplane instructions tell me to do; I may not care to do what my parents tell me to do. Yet it remains true that certain actions were prescribed, even when this prescription is not fulfilled.

Somehow we must allow for the possibility of misunderstanding and disobedience while at the same time recognizing that the speaker intends for the hearer to do what he tells him. The obvious way is to say that to prescribe an action is to try to cause it verbally. What gives directive meaning to a sentence is not the results it actually produces as much as the intention of the speaker to bring about certain results. To tell someone to do something is not necessarily to get him to do it, but it is to attempt to do so.

The person who utters a directive sentence is attempting to produce, modify, or give direction to action.

The effectiveness of this attempt depends upon the context within which the language is used. The use of language to direct action is continuous with other means. For this reason there are various ways of prescribing, various ways of trying to get someone to do something. In commanding, the telling is backed up by the will and force of the speaker, for to command is to be prepared to enforce one's commands. In ordering, what backs up the telling is not mere force, but the authority of the speaker. The army officer need not personally overpower the private with his brawn; he can appeal to his position in the army. By authority I mean the recognized right derived from one's special position in some organization to tell others what to do; to what degree this simply reflects the power of the organization is a nice question which I beg to beg. In requesting, the telling is backed up by the good will of the person asked. The appeal is to his friendship, desire to help, or desire not to be unpleasant. In suggesting, it is assumed that the agent would welcome some suggestion because he is bored or undecided and that a verbal cue will set him off. In advising, one tells another what he should do to further his own purposes. Advice is usually about the means someone might choose to pursue his own goals. In the few cases where one person advises another to choose a certain goal, it is still assumed that this is what the advisee would really want if he only understood. In exhorting, a person who is already tempted or trying to do something is encouraged to go ahead with his action. In instructing, one tells another what detailed acts to do in order to do some over-all act. Suppose, for example, that someone wants to build a model airplane or bake a cake. Such processes are rather complex activities made up of many smaller segments. One tells the person what each of these subacts is and the correct order in which to do them. Instructing is telling a person how to do what he already intends to do. Thus we must distinguish at least commanding, ordering, requesting, suggesting, exhorting, advising, and instructing from each other. These are various forms of prescribing. Presumably there are corresponding forms of prohibiting and permitting as well, but I shall not go into these.

It is important, although hardly surprising, to notice that in every case there is both a prescriber and a prescribee. I have spoken as though directive sentences tell someone to do something, but this figure of speech is possible only because these sentences are used by a prescriber. There is always *someone* telling *someone* to do something. The fact that for every directive there is someone doing the telling and someone being told is basic to the kind of telling involved in these sentences. This fact is reflected in the grammar of the imperative mood, for imperative sentences are normally in the second person. A directive without both a director and a directee would make no sense.

There seem to be two qualifications to the principle that in direction there is always someone telling someone what to do. First, there may be several directors or directees or both. The someone doing the telling or being told may be more than one. There must, however, be at least one person on each end of the telling–being told relation. Second, the director and the directee might be the same person. Someone can tell himself what to do. For example, I might encourage myself to type faster or write some instructions to remind me how to fix the toaster the next time it burns the toast. Such reflexive directing seems to be a degenerate case, however, for it is not clear how I could command, request, or advise myself to do something.

The three basic features of directive meaning, then, are

indication, quasi-comparison, and prescription-prohibition. Every directive sentence refers to one or more objects which would be involved in the action directed. At the very least, one or more agents must be indicated to perform the action, but there may be other objects as well. Unless it is to be empty, every directive sentence must specify what kind of action is called for. Thus it is quasi-comparison which gives content to the directive. Finally, every directive sentence either prescribes, prohibits, or permits the action it characterizes. This prescription-prohibition dimension always involves both a person doing the telling and a person being told what to do, that is, one person using language in an attempt to cause another person to act in a certain manner.

4. *Comparison with Other Kinds of Meaning*

It will help to clarify the nature of directive meaning and to show its distinctness if we compare it with the other kinds of meaning we have distinguished. The obvious place to start is with descriptive meaning. All directive sentences share with descriptive sentences the feature of indication. In both cases the sentences refer to one or more objects. Almost all directives share the feature of quasi-comparison with descriptions. With a very few exceptions directive sentences specify what kind of action is called for. It is these two similarities which have led some to suggest that corresponding descriptive and directive sentences should be said to have the same content. For example, "you will soon shut the door" and "shut the door soon, you" are about the same objects and characterize them in the same way.

It is in what grammarians call their mood that these sentences differ. Descriptions fall along the assertion-denial dimension. They take some stand on the claim that the quasi-comparison is in fact appropriate to the indicated objects. Directives fall along the prescription-prohibition dimension. They call upon the agent to do an action of the kind specified. These two, telling what an action is like and telling someone to do the action, are fundamentally different.

There is one argument sometimes used to establish this difference which seems to me rather weak. Directives must be fundamentally different from descriptions, it is claimed, for they have a very different logic. An assertion and its negation are contradictories, but a prescription and its negation are only contraries. To deny a proposition p is to affirm not-p. Any assertion is either true or false; there is no third alternative. But between the prescribed and the prohibited is the permitted. We must not identify the negation of a prescription with a prohibition. This distinction between "not do A" and "do not-A" is reflected in the everyday expressions "don't bother" and "don't do." It would seem that directive sentences flaunt the law of excluded middle held sacred by the logic of descriptive sentences.

The difference is, however, more apparent than real. No doubt being permitted is a middle ground between being prescribed and being prohibited. But so is being entertained as possible a middle ground between being asserted and being denied. Just as a prescription can be negated in two ways (by being withdrawn or by a contradictory directive), so an assertion can be negated in two ways (by being withdrawn or by a contradictory description). It is true that the law of excluded middle holds for descriptive sentences, provided one prepares the way for a two-valued logic by considering only assertions and denials. But there is no reason there could not be a corresponding law of excluded middle for directive sentences, provided one prepares the way for a two-valued logic by considering only prescriptions and prohibitions. Just as every description is either true or false, so every directive would be either fulfilled or violated. The parallels between the logic of directives and the logic of descriptions need not be denied.

Yet the distinction between the assertion-denial dimension and the description-probibition dimension should not be denied either. Basically the difference between them lies in what the speaker is intending to do with the sentences. In describing an action he is accepting it as something which is or will be actual and is attempting to classify it correctly. In directing an action he is envisaging it as something which might be actual and attempting to bring it about or prevent its happening. It seems clear that telling what the action is like is not the same as telling someone to do it.

It may be thought, however, that we have concentrated too exclusively upon the action. To be sure, describing the action is not telling anyone to do it. But it is possible to call for an action by describing something other than the action, the speaker's desire that it be done. To say "open the window, you" is really to say "I want you to open the window." There may well be contexts in which these two sentences would mean the same thing. But this is because the latter sometimes has directive meaning, not because the former is a disguised description. If "I want you to open the window" really is intended only as a description of the speaker's desires, it is not a directive. This can be seen from the fact that rejecting it would involve disagreement rather than disobedience. If the meaning of the sentence is merely descriptive, then rejecting it would involve saying otherwise, trying to disprove the statement, refusing to believe it, and so on. Rejecting a sentence like "open the window, you" does not involve trying to disprove the imperative or refusing to believe that the speaker wants you to open the window. Rejecting a directive sentence involves, rather, refusing to obey it and resisting any efforts to make one obey it.

It seems clear that the prescription-prohibition dimension is quite different from the assertion-denial dimension. A directive does more than describe an action or the speaker's desire for that action. Unless a sentence tells the agent to do the action, the agent can hardly be said to obey or disobey it. Such directive telling is quite different from telling what the action is like or telling what one wishes. It is using language with the intent of producing the action. A speaker might attempt to produce the action he desires indirectly simply by describing his wishes. But if he *meant* only to describe his wishes, he could never complain that he has been disobeyed; his only complaint could be that his wishes have been disregarded. That these are not the same can be seen from the fact that it is possible to disregard unexpressed wishes but impossible to disobey an unexpressed directive.

Similar considerations apply to the view that directive sentences have a special sort of emotive meaning. It might be thought that they express, rather than describe, the speaker's wishes. I have already rejected this suggestion on the grounds that directive sentences can have no past tense. Thus it makes sense to say "Oh how I wish that you had shut the window five minutes ago" but it is meaningless to say "shut the window five minutes ago."

In fact, the basic features in directive meaning are quite different from those in emotive meaning. To be sure, most emotive sentences do share indication with directive ones. However, emotive sentences have neither of the two remaining features of directive meaning, quasi-comparison and prescription-prohibition. Instead emotive utterances have emotionality, and expressiveness. It seems hardly worth underlining such great differences. Directive meaning is not at all the same as emotive meaning.

The remaining feature of many emotive sentences, partiality, calls for more consideration. It might be thought that the opposition between prescribing and prohibiting might be reduced somehow to that between positive and negative partiality. Since partiality is the central feature of evaluative sentences, I will try to explain the relations between evaluative and directive meaning in some detail.

It might be suggested that to say "do" or "don't do" is to assert one's partiality toward the action specified. No doubt the utterance of a prescription is a sign that the speaker favors the act, and one would be unlikely to prohibit an action he did not disfavor. The person who issues a directive normally does so because of his attitude toward the act in question. Still, prescribing and prohibiting cannot simply be identified with asserting favor and disfavor respectively, for one can favor all sorts of objects but can prescribe or prohibit only actions. The picture may be beautiful and the dinner good, yet it makes no sense to say "do the picture" or "do the dinner." One can, of course, say "paint the picture" or "eat the dinner," but these prescribe the painting and the eating not the picture and the dinner. Obviously direction cannot simply be identified with evaluation.

However, directives might be a special case of evaluations, those which evaluate actions. Alas, matters are not that simple either. To say that an action is good is not to prescribe it, for there may be a better one which one would prefer to see done. Or, to say the same thing in other words, there may be several good actions among the alternatives, but only one can be prescribed at a time.

Even this difficulty might be overcome. Perhaps to say "do A" is to say that A is the best possible action under the circumstances. But here trouble appears in our negative utterances. To prescribe A is to preclude all alternative

239

ways of acting, but to say that *A* is the best action is not to say that all others are bad. The difficulty is that there are degrees of partiality while the "do" or "don't" of direction is an all or nothing affair. While the pro and con of partiality clearly seems connected with the prescription-preclusion dimension, they are not the same.

That direction and evaluation are distinct kinds of meaning can be recognized as easily by approaching the matter from the opposite direction. Evaluative sentences fall upon the assertion-denial dimension. This implies that in some sense every evaluation is either true or false. However, it has long been recognized that imperatives, which are the most obvious illustrations of directive language, have no truth value.

It would appear, therefore, that directive meaning cannot be reduced to evaluative meaning. Although it shares the feature of indication, this is where the similarity ends. Directive sentences normally involve quasi-comparison and always fall upon the prescription-prohibition dimension. Evaluative sentences involve partiality and fall upon the assertion-denial dimension.

5. *Semantical Presuppositions*

Since directive sentences have a distinct kind of meaning, it is to be expected that their semantical presuppositions will differ somewhat from those of descriptive, emotive, or evaluative sentences. For example, every description which is asserted or denied semantically presupposes that the objects it purports to name actually exist. With the exception of the indicated agent, this is not true of directive sentences. When I say "open the window, John" both John and the window exist. But when I request my wife to "please bake me a cake," the cake does not yet exist and may never come into existence. With regard to indication, therefore, the semantical presuppositions of directive language are much more complex than is the case with description. (1) The agent or agents which the directive sentence purports to indicate must exist. It is meaningless to say "open the window, John" unless there really is a John. (2) In most cases the other objects involved in the action must also exist. It is equally meaningless to tell John to open a nonexistent window. (3) In the special case of directing someone to produce something, the directive remains meaningful even though the product is never created. Thus the existence of the indicated objects is usually, but not always, semantically presupposed by a directive sentence.

Sometimes it is said that directives never semantically presuppose that the objects they purport to indicate exist. Mayo, for example, has suggested that imperatives are not about anything in the strict sense.[1] His reason appears to be that the action they call for is always in the future and, therefore, not in existence at the time the sentence is uttered. On the same grounds he denies that future indicatives really refer to anything. One supposes that he would extend this suggestion to indicatives in the past tense as well, for most of the statements we make about the past purport to indicate objects which have ceased to exist.

Although I cannot agree with this suggestion, it does point out the need for me to clarify what I mean by saying that the existence of the indicated objects is presupposed in certain cases. No doubt the objects which descriptions in the past or future tenses purport to indicate may not now exist. At the present moment, they are non-existent.

[1] B. Mayo, "The Varieties of Imperative," *Aristotelian Society*, Suppl. 31: 165–167 (1957).

But if the descriptions are to be meaningful they must exist in the past or the future as the case may be. Similarly, Mayo is quite right that imperatives need not refer to anything which exists *at the time of utterance*. But in most cases they semantically presuppose that the objects they purport to indicate will exist at the time when the action is called for. What is presupposed is that the indicated objects exist at the appropriate time, not at the time of utterance.

The second semantical presupposition of directive sentences concerns the nature of the directee. Directive language always involves someone telling someone to do something. Thus every directive sentence must be addressed to one or more directees; there must always be somebody being told what to do. It is meaningless to utter a directive aimed at nobody, although one can address a directive to people in general. The sign "keep off the grass" semantically presupposes that someone will be walking in its vicinity.

I have said that direction always involves telling some-*one* what to do. Must the directee be a human being? It does not seem meaningful, except figuratively or animistically, to request the trees to wave their branches or to command the stars to stand still. Yet it is not uncommon to request a cat to come here or to command a dog to lie down. It is not impossible that such sentences addressed to animals differ from genuine directives in important respects, but they seem prima facie to have fundamentally the same kind of meaning. Therefore, I do not think that directive sentences semantically presuppose that the directee is a human being. They do, however, presuppose that the directee is capable of doing as he is told, that he is capable of acting. While a directive need not be addressed to a moral agent, it must be addressed to some agent with the capacity for responding to linguistic stimuli in the appropriate manner.

The third semantical presupposition of directive language is that the quasi-comparison must be conceivable. It is meaningless to tell someone to do an action which is logically impossible, for example. Even a lowly private cannot be ordered to stand at attention and at rest simultaneously. However, it does seem meaningful, although rather silly, to order an air force officer who has just crashed his plane to fly back to the base by flapping his arms. The fact that the directee is unable to obey the directive does not make it meaningless, although it would seem a bit harsh to charge that officer with disobeying the command. It seems to be logical, not physical, possibility which limits meaningful direction. At the very least the quasi-comparison which specified the act called for must be conceivable.

The fourth semantical presupposition of directive language concerns its tense. Since it is impossible to change the past, it makes no sense to tell someone to have done something. Meaningful direction is limited to actions which lie in the future at the time when the directive is uttered. This limitation is reflected in the grammatical fact that imperatives have no past tense. This is not, as Hare seems to suggest, simply an accidental feature of English grammar which might be corrected in an "enriched" imperative mood.[2] It is essential to the nature of any sentence that means to tell someone to do something that it be uttered not later than the time at which the action is called for. One of the semantical presuppositions of every directive sentence is that at the moment of utterance there is still time for it to be fulfilled.

[2] R. M. Hare, *The Language of Morals* (Oxford: Clarendon Press, 1952), pp. 187–188.

These seem to be the four basic semantical presuppositions of directive language. In most cases, but not all, the objects which the sentence purports to indicate must exist at the appropriate time. The directee must be capable of responding appropriately to directive language, although he need not be a moral agent. The quasi-comparison must specify a conceivable action. And the sentence must be uttered before the action which it calls for is supposed to take place.

6. *Hypothetical vs. Categorical*

Before we leave the subject of directive meaning, there is a distinction which calls for some consideration. Many of those who assign directive meaning to judgments of obligation place a great deal of emphasis upon the distinction between categorical and hypothetical imperatives. As a rule these are ethicists who have accepted Kant's thesis that only a categorical imperative could be genuinely moral. Unfortunately they do not explain carefully what they mean by being categorical. Sometimes they seem to mean (1) that any genuinely moral imperative must be binding upon all rational beings. On this interpretation a categorical imperative is one which is universal within the universe of moral agents. At other times they seem to mean (2) that some or all moral imperatives are epistemologically ultimate. On this view a categorical imperative would be one which cannot be derived from any other judgment. Finally, they sometimes seem to mean (3) that it is always wrong to exempt oneself from the burden of those obligations which he requires of others. Here a categorical imperative is one which allows for no exceptions. Discussion would be helped if it were realized that the dichotomy categorical-hypothetical really covers several distinctions which are both distinguishable and separable. A few words seem in order on each of these distinctions.

Every descriptive sentence tells what some object or objects are like. Thus it is possible to distinguish various degrees of universality in terms of the range of indicated objects of which some quasi-comparison is asserted. Similarly, evaluative sentences, or any other sentences which fall along the assertion-denial dimension, can be more or less universal depending upon the range of objects about which they make an assertion. But since directives neither assert nor deny, one cannot extend this concept of universality to them.

At the same time there does seem a sense, or perhaps several senses, in which one directive can be more universal than another. "Always tell the truth" seems more universal than "sometimes tell the truth," for the former applies to every situation when one might be tempted to lie and the latter applies only to some of these situations. Again, "everybody leave the room" seems more universal than "some of you please leave the room," for the former is addressed to all the people in the room and the latter to some of them only. As Ladd has pointed out one could classify directives as more or less universal either in terms of the range of occasions to which they apply or the range of agents to which they are directed.

There is a real point in insisting that every moral directive must be universal with respect to indicated agents. The rightness or wrongness of an action does not depend upon who is doing it. Thus an action which would be obligatory for one person would be equally obligatory for any other person under the same circumstances. Whether or not saying that someone *ought* to do something is the same as *directing* him to do it is another question which may be postponed for the moment.

It does not seem so plausible, however, to insist that every moral directive must be universal with respect to the occasions when it is applicable. "Do not lie" probably prohibits everyone from lying on all occasions, but it would be perverse to interpret "tell the truth" as prohibiting silence or writing novels. This prescription is tacitly restricted to those occasions when the agent purports to be speaking informatively. Most directives, in fact, have some explicit or implicit limitations upon the circumstances under which they are to be fulfilled. It is hard to see why this should make them or the acts which fulfill them any less moral.

On the other hand, there is one kind of limitation upon the universality with respect to the occasions of applicability which does seem out of place in a moral imperative. "If you want to, tell the truth" seems to lack the bindingness which one would expect in a dictate of obligation. It is the special nature of the reservation, however, which introduces the leniency. Whether or not one ought to do an action does not depend upon whether he happens to want to do it. Still, the fact that moral directives are not limited to those occasions when we feel like obeying them should not lead us to refuse to admit any specification of the circumstances into a moral imperative.

If by a categorical imperative one means a directive which tells one to do some morally obligatory action, then he should not insist the categorical imperative is completely universal. It is essential to distinguish between universality with respect to agents and universality with respect to occasions. Perhaps the dictates of morality are directed at every moral agent, but they are not addressed to every agent including dogs and cats. While some moral imperatives seem to apply to every situation in which one might find himself, others seem to apply only in certain circumstances.

A second characteristic often taken as definitive of a categorical imperative is ultimacy. Somehow, it is felt, one undermines morality by asking why one should do his duty. There can and should be no reasons to support a genuinely moral directive. Thus a categorical imperative is one which is epistemologically ultimate in that it is not justified by anything outside of itself.

Not every directive is ultimate in this sense. Presumably "never tell white lies" can be deduced from "never tell lies." Again, "close the window" can be supported by "I am cold," "the wind is blowing my papers about," or "the noise is dreadful." While the inference of one directive from another would seem to follow rules analogous to those of ordinary logic, the inference of directives from descriptions or evaluations does not fit these familiar patterns. In either case, however, it seems that many directives can be justified.

This provides a basis for distinguishing between ultimate and derivative directives. A genuinely ultimate directive would be one whose acceptance or rejection is without any grounds whatever. A derivative directive would be one which could be supported either by other directives or by some other considerations. It is useful to have the more restricted notion of systemic ultimacy as well. Just as it is possible to draw up a moral code of prescriptions and prohibitions, so it would be possible to systematize this moral code so that most of the directives could be deduced from a few logically primitive ones. A directive would be ultimate in a given system if it were accepted without proof in that system. A derivative directive in the system would be one which could be deduced from the ultimate directives in that system.

I doubt whether there are any directives which are ultimate in the strict sense. It always seems possible to advance at least some considerations which have a bearing upon the acceptance of any directive. I believe, therefore, that it is a mistake to insist that moral imperatives must lie beyond all justification. At the same time, within any given system of directives there will always be at least one which is ultimate in that system. This fact, however, seems of logical rather than moral interest. Thus it does not seem very fruitful to conceive of a categorical imperative as one which is ultimate.

A third manner of conceiving of a categorical imperative is as one which does not allow of any exceptions. But in this view every directive would be categorical. It is a mistake to think that one can distinguish between those directives which allow of exceptions and those which do not. It is the people who issue directives who allow exceptions when they fail to enforce them; the directive itself does no more than prescribe, prohibit, or permit an action. An exception exists when a directive prescribes or prohibits a class of actions, when most of the agents at whom the directive is addressed conform to it, but when one or a few indicated agents fail to act in the directed manner without being penalized. The directive applies equally to those who conform and to those who do not. If it did not apply to those who flaunt it, they could hardly be considered exceptions to it. It is those responsible for the enforcement of the directive who allow the exceptions by tolerating those who disobey it.

A directive may, of course, be more or less universal with respect to agents. The directive that all men between the ages of seventeen and thirty-five are to register for the draft is less universal than the directive that all men of all ages are to do so. The former exempts men outside the specified age range, however, only in the sense that it is not addressed to them; it does not command them to register and then allow them to disobey with impunity.

In short, a directive either does or does not call for

someone to do a given action, and that is the end of the matter. It is the person who disobeys a directive who makes an exception of himself and the person who issues the directive who allows him to get away with it. Allowing exceptions is not an epistemological property which distinguishes certain directives from others; it is not a characteristic of a sentence telling someone to do something. Rather it is a relation between the person doing the telling and the person being told which arises only after the telling. It does not seem possible, therefore, to distinguish between categorical and hypothetical imperatives in terms of whether or not they allow exceptions.

7. *Summary*

In this chapter I have been struggling with the nature of directives. A directive sentence tells someone to do some action. Every directive must indicate one or more agents at whom it is directed. It may also indicate other objects which are to be involved in the action called for. In addition to their indicative meaning, most directives have quasi-comparative meaning. A directive must specify what kind or sort of action is called for by the agent. Thus, with a few exceptions, every directive sentence has some descriptive content. This is neither asserted nor denied, however, but only conceived. Instead, every directive sentence falls somewhere along the prescription-prohibition dimension. It either prescribes, prohibits, or permits (or entertains or pretends to prescribe, prohibit, or permit) the specified action. There are many ways of prescribing: commanding, ordering, requesting, instructing, advising, and so on. In every case the prescriber is trying to get the prescribee to do something. This attempting to produce, avoid, or give direction to action by the use of language is the core of directive meaning.

— X —

Critical Meaning

The fifth and last kind of meaning which I wish to distinguish is critical meaning. I borrow the label from Castell, but my characterization has more in common with suggestions made by Austin, Hart, Strawson, and Toulmin. As examples of critical sentences let us take the following.

"Snow is white" is true.
Your argument is invalid.
His statement was groundless.
Probably Mars is uninhabited.
Stealing is wrong.
You ought to be more careful next time.

I group these sentences together because in each case the main point of the sentence seems to be to criticize something or other. The objects which are criticized vary considerably. Some are statements, some are arguments, and some are actions. However, all of these various objects are criticized, and on the same basis. Each of these sentences qualifies, accepts, or rejects the claim of its object to be rationally justified. It is this criticism of the claim to rationality which gives these sentences their meaning.

1. *Indication and Assertion-Denial*

The first feature of critical meaning is indication. Every critical sentence picks out one or more entities to be the object of its criticism. The sentence " 'snow is white' is true" is about the sentence (or possibly the proposition) "snow is white." "Stealing is wrong" refers to acts of stealing. The indicative nature of these sentences raises no new problems, although there are many questions one could ask about the nature of the objects referred to in criticism. For example, is it really the sentence, or the thought in the speaker's mind, or a proposition in Plato's heaven, or the act of uttering the sentence which is being criticized? In any event, every critical sentence indicates some object or objects which it can be said to be about.

The second feature of critical meaning is also a familiar one, assertion-denial. Critical judgments can be asserted, denied, doubted, pretended, entertained, or hypothesized. For example, one can say "your argument was invalid," "your argument was not invalid," "was your argument invalid," and so on. Thus every critical sentence falls somewhere along the assertion-denial dimension. Always some stand is taken on the claim that the critical predicate correctly applies to the indicated object.

2. *Criticism*

It is in the special nature of the predicates involved that the new feature of critical meaning lies. Words like "true,"

251

"false," "valid," "incorrect," "unjustified," "reasonable," "right," and "ought" derive their meaning from the role which they perform in the process of criticism. These predicates criticize the objects to which they are applied. Moreover, they criticize their objects in a particular way, in terms of their claim to rationality. By criticism I mean the use of language to modify, challenge, concede, reaffirm, or withdraw a claim to rational justifiability. To understand the nature of criticism, therefore, we must gain some conception of the nature of reasoning.

Reasoning is a process of giving reasons for or against something. It may be a social process in which several people argue with one another about some conclusion, or it may be an individual process in which a single person turns over the pros and cons in his own mind. Ideally this process of presenting and considering reasons and counter-reasons goes on until the weight of evidence is clearly recognized to be on one side or another, but often the reasoning is discontinued by the participants or interrupted by outside causes before any final conclusion is established.

In many ways, to borrow an illustration used effectively by Hart,[1] reasoning is like a trial. Both are procedures by which the arguments for and against some claim are weighed and some conclusions reached. In both a trial by jury and a trial by reason there is a difference between correct and incorrect procedure. Just as there can be a mistrial, so there can be mistaken reasoning. In both cases the goal of the procedure is to reach some verdict which will decide for or against the claim being made.

To be sure, there are important differences as well. The correct legal procedure is established either by custom or by legislation, but the differences between correct and in-

[1] H. L. A. Hart, "The Ascription of Responsibility and Rights," *Aristotelian Society Proceedings*, 49:172–183 (1948–49).

correct reasoning cannot be established by such human actions. In the courtroom there are individuals specifically appointed to be the judge and the jury. In a trial by reason each person is ultimately his own judge and jury. The authority of a legal verdict is derived partly from the force which stands behind it and partly from the respect which the citizens have for the courts. The authority of reason seems ultimately to be free of either of these sanctions.

In spite of these points of difference, the analogy remains useful if not pressed too far. One of the things it can teach us is that criticism is distinct from description. Suppose that a burglar enters my house, steals as many valuables as he can carry, but wakes me as he blows open my wall safe. After a hot pursuit, I manage to capture him and turn him over to the proper authorities. In due course the court will render the verdict of guilty. Now the importance of the judge's assertion "he is guilty" does not lie in the fact that it characterizes the burglar's act as of a certain sort, but that it is the outcome of legal proceedings and possesses the sanction derived from its mode of origin. For weeks I have been anxiously awaiting this verdict. I am interested in it, not as the formulation of a quasi-comparison in which the judge informs me of the nature of the act, but as the verdict of a duly constituted court which will return my property to me and result in punishment for the culprit. Words like "true" and "false" can no more be understood dsecriptively than words like "guilty" and "innocent" can.

A second thing we can learn from this analogy is that the meaning of a critical predicate varies with the place which it has in the process of reasoning. Consider how the word "guilty" can change its meaning as the trial proceeds. When I charge the burglar with being guilty of theft, I am demanding a trial and promising that I can produce enough evidence to make good my accusation. When the judge asks the accused man, "do you plead innocent or guilty," he is asking him whether he is prepared to defend his innocence or whether he will concede without a legal fight. When the prosecution lawyer begins his case by saying "this man is guilty," he is boasting that he will win the trial. When the defense lawyer answers "this man is not guilty," he is not so much contradicting what was said as challenging the prosecution to make good or withdraw its boast. When the judge finally says "this man is guilty," he is rendering a verdict which declares that the prosecution has made good its boast. Thus at one time the word "guilty" can be a challenge to undergo a trial, at another a boast that the trial is going in favor of the prosecution, and finally the verdict of a completed trial. If said by the defending lawyer at the start of the trial, "not guilty" is a challenge to the prosecution to make good its claim; if said by the judge at the end of the trial, it is a dismissal of that claim.

Similarly, critical words alter their meaning somewhat with the stage of the reasoning process at which they are uttered and with the person doing the speaking. "That is false" uttered by Jones just after Smith has made a statement is a challenge to Smith to support his statement with evidence if he can. Probably it is also a boast by Jones that he can present reasons to disprove the truth of the statement. If Jones repeats his charge of falsity after both men have given their reasons, it is not so much a challenge and a boast as a claim that the statement has been disproven and an invitation to Smith to admit defeat. If Smith says "that was false" during the discussion, he is withdrawing his original statement and conceding Jones's point. Throughout this variation in meaning, however, there is the continuing thread of claim being made, challenged, reaffirmed, or withdrawn.

The third thing we can learn from our analogy is the

difference between criticizing and justifying. In a legal trial one can distinguish between the charges being made or rejected and the arguments being presented to prove or refute these charges. Words like "guilty," "negligent," or "innocent" are used to make or repudiate charges and to pass verdicts. But making a charge is one thing and defending it another. The statements of fact made, the documentation presented, the exhibits entered as evidence are the means used in supporting or refuting the indictment. Similarly there is a distinction between the critical and the justificatory uses of language in reasoning. Words like "true," "false," "valid," "incorrect," "right," and "groundless" are used critically; they make, withdraw, reaffirm, or challenge the claim to rationality. Words like "therefore," "if . . . then," "since," and "because" are used in justifying; they introduce and show the relevance of the reasons which are presented for or against the claim to rationality. These are very different uses of language, although they are tightly interwoven in the fabric of reasoning.

Reasoning is much like a trial in the sense that jousting tournaments and ordeals by fire, as well as court proceedings, are trials. A trial is something to be done or undergone, a test which renders a verdict in favor of one party and against the other. Tests of strength were long thought to be one way of obtaining a verdict from God in any dispute. The analogy between reasoning and competitions of strength are illuminating in the case of critical terms. In fact, we often describe reasoning in terms derived from such contests; reasons "attack," or "defend" the statement being considered. When a child on top of a heap of snow chants "I'm the king of the castle," he is not primarily concerned with describing his location a few inches above his playmates, but with challenging them to try to push him off and with boasting that he will be successful in resisting their most valiant efforts. Similarly, to say that a statement is true is much like boasting that one is prepared to defend it with reasons against the reasons of all who disagree. The word "true" does not describe the statement as having a relation of correspondence with reality, but it declares the readiness of the speaker to defend the statement in the lists of reasoning. It is much like the "I'll take all comers" said by a boxer or a chess player. This is more of a boast or challenge than a prediction. Boasts are fulfilled and challenges met; they are not verified or disconfirmed.

"You are wrong" is a preliminary to showing the mistake, a boast about the arguing one is about to do and a challenge to the author of the statement to defend his position. "I was wrong" said at the close of such a contest of reasoning is a retracting of this proud boast or a withdrawing of the claim to rationality originally made on behalf of the statement. "That is false" is much like "draw for your guns." It is a warning of shooting to come and a challenge to the opponent to shoot first if he can; but in reasoning the weapons are bits of evidence not bits of lead. In spite of its grammatical form "draw for your guns" is not really an imperative. You will not have disobeyed me if you refrain from drawing; you will simply have let my challenge-boast go by default. Challenges are not disobeyed; they pass unheeded. Boasts are not disobeyed; they are disregarded. Toulmin seems to have failed to notice this, for in *The Uses of Argument* he appears to identify the force of a modal term with directive meaning.[2] Actually, critical meaning is quite distinct from directive meaning. Challenging someone to do something is not the same as telling him to do it. The boy chanting from the top of the heap of snow

[2] S. E. Toulmin, *The Uses of Argument* (Cambridge: Cambridge University Press, 1958), p. 30.

256

is not commanding his playmates to push him off, he is daring them to do so.

Of all the forms which trials of strength can take, the duel or fight to maintain one's honor is particularly illuminating. It is assumed without question that every gentleman is prepared to defend his honor; that is, as it were, implicit in being a gentleman. In similar fashion it is assumed that every rational man is prepared to defend his assertions and his actions with justifying considerations; that is implicit in asserting seriously or acting responsibly. Just as gentlemen do not go about fighting one another all the time, so we do not need to be continually justifying our sayings and doings. A duel takes place only when one person perceives an insult in the other's speech or conduct and provokes a fight by some symbolic gesture. Analogously two people argue with one another only when one perceives an error in the other's assertions or actions and provokes an argument by some critical challenge. However, unless a man is prepared to fight when challenged, he is no gentleman; and unless a man is prepared to justify himself when criticized, he is not fully rational. In this way the claim to rationality is implicit in all asserting and acting.

"That is false" or "you are wrong" is analogous to slapping a man's face with one's gloves; only it is a challenge to rational debate rather than mortal combat. "Yes, I was mistaken" is like throwing down one's sword in submission to terminate a duel. The critical use of language is closely analogous to the challenge, the acceptance of the challenge, the admission of defeat in dueling. The justificatory use of words should be compared to the actual thrusting and parrying with swords. Just as the very meaning of the signs and gestures by which one expresses his claim to honor cannot be understood apart from the institution of dueling, so the meaning of critical language cannot be understood apart from the activity of reasoning.

3. *The Claim to Rationality*

Critical sentences challenge, reaffirm, or withdraw the claim to rationality. Exactly what is involved in this claim? To be rational involves being reasonable, being able to reason. In making any assertion one tacitly claims that he is in a position to give reasons for it. This is possible, of course, only if such reasons exist and if the asserter possesses the intellectual ability to recognize and present them. But being reasonable includes more than being able to reason; it also includes the exercise of this ability. The unreasonable man is not simply the one who is without the capacity for reasoning, but the one who refuses to do so. To judge without evidence is to be unreasoning, but to ignore evidence which is at hand is to be unreasonable. The claim to rationality includes the claim that one is in a position to justify himself with reasons and that he has not overlooked or contravened more weighty reasons against him. It is the claim that one is judging responsibly.

To judge responsibly is to be able to respond, to be prepared to defend one's judging. It is also to be liable to respond. One judges responsibly only when he recognizes the legitimacy of the demand to defend his judgment. This liability to respond is not a demand forced upon one from without but is taken upon oneself in the act of judging; in committing oneself to any assertion or action one assumes the liability to be called to account. Thus the claim to rationality is the claim that one can support his assertion or action with reasons, that he has not done violence to the opposing reasons, and that he recognizes the liability to be called before the court of reason.

So far I have spoken only of *the* claim to rationality as though there were only one form which such a claim could take. And, in a sense, this is so. The claim is always that reasoning will bear out the judgment, that the critical consideration of all relevant factors will show that this is the only rationally justified judgment. This common claim does have two distinct forms, however. These are the claim to actual truth and the claim to necessary truth.

Any assertion (descriptive, evaluative, or critical) claims that it is correct and that all contrary assertions are mistaken. However, the fact that for any given assertion there are other incompatible assertions requires the judger to have some reason or grounds to judge in one manner rather than another. The question of which of the alternative assertions is to be accepted and which denied can be rationally determined only by appeal to the relevant considerations. The claim to actual truth is the claim that the assertion made, while only one among several conceivable alternatives, can be shown to have the weight of evidence on its side. This claim can be made good by showing that the given assertion can be supported by more or stronger reasons than any of its alternatives and that any opposed considerations are either mistaken or inconclusive.

When a judger presents considerations to support this claim to actual truth, however, a new sort of claim emerges. Suppose that someone offers p in support of q. Now p really supports q only if it is itself actually true and is logically relevant to q. Let us ignore the claim that p is actually true, since this is simply the same form of the claim to rationality made on behalf of another judgment. The claim that p really does confirm q, on the other hand, is quite a different sort of claim. This is not a claim about the actual truth of a judgment, but about the necessary validity of an argument. The claim is that one judgment determines the other, that it is inconceivable that the first be true and the second false. The reasoning which defends this claim to necessary truth is not the presentation of additional grounds for judgment but the complete understanding of the judgments already involved. This claim that the assertion of p and the denial of q cannot be thought together is supported by thinking itself.

The claim to rationality, the claim that reasoning will show the given judgment to be correct, takes two primary forms. The claim to actual truth is the claim that there are good reasons or determining grounds for the acceptance of one judgment among conceivable alternatives. The claim is that while there are a variety of possibilities presented to thought the one which is actualized can be known by an appeal to other judgments and, finally, to experience. This claim is challenged and defended, refuted or made good, only by presenting the relevant considerations, by appealing to all known facts with any logical bearing on the issue. The claim to necessary truth, on the other hand, is the claim that there are no alternatives conceivable, the claim that the acceptance of one judgment removes the freedom to accept or reject another. This claim that thinking one judgment necessitates thinking another, or that the acceptance of one and denial of the other is unthinkable, is tested by the thinking of the judgments in question. If alternatives are found, the claim to necessary truth is mistaken; if one finds himself unable to conceive of any alternatives, the claim is vindicated.

Critical meaning, we may now say, has three main features—indication, assertion-denial, and criticism. Every critical sentence refers to one or more objects of criticism. A critical sentence asserts, denies, pretends, entertains, or hypothesizes the claim that some critical predicate is appropriate to the indicated object. Finally, every critical sentence modifies, reaffirms, challenges, withdraws, or repudiates the claim to rationality implicit in that object.

There is one set of critical words which I have hardly mentioned as yet. These are the expressions which Urmson has called "parenthetical verbs" and which he has characterized in a way which I find very suggestive. "I know," "I believe," "I think," and "I guess" belong in this category. Expressions such as these do not serve to describe what is going on in the speaker's mind at the moment of utterance but to underline and modify the claim to rationality he is making on behalf of his utterance.

4. *Performatory Meaning*

One of these ("I know") has received a considerable amount of attention by Austin in his now famous "Other Minds" article.[3] This raises the question of whether what I have called critical meaning is not simply performatory meaning under a new flag. To be quite honest I do not know, for I have never been able to find a clear statement of the nature of performatory meaning. The model for performatory meaning would seem to be "I promise" said by a person making a promise. To judge by his article Austin seems to have wished to make three points by labeling such expressions "performatory." (1) They are nondescriptive. To say "I promise" is not to describe a mental act of promising which is somehow like resolving but more internally binding. Promising is not some hidden mental process of a peculiar kind which is simply reported by the speaker. (2) These expressions are used in the actual performance of some action. Saying "I promise" *is* promising. Uttering the words is actually doing the promising; to make a promise is

[3] J. L. Austin, "Other Minds," *Aristotelian Society*, Suppl. 24:148–187 (1950).

to say "I promise" in the appropriate context. It is this public saying which is the origin of the bindingness involved. Presumably such expressions are called "performatory" to emphasize the fact that in these cases uttering the words is performing the activity in question. (3) The exact expressions one uses in these linguistic performances are certain established formulae. It is important to say "I promise to return your book" not simply "I will return your book." By uttering the special formula "I promise" one binds himself more firmly. This seems to be implied by Austin's frequent references to the language of ritual.

If this is accepted as an accurate account of performatory meaning, should it be said that critical predicates have performatory meaning? I would agree (1) that they are non-descriptive. The peculiarities of critical language do not come from the fact that it describes a very special subject matter but from the fact that it is concerned with claiming rather than describing. (2) I would also agree that uttering critical language is performing some activity, but I can see no special significance to this point. Uttering any kind of language is doing something; this is not restricted to any particular kind of meaning. The important question is not whether one is doing anything when he uses certain words but what he is doing. There seems no point in labeling certain expressions performatory unless one specifies exactly what kind of performance they involve. The only hint which Austin gives is that in saying "I know" one is giving others his authority to make the statement which accompanies these words. No doubt this is part of the meaning of this expression. But I have tried to show that there is more to it than this; what one is committing oneself to in the use of critical language is some stand on the claim to rationality. Besides, unless more is said about what is involved in "giving one's authority," to be told this much is to be told very little. I probably would not agree (3) that critical language employs formalized language. In one sense all language is formalized. In order to say anything in ordinary language one must use the word or words which are ordinarily used for that purpose; there is always a difference between correct and incorrect word choice. But when we speak of the language of ritual as formalized we mean more than this. We mean that although there are several ways of saying what would ordinarily amount to the same thing, only one of these is considered ritualistically effective or proper. This does not seem to be true of critical language. Expressions like "I know," "is groundless," and "is true" seem no more stylized or traditional than any other part of language. In short, I would not strenuously object to the contention that critical sentences have performatory meaning. On the other hand, the label "performatory" does not seem to be clear enough to be very helpful; and when its significance is spelled out, it does not seem to tell us very much about critical language. I have tried to give both a more restricted application and a more fully developed content to my own label.

5. Aspects of Critical Meaning

There are a number of aspects of critical meaning which it is important to distinguish. Critical sentences modify, reaffirm, challenge, withdraw, or reject the claim to rationality. In so doing they pass judgment upon the claim made by their objects. Clearly it is possible to declare either for or against the claim. Every critical sentence takes some stand on whether or not the claim to rationality of its object is tenable. "P is true" declares that p's claim to rationality is tenable. "That is false" maintains that the claim of the assertion being criticized is untenable. Similarly, to call an action "right" is to reaffirm its claim, but to call it "wrong" is to challenge or reject its claim to rational justifiability. Critical sentences might be said to be positive or negative depending upon whether they uphold or reverse the claim which they criticize.

The second aspect of critical meaning is its explicitness. Every serious assertion or responsible action involves a claim to rationality. To say "snow is white," for example, is to be prepared to establish the whiteness of snow or to withdraw the statement. Normally one does not bother to emphasize this claim. It is implicit in the act of asserting and reveals itself only in the word order, the tone of voice, and the facial expression. If this claim should be questioned, however, it becomes the center of attention. To say " 'snow is white' is true" is to endorse the claim explicitly; and to say " 'snow is white' is false" is to challenge or reject that claim explicitly. Critical sentences, then, make explicit the claim to rationality which is implicit in all assertions or actions. In fact, the assertion-denial dimension which we found in description and evaluation is simply implicit critical meaning. There can be degrees of explicitness. Between "snow is white" and " 'snow is white' is true" stands "snow is truly white."

To the extent that the claim to rationality is the primary concern in judging, it is explicit; to the extent that the claim is secondary to the content being judged, it is implicit. Whenever the question of accepting or rejecting a judgment comes up, one may pay particular attention to *what* one might accept or reject or to *whether* one is to accept or reject it. I cannot judge without committing myself to the correctness of my judging; I cannot maintain a claim to correctness without specifying what I take to be correct. The content judged and the claim to correctness are inseparably united in the judging. Yet one may be emphasized more than the other. To the degree that a sentence emphasizes a claim to correctness it can be said to have explicitly critical meaning.

It will be noticed that the claim to rationality which a critical sentence judges is that of something other than that sentence itself. The sentence " 'snow is white' is true" explicitly criticizes the claim to rationality of the sentence "snow is white." At the same time it makes its own implicit claim to rationality. Since one could equally say " 'snow is white' is not true," the sentence " 'snow is white' is true" falls within the assertion-denial dimension. Like any assertion it claims that it can be supported by evidence more strongly than any of its alternatives. Thus a critical sentence possesses its own implicit claim to rationality and at the same time makes explicit the claim to rationality of its indicated object.

This raises the perplexing question of the synonymy of a judgment in which the claim to rationality is merely implicit with one whose noncritical content is the same but in which the claim is explicit. Do "snow is white" and " 'snow is white' is true" have the same meaning? I would suggest that a critical judgment is not synonymous with its corresponding uncritical judgment, but that the difference of meaning lies exclusively in the degree to which the critical meaning is explicit. "Snow is white" functions primarily to describe; it may be used to inform, amaze, deceive, and so on. " 'Snow is white' is true" functions primarily to criticize; it may be used to invite reasoning, to repeat a previous assertion, or to concede a claim to rationality. This difference is sufficient to keep the two judgments from being identical. The critical judgment is not the same as, but is about, the object it indicates. The difference of meaning, however, is limited to critical meaning. The critical judgment has no additional descriptive or evaluative meaning. " 'Snow is white' is true" says no more than "snow is white" does in the way in which "snow is white and cold" might be interpreted to say more. There is nothing which one states or claims which the other does not state or claim. The difference lies exclusively in the degree to which the claim to rationality is explicit. Yet this difference is important enough to lead us to classify critical sentences as having a distinct kind of meaning.

The third aspect of critical meaning which I wish to point out is its strength. Just as a boast may be made in a loud voice so that everyone can hear or uttered softly to those close at hand and a challenge may be issued with assurance or trepidation, so the claim to rationality may be made confidently or hesitantly. Here is where our friends the parenthetical verbs come into the picture. Increasing degrees in the strength of the claim to rationality are shown by the expressions "I guess," "I think," "I believe," and "I know." Expressions like "probably," "certainly," and "possibly" function in the same way. They show the degree to which one is confident of the claim he is making and the extent to which he is prepared to defend it under criticism.

The fourth aspect of critical meaning is its width. One may criticize in the light of a wider or narrower range of considerations. To say "that is false" is to say that the claim cannot be upheld in the face of all the evidence. To say "that is groundless" is merely to deny that the person who made the statement being criticized had any evidence when he spoke; it is not to say that there is no evidence for it at all. Criticism may be limited to the considerations which the speaker is actually aware of, or it may be based upon all those considerations which he could have been aware of with a certain amount of effort, or it may take account of all possible considerations. Differences of width are shown by the philosophically commonplace distinctions of correct and reasonable conjecture, true and credible belief, and objective and subjective rightness of action.

At least these four aspects of critical meaning must be distinguished. A critical sentence can be positive or negative; it can say that the claim it is judging is tenable or that it is untenable. A critical sentence makes explicit the claim to rationality which is implicit in some other assertion or in some action. The claim to rationality may be made more or less strongly; one may commit himself with various degrees of completeness to the defense of some claim to rationality. Criticism may be in the light of more or less evidence; the width of the criticism may vary.

6. *Semantical Presuppositions*

What are the semantical presuppositions of critical meaning? Under what conditions can one meaningfully use critical sentences? The first condition seems to be that the indicated object must exist. Something has to be before it can be criticized. It makes no sense to say "that is false" unless someone has just asserted something. "What you did was right" semantically presupposes that you actually did some action.

But surely we can criticize imaginary actions. We can say, for example, that it was wrong of Oedipus to taunt Tiresias, although the action of taunting never really existed. This same problem arises over descriptive and evaluative sentences as well. We can say that Oedipus was easily provoked or that he was a basically good man. One could regard these as tacitly hypothetical. To say that what Oedipus did in the play was wrong might be to say that if anyone actually did the same action it would be wrong. Probably a better way to treat these critical judgments is as pretended rather than actually asserted. When one criticizes a make-believe action, he is for the moment himself becoming part of the make-believe world. It is only from a standpoint within the context of the play that one can describe, evaluate, or criticize Oedipus.

The second semantical presupposition of critical language is that the indicated object is of the kind which could make a claim to rationality. It is meaningless to say that a tree is true or that a sensation is false, for these are not the kinds of things which can be correct or incorrect. At the same time it is not necessary that the object criticized actually make a claim to correctness. My impulsive act of retaliation was done in a rage so fierce that I did not stop to think what I was doing. Yet I could have deliberated, and this is enough to make my action subject to criticism.

What kinds of things are subject to criticism? There seem to be two conditions which must be fulfilled before anything can claim rationality. (1) There must be some choice involved. One can describe the book as red or as blue. One could steal the money or not steal it. One could favor or disfavor the painting. There must be conceivable alternatives before the question of which one is more rationally justified can even be raised. This question is pointless, however, unless there is some reason to answer it in one way rather than another. (2) There must be some possible reasons for or against each alternative. Only where the choice can be made in the light of relevant considerations can it claim to be rational.

I am not sure how many kinds of things meet these requirements but at least statements, human actions, and human emotions seem to do so. Asserting or denying any description, evaluation, or criticism is always subject to criticism. Human actions are also criticizable as right or wrong, rational or irrational. Animal actions, however, do not seem subject to criticism. It does not seem to make sense to say that Fido did wrong when he chewed up my best slippers. Probably this is because Fido cannot be said genuinely to choose, much less to choose in the light of relevant considerations. Finally, human emotions appear to be criticizable. One can say that John's love is irrational or that Mary's fears are unreasonable. The given in experience, on the other hand, seems below the level of criticism. That is why it provides an ultimate basis for judgments of actual truth.

The third semantical presupposition of critical language is that the critical predicate cannot be both positive and negative in the same respect. It makes no sense to say that a certain statement is "true and false." One can apply both positive and negative critical predicates, however, if they differ in width. One can legitimately say that a lucky guess is both true and unfounded or that an action is both subjectively right and objectively wrong. One cannot say that a belief is both reasonable and groundless, but he can say that it is both reasonable and mistaken.

The fourth semantical presupposition of critical language is that there be some possible evidence to support any meaningful criticism. Since critical sentences fall within the assertion-denial dimension, they presuppose that the claim to rationality which they make can be defended by appeal to some relevant considerations. In a way this semantical presupposition is redundant; for if the second presupposition is fulfilled, this one will be also. Thus, if the object of criticism is such that its claim can be supported by relevant considerations, then the critical judgment can appeal to these same considerations to support its own claim to rationality.

These, then, are the four semantical presuppositions of critical language. The object which any critical sentence purports to indicate must exist, unless that sentence is only entertained or pretended. The indicated object must be of the kind which is subject to criticism; that is, it must involve a choice for or against which reasons could be given. No critical sentence can apply both positive and negative critical predicates of the same width to its object. Finally, there must always be possible evidence to support any meaningful criticism.

7. Judgments of Obligation

I have stated, rather dogmatically so far, that among the legitimate objects of criticism are human actions. This suggests that judgments of obligation might well be regarded as a species of critical judgments, those dealing with actions. I am prepared to argue that in fact this is the most enlightening way of interpreting this kind of ethical sentence. To say that an action is right is to assert that its claim to rationality is justified; to say that an action is wrong is to assert that the claim is mistaken. Again, to say that one ought to do an action is to assert that leaving it undone would be unjustified; to say that one ought not to do an action is to assert that doing it would be unjustified. Words like "right," "wrong," and "ought" function very much like the words "true," "false," and "unreasonable."

On my view, judgments of obligation are simply one species of the genus critical judgments. Any critical judgment whose indicated object is a human action may be said to be a judgment of obligation. Within this species, however, there is a very important subspecies, that of judgments of moral obligation. "One ought not to eat peas with his knife" might be said to be a judgment of obligation, but it hardly seems to formulate a genuinely moral obligation. What is it that distinguishes certain judgments of obligation as being specifically moral?

Presumably it is the kind of criticism which they formulate. Only certain kinds of criticism of action are thought to be specifically moral. No doubt there are many factors which distinguish moral from nonmoral criticism, but I will mention three which particularly impress me. (1) The reasons for or against the action are strong ones. Where the relevant considerations are trivial the obligation is not moral. (2) Characteristically, but probably not always, these considerations involve the welfare of others. Criticizing an action morally usually involves considering its impact upon the lives of others. To the extent that an action will affect only the agent himself we are inclined to say that no specifically moral obligation exists. (3) Often there is a temptation to act in a manner contrary to the preponderance of reasons. As Kant emphasized, the oughtness of morality comes out most clearly when inclination is in conflict with reason. There seems, however, to be no sharp line separating specifically moral criticism from nonmoral criticism of action. For this reason I do not regard judgments of moral obligation as essentially different from judgments of obligation in general. In fact, judgments of moral obligation appear to be less distinct from other judgments of obligation than judgments of moral value are from other value judgments.

In my opinion judgments of obligation are simply those critical judgments which deal with human action. There are those, however, who would argue that their meaning is not critical. I must explain why it seems better to say that judgments of obligation have critical meaning than any of the other kinds of meaning which I have distinguished. In so doing I will at the same time be showing that critical sentences have a kind of meaning which is distinct from the others which I have discussed.

Some contend that to say that an action is right or wrong is to describe the action as possessing the characteristic of rightness or wrongness. Judgments of obligation are a special class of judgments which tell what actions are like. My objection to this interpretation is essentially that it commits the naturalistic fallacy. That is, it treats the question "should I do the action?" as though it were the question "what is the action like?" Suppose the action does have the characteristic of rightness, why should I do it? The question of what one ought to do cannot be identified with the question of how one ought to describe an action. The real ethical problem is what reasons there are to do or not to do the action in question. This is precisely the question which a critical judgment considers.

Others contend that judgments of obligation have emotive meaning. To say that an action is right or wrong is to express one's feelings for or against it. But emotive sentences do not fall along the assertion-denial dimension. Therefore, this interpretation fails to explain why we consider it possible for a person to be mistaken in his ethical opinions. It also fails to explain why we do not regard every ethical argument which proves persuasive as a logically correct bit of reasoning.

Perhaps judgments of obligation have evaluative meaning. To assert that an action is right or wrong would be to assert a pro or con attitude toward the action. But then what does one do with the commonly recognized distinction between judging an action wrong and judging it evil? Suppose that a mother who knows that her child has eaten several green apples during the day gives the child some pills to cure its stomach-ache. The next morning the child is dead from appendicitis. Surely it is not meaningless to say that while the mother did what was wrong she is not wicked. Another reason that I hesitate to identify judgments of obligation with judgments of value is that we often support the former with the latter. But one statement cannot be a reason for another when they both have the same meaning; reiteration is not justification. Since it seems to be legitimate to argue that an action is wrong because it is bad, saying that it is wrong cannot mean the same as saying that it is bad.

Perhaps the most tempting alternative is to hold that judgments of obligation have directive meaning. One could explain the practical import of judgments of obligation by maintaining that they call for action as well as by claiming that they criticize action. However, directive sentences tell someone to do something. This is reflected in the grammatical fact that imperatives are normally in the second person. On the other hand, judgments of obligation can be put in the first or third person just as naturally as in the second. Also, judgments of obligation are frequently in the past tense, but there is no past tense to the imperative mood. While it makes perfectly good sense to say that a person ought not to have done an action, it is meaningless to tell him not to have done it. Finally, directive sentences can be addressed to animals, but the actions of animals do not seem subject to criticism. One can tell a dog to lie down or a horse to whoa, but it does not seem meaningful to say that the dog ought to lie down or that the horse ought to stop. Judgments of obligation cannot be interpreted as having directive meaning.

So far my argument has been essentially negative. Judgments of obligation do not have descriptive, emotive, evaluative, or directive meaning. But what positive reasons are there to suggest that they do have critical meaning? I can think of five.

(1) One might, of course, admit the existence of critical

meaning but wish to limit its applicability to propositions or statements. One might contend that, while statements are obviously true or false, actions cannot be properly said to be either. What is more, there is not a sufficient parallel between the two to make it helpful to suggest that actions are correct or incorrect in at all the same sense that statements of fact are. Unfortunately, this tempting restriction of rational criticism seems to mean the end of ethics. If the action itself cannot literally be said to be correct or incorrect, what could it mean to predicate rightness or wrongness of it? More important, what becomes of the problem of choice? Choice constitutes a problem, rather than a merely psychological process, only when it is presupposed that one alternative is more justified rationally than another. If the distinction between correct and incorrect really does not apply to actions, then there are no genuinely practical problems at all. I doubt whether anyone seriously accepts this consequence of denying that human actions are subject to criticism. But, if critical meaning can apply to actions, the obvious candidates for this task are judgments of obligation.

(2) The key words which occur most frequently in judgments of obligation are "ought," "right," and "wrong." These same words also occur in sentences whose meaning seems obviously to be critical. "That statement is quite right." "Your reasoning is all wrong." "From the looks of those clouds, it ought to rain before morning." Although it is possible that these words are ambiguous and have different kinds of meaning in the two contexts, it is more probable, in the absence of strong contrary evidence, that this verbal identity reveals a semantical similarity. This probability is vastly increased by the fact that so many, not just one or two, of the key words in which judgments of obligation are formulated also occur in undeniably critical sentences.

(3) Many of the sentences formulating judgments of obli-

gation fall into two groups, those using the words "right" or "wrong" and those using the words "ought" or "ought not." While the first pair of words are logical contradictories, the second pair are not. By interpreting both pairs of terms as having critical meaning it is possible to explain both their essential similarity of meaning and their logical difference. To say that an action is wrong is like saying that it ought not to be done; both challenge the claim to rationality implicit in the action. But saying that it is right is not at all the same as saying that it ought to be done. Exactly what is the difference? To say that an action is right is to concede its claim to rationality; it is either to withdraw a challenge made or to grant that no challenge will be made. To say that an action ought to be done is not simply to concede its reasonableness, but to press the unreasonableness of leaving it undone. This interpretation makes it clear why "ought" is a stronger word than "right" even though "ought not" is equivalent to "wrong."

(4) Most judgments of obligation seem to be binding in some way upon the person to whom they are addressed. To explain this element of constraint Kant and others have interpreted ought sentences as one class of imperatives. We have seen, however, that judgments of obligation cannot have directive meaning. How, then, can we explain the sense in which they are binding? By interpreting them as one class of critical sentences. To say that an action ought to be done is to press the claim that it would be unreasonable to leave it undone; to say that an action ought not to be done is to press the claim that it would be unreasonable to do it. Such sentences speak to the potentially irrational man. They challenge that man to stop and reason in spite of his impulses urging him to act, and they claim that in the end this reasoning will lead to an action opposed to what he is now tempted to do. Thus by assuming that judgments

of obligation possess critical meaning we can explain just what Kant wanted to explain, the sense in which ought sentences are constraining. We can also explain far better than Kant did exactly why ought sentences speak only to one who is rational but imperfectly so.

(5) To assume that judgments of obligation are critical also explains their logical redundancy. Falk has pointed out that we appeal to judgments of obligation when trying to justify some course of action but that these judgments do not seem to replace or supplement the reasons we give for doing the action. "You ought to" seems to be part of the process of reasoning, but a logically redundant part.[4] This can be readily explained in terms of my distinction between the critical and the justificatory uses of language. Both kinds of language function within the process of reasoning, but in very different ways. Critical language makes, modifies, presses, challenges, rejects, reaffirms, withdraws, or concedes some claim to rationality; justificatory language presents reasons for or against such a claim. Thus to interpret judgments of obligation as critical explains both why they occur in the process of reasoning and why they seem to add nothing to the reasons offered.

There are several positive considerations to support my claim that judgments of obligation are that class of critical judgments which pertain to actions. Human actions are subject to genuine criticism. Many words which are typical of judgments of obligation also occur in obviously critical sentences. This interpretation explains both the essential similarity and the logical difference between the pairs of words "right, wrong" and "ought, ought not." It also explains the sense in which ought sentences are binding upon the person to whom they are addressed. Finally, it explains the logical redundancy of judgments of obligation.

[4] W. D. Falk, "Goading and Guiding," *Mind*, 57:165–166 (1953).

8. *Summary*

Critical meaning is quite distinct from descriptive, emotive, evaluative, or directive meaning. Its main features are indication, assertion-denial and criticism. Every critical sentence indicates one or more objects to be criticized. Each asserts, denies, entertains, pretends, hypothesizes, or questions that some critical predicate is appropriate to the indicated object. These critical predicates serve to emphasize, modify, challenge, withdraw, reaffirm, or reject the claim to rationality made by the object being criticized. It is within the context of the give and take of reasoning that one can most fully realize all that is involved in such criticism. The most important kind of criticism, for our purposes, is that dealing with human actions. This, I have suggested, is formulated in judgments of obligation.

The Vocabulary of Ethics

I have distinguished five kinds of meaning—descriptive, emotive, evaluative, directive, and critical. A descriptive sentence tells what some object or objects are like. An emotive sentence expresses some emotion which the speaker does or might feel. An evaluative sentence asserts a pro or con attitude towards its object. A directive sentence tells someone to do something. A critical sentence modifies, challenges, reaffirms, withdraws, concedes, or rejects its object's claim to rationality. I would not dream of suggesting that these are the only kinds of meaning a sentence can have. Still, I hope that these five will be sufficient to throw considerable light upon the nature of ethical language.

I cannot, of course, discuss in detail all the words, phrases, and sentences which constitute the texture of our ethical language. I propose to begin, therefore, by attempting to characterize the meaning of the words "good," "bad," "right," "wrong," and "ought" in terms of the kinds of meaning which I have distinguished. I choose these particular words because they have been much discussed in the recent literature and because they occur frequently in sentences which everyone would admit to be typically ethical.

With luck I can accomplish several things by applying my semantical categories to these particular linguistic specimens. First, I may help to clarify the meaning of certain words which have not always been properly understood by philosophers. Second, I can test the adequacy of my semantical categories by seeing how well they apply to these examples of ordinary language. Third, I hope to round out my characterization of these five kinds of meaning by supplying some concrete illustrations of each.

1. *"Good" and "Bad"*

Let us start with these sample sentences:

That movie was good.
This soup is not very good.
The tight-rope artist is good.
That man is bad.

I think that it can safely be said that such sentences would have almost purely evaluative meaning under normal circumstances. Each possesses indication, partiality, and assertion-denial. Aside from the obvious fact that they are about different things, they differ mainly in the kind of attitude which they assert. To say that a movie is good is to put one's liking into words, and to say that soup is not very good is to formulate one's mild disliking. To call a tight-rope artist good, on the other hand, is probably to assert one's admiration. Finally, to say that a man is bad is to assert moral disapproval of him. While all four sentences are evaluative, only the last is a moral evaluation.

It is quite normal for a sentence to have predominantly evaluative meaning without losing all of its descriptive meaning. "He is a good man" asserts that the indicated object is a man as well as good. Although the word "good" adds nothing to the descriptive meaning in this context, the word "man" does assert a quasi-comparison of the object indicated. However, "he is morally good" should not be said to have descriptive meaning. While calling something morally good semantically presupposes that it is human, it does not actually assert this. Similarily "that man is good" need have no descriptive meaning, unless it means to assert "man" of its object. Probably a descriptive predicate occurring in the grammatical subject is an unasserted auxiliary to indication in most cases. That evaluative and descriptive meaning can be conjoined in the same sentence is hardly news.

That the word "good" itself can function descriptively may seem more surprising. To say "it is good weather today" is probably intended by the speaker more to inform the hearer about what kind of weather it is than to formulate his pro attitude toward it. (In other contexts, of course, this sentence would have emotive meaning, for it would be meant to express the speaker's good will toward the hearer. I am assuming that the sentence occurs in some other context such as a newspaper report or a letter.) In "Jones has a good reputation" the word "good" has hardly any evaluative meaning. To say that a man has a reputation for goodness is neither to say that his reputation is deserved on the basis of the moral code of those who praise him nor to accept this moral code. "It hasn't rained for a good week" and "we had a good deal of trouble finding your house" are examples of sentences where the word "good" seems to have no evaluative overtones whatever. Here it simply describes the amount of time or trouble involved.

It appears that the word "good" has many uses ranging from those with purely evaluative meaning to those with purely descriptive meaning. This gradation from evaluative to descriptive meaning can be illustrated more fully by a selection from the entire sweep of our vocabulary. To call something "fine" or "nice" is normally not to describe at all; usually one can get no clues about what the object is like from the application of such words. Yet "fine" may be used to describe delicacy of surface or intricacy of texture, and "nice" can characterize one's sexual behavior. At the other extreme, "tender" usually describes the sort of treatment or texture and "tall" quasi-compares with respect to height. When applied to a woman or man respectively, however, these words probably include evaluation. This fusion of evaluative and descriptive meaning which exists precariously at the ends of the spectrum is an obvious feature of the middle ranges. A host of words such as "cruel," "selfish," "cultured," "cowardly," "manly," and "unscrupulous" combine both kinds of meaning.

There is one particular use of the word "good," its attributive use, which poses certain interesting problems about the relation of evaluative and descriptive meaning. Consider these examples:

He is a good doctor.
He is a good burglar.
I have a good knife.
I have a bad cold.
He has a good case of jaundice.

All of these sentences have some descriptive meaning, of course; for in each some descriptive predicate such as "doctor" or "jaundice" is asserted of the indicated object. But does the word "good" add to the descriptive content of such sentences or is its function purely evaluative?

It has been suggested that in its attributive use the word "good" is ambiguous. A good doctor can be either an excellent doctor or merely a successful one. While to call a man a good doctor may be to assert a pro attitude towards him with respect to his doctoring, it may be simply to describe him as the kind of a doctor who has succeeded in fulfilling the normal goals of doctoring. That this latter use of the word "good" to describe a man as successful or efficient at his task has no evaluative meaning is supposedly shown by the fact that it makes sense to speak of a good burglar. Surely we do not mean to say that burglars have positive value! In other examples of the attributive use of the word "good" another ambiguity emerges. A good knife can be either an excellent knife or a typical one. That the expression "a good so and so" can mean only typical or normal without a hint of praise might seem to be shown by the fact that we speak of such things as a "good case of jaundice."

I suspect, however, that the attributive use of the word "good" seldom if ever has a purely descriptive meaning. Notice that while I have a good knife I have a bad cold. Such sentences presuppose a prior evaluation of the class involved; knives are usually useful and colds customarily annoying. To characterize an entity as good of its kind is generally to evaluate it positively or negatively in cases where its kind is normally valuable or disvaluable. I doubt whether we would use the word "good" to mean typical where there is no evaluative aspect to its meaning. This need not imply that to speak of a good case of jaundice is to assert the value of that painful disease. What makes this a good case is its value as an example of the species; for the purpose of coming to know about jaundice this case presents a fine opportunity. Similarly, to speak of a good doctor is not simply to describe him as successful without approving of his aims. In fact we do think that the successful doctor accomplishes much of real value. This is why we so seldom speak of good burglars. When we do speak of a good burglar it is because we feel that there is positive value in certain aspects of his craft. Careful planning, skill in opening locked safes, and wealth easily obtained are genuine values; that they are outweighed by the harm done in burglaring need not lead us to deny their goodness. I conclude that the attributive use of "good" normally possesses predominantly evaluative meaning. To call anything good of its kind is either to suggest that since the kind is good this one must be also, or that this one is better than the average of its kind, or that it is a good example of its kind, or that it achieves some genuine values.

It appears to me that the word "good" has evaluative meaning in most contexts. Sometimes it can be said to have purely evaluative meaning. Often it has both evaluative and descriptive meaning. And on rare occasions its meaning seems to be purely descriptive. There is a similar spectrum of uses of the words "good" and "bad" ranging from the evaluative to the emotive.

Quite frequently I murmur "good" when I see the meal which my wife has prepared for me. While I might be intending to assert that a pro attitude is appropriate to such excellent food, it is more likely that I am simply expressing my approval and appreciation. When I say "good" as the dentist informs me that he has finished drilling, it is more a sigh of relief than an evaluation of the situation. The bellowed "good" at the football game is little more than a shout of jubilation. The "too bad" said to a friend in trouble typically expresses sympathy and even sorrow. It is not at all uncommon for "good" and "bad" to be used with purely emotive meaning.

It is even more common for them to be used with a mixture of emotive and evaluative meaning. Probably a great deal of evaluative language is incidentally emotive. To the extent that we feel strongly about good and bad, and what things are more deserving of deep feeling, our emotions become involved in our value judgments. The fact that emotive meaning so often accompanies evaluative meaning, however, should not lead us to ignore or minimize the distinction between them.

There is a similar affinity between the evaluative and directive uses of language. To say "it is a good play" is almost to say "go to see it." It is not easy to draw the line between those cases where the directive is merely suggested by the evaluation made from those in which the speaker actually meant to direct. It seems likely that the words "good" and "bad" serve to issue veiled prescriptions or prohibitions in many cases. That there are times when direction is included in what the speaker intended to say can be seen when one disregards such veiled advice. One way of prohibiting stealing is by saying "stealing is evil." Probably the directive meaning of the words "good" and "bad" emerges most obviously when one is speaking to a young child. To say "good boy" is surely to encourage the little fellow to continue what he is doing; to say "that's bad" is to prohibit such activity.

Finally, there are the uses of "good" and "bad" with critical meaning. To admit that a person has a "good excuse" is to concede that his excuse is both relevant and of some strength. A "bad argument" is one in which the reasons presented on behalf of the conclusion are either irrelevant or themselves incorrect. On the other hand, a "good reason" is one which genuinely supports the conclusion being drawn from it. These examples seem to illustrate the use of "good" and "bad" in criticism. They may not, however, be entirely without evaluative meaning; for cogent reasoning has a real value both for the intellectual satisfaction it gives and for the practical value of being aware of the truth. When one speaks of a "good chance" that something will happen, the word "good" modifies the claim to rationality with respect to strength. While we would usually speak of a good chance when it is probable that something good will happen, one can say "there is a good chance I will lose my shirt on the next race."

We must conclude that the meaning of words like "good" and "bad" is not as simple as some suppose. Certainly there can be no question of defining *the* meaning of such words. Although the words "good" and "bad" have predominantly evaluative meaning, they can also have descriptive, emotive, directive, or critical meaning. What is worse, these divergent kinds of meaning are not restricted to different occurrences of the words, but any given utterance can function in two or more ways. However, this fact that a single utterance can function in many ways does nothing to destroy the distinctness of the various kinds of meaning. It is only by distinguishing carefully between one kind of meaning and another that one can grasp something of the complexity of our ethical vocabulary.

2. *"Right" and "Wrong"*

This complexity can be seen just as well in our use of the words "right" and "wrong." When it is said that someone has the "wrong answer," it is being said that he is mistaken. To admit "your guess turned out to be right" is to concede that the guesser was correct in his conjecture. To object to someone's reasoning as "all wrong" is to criticize it as lacking in cogency. These examples illustrate a use of the words which is almost purely critical. Although we have a special vocabulary of words like "true" and "valid" for epistemological purposes, the words "right" and "wrong" often function in this way also. In fact, it seems to me that in most cases these words have predominantly critical meaning.

This is as true of their ethical as of their nonethical uses. "You did exactly right in hitting him back" concedes and even reaffirms the claim to rationality of this act of retaliation. Each human action makes, or could make, a claim that it is the reasonable thing to do in the light of the relevant considerations. Because action involves a choice for and against which reasons can be given, it is subject to criticism. To call an action "right" or "wrong" is to challenge, reaffirm, withdraw, concede, or reject this implicit claim to rationality. These words have much the same meaning when applied to actions that the words "true" and "false" have when applied to statements. To say "stealing is wrong" is to claim that there are weighty reasons against stealing and that any reasons which could be given in its support would be insufficient to justify it. The primary meaning of the words "right" and "wrong" is critical.

At the same time sentences containing these words often have directive meaning. To say "stealing is wrong" may be to prohibit stealing. Sometimes this direction may be merely suggested by the speaker's criticism, but at others it is part of what he meant to say. One might well put advice on how to live in the form of a set of sentences about which actions are right and which ones wrong. This directive meaning comes to the fore and the critical meaning of the words "right" and "wrong" recedes into the background particularly when one is speaking to small children or to unreasonable adults. Although one uses words which are normally used in criticism, in such cases one is probably telling someone what to do or what not to do. Again, whenever one says that it is "all right" to do something, he is simply giving his permission. There appears to be nothing but direction involved in most such cases.

To say "stealing is wrong" also seems to suggest that stealing is morally evil. I must admit that I am not at all sure whether the evaluation is actually part of the meaning of the sentence or only suggested by it. When a baseball coach shouts approvingly "that's the right way to swing a bat" he seems to be praising the player as well as asserting that he is acting in the correct manner. Probably there is a mixture of evaluative and critical meaning here, with just a dash of emotive meaning thrown in to confuse the eavesdropping epistemologist. To say that a cake is "done just right" would seem to amount to a positive evaluation. It appears that many uses of "right" and "wrong" have at least some evaluative meaning.

These words can also have considerable emotive meaning. To say "telling the truth is right" may be primarily to criticize, but incidentally it expresses the speaker's approval. Since we tend to feel strongly about what is right and wrong, it is only natural that we should give our emotions linguistic expression. In most cases "wrong" probably has stronger emotive meaning than "right," because our negative emotions seem to have more felt intensity than our positive ones. The emotive meaning which so often accompanies critical meaning occasionally occurs in almost pure form. When my bleary-eyed friend in the bar murmurs "you're all right," his lack of critical faculties suggests that his meaning is largely emotive. When the exasperated mother shouts "that's wrong" at her wayward child, her utterance may express her feelings more than prohibiting or directing the action.

287

Like most words in our ethical vocabulary, "right" and "wrong" can be used with varying degrees of descriptive meaning. Consider these examples:

This shoe is the wrong size.
He took the right road.
You must have the wrong number.

I am informing the salesman when I tell him that the shoe does not fit; I am describing the geometric relation between my foot and the shoe. There remain, of course, evaluative, critical, and directive overtones to what I say. I am suggesting that this shoe would be bad for my foot, that his decision to bring it to me was mistaken, and that he bring me another. Yet the descriptive element is undoubtedly there and, in some cases, predominant. When a person asks "am I on the right road to Green Bay?" he primarily wishes to know whether the road he is now on leads in a relatively direct manner to that longed-for city. Although the answer will involve some positive or negative criticism of his decision to take this route, this seems secondary to its informative significance.

This descriptive function becomes almost the sole kind of meaning in sentences such as these:

This is my right hand.
Answer me right here and now.
I came right home.
There are ninety degrees in a right angle.
I was sick, but I feel all right now.

Here "right" is used almost entirely for quasi-comparison. The right hand is simply the one which the body is to the left of, and a right angle is any angle containing ninety degrees. That these purely descriptive uses of the word "right" may not be entirely unrelated to its critical

288

uses is suggested by the fact that, since most people are right-handed, one generally makes fewer mistakes with his right hand than with his left. Also notice that we characterize the man who acts as he should as being "upright" and say that the reformed criminal is now "going straight." Still, it is interesting that there do not seem to be any uses of the word "wrong" that are as purely descriptive as these.

It would appear, then, that the words "right" and "wrong" have predominantly critical meaning. As a rule, to use these words is to criticize the claim to rationality implicit in the object to which they are applied. This is so whether the object criticized is a statement or a human action. At the same time these words often have other kinds of meaning which may sometimes become primary. The directive, evaluative, emotive, or descriptive meaning which is normally incidental to the critical meaning becomes the dominant or even exclusive meaning of "right" and "wrong" in certain circumstances. Like the other terms in our ethical vocabulary, these words have a complexity of meaning which has been insufficiently recognized.

3. "Ought"

Something of the same variety of related uses will be found in the case of the word "ought." Let us start with some examples of this word occurring in typically ethical sentences.

You ought not to have stolen the money.
I ought to give more to charity.
No one ought to lose his temper under any circumstances.
Everyone ought to respect the rights of others.

It is my contention that these should be taken to be critical sentences. To say "you ought not to have stolen the money" is to challenge the stealer to defend his action with justifying reasons and to boast that one can show by reasoning that the preponderance of considerations lies on the other side. To say "I ought to give more to charity" is both to concede that the claim to rationality implicit in my present mode of behavior could not withstand the scrutiny of reasoning and to boast that one could rationally justify more generous actions. In its normal ethical context the expressions "ought" and "ought not" serve to underline, challenge, reaffirm, withdraw, concede, or reject the claim to rationality implicit in some action or class of actions.

Because the word "ought" is most frequently used in criticizing human actions, it is often thought that its meaning must be directive. Ought sentences are obviously meant to be practical. The meaning of directives is clearly practical. Therefore, ought sentences must be directives. But this assumes that there is only one way in which a sentence can have any direct bearing upon action. In fact there are many ways. A sentence can describe, evaluate, criticize, or express an emotion toward action as well as tell someone to do it. That ought sentences are usually not directive in meaning can be seen from the fact that, while directives semantically presuppose that the action called for lies in the future, it makes perfectly good sense to say "you ought not to have stolen the money."

One reason that this distinction between the criticism and the direction of action has been so frequently overlooked is that they are so closely related. To say "you ought not to lie" comes very close to saying "do not lie," for the person who would say the former would normally be inclined to say the latter also. In fact, when one is prepared to justify his admonition with reasoning, it would be only natural to formulate one's directive in the language of criticism. I am quite willing to grant that ought sentences may occasionally have an almost purely directive meaning and that they frequently have incidental directive meaning. We do sometimes say that someone ought to do something when we mean to tell him to do it. Still, I would suggest that the primary meaning of most ought sentences is critical rather than directive.

The failure to realize that the word "ought" usually has critical meaning has often led to misunderstandings. Prichard, for example, has gone so far as to declare that the expression "ought to be" is meaningless.[1] The origin of this mistake probably lies in Kant's interpretation of ought sentences in term of a special kind of imperative. That not all ought sentences in ordinary language are imperatives can be seen from the following examples.

There ought to be a cure for cancer.
There ought not to be any racial discrimination.
Professors ought to be paid more!
A beautiful world ought to exist even if there were no perceiver.

I suggest that in sentences such as these the "ought" functions critically. To say "there ought to be a cure for cancer" is much like saying "oh that there were a cure for cancer." To say "there ought not to be any racial discrimination" is much like saying "how I wish that there were no racial discrimination." In each case the "ought" serves to emphasize the fact that the sentence is no mere expression of a personal desire or aversion but that it claims objective validity.

This parallel between certain ought sentences and the corresponding sentences in the optative mood should re-

[1] H. A. Prichard, "Does Moral Philosophy Rest on a Mistake?" *Mind*, 21:24 (January 1912).

mind us of the relation between evaluative and emotive meaning. While evaluative sentences fall upon the assertion-denial dimension, emotive sentences merely express an emotion without claiming that it is rationally justifiable. This suggests that ought-to-be sentences have primarily evaluative meaning. To say "professors ought to be paid more" is to say that it would be a good thing if professors were given higher pay. The word "ought" underlines the fact that such sentences are genuine evaluations and not mere emotive utterances. Once this critical function is recognized, ought-to-be sentences lose their air of illegitimacy.

There is another class of ought sentences which is frequently misinterpreted for much the same reason. Here are some examples:

You ought not to be angry with me.
I ought not to become depressed so easily.
Husbands ought to love their wives more faithfully.

It is often said that sentences like these are, strictly speaking, meaningless. It is assumed that it makes no sense to tell anyone to do anything he is absolutely incapable of doing and that our emotions, at least upon any given occasion, are beyond our voluntary control. It is concluded that it is meaningless to assert that someone ought to feel a certain emotion in the sense in which we can say that he ought to pay his debts or speak the truth.

This conclusion follows from the given premises provided it is granted that all ought sentences have directive meaning. This should not be granted, however. In saying "you ought not to be angry with me" I am not telling you to feel differently but criticizing the way you do feel. I am challenging you to show that you have reasons to justify your anger and boasting that I can show that your feelings towards me are unreasonable. In saying "I ought not to become depressed so easily" I am conceding that my reasons for feeling depressed are insufficient and declining to defend my feelings before the court of reason. No doubt one's feelings are not subject to his voluntary control, but criticism does not presuppose such control. Beliefs can be significantly said to be true or false, reasonable or groundless, in spite of the fact that one cannot believe something simply by deciding to do so. It is not in this sense that critical language semantically presupposes that the indicated object presents a choice.

There is one class of sentences in which the critical meaning of the word "ought" seems particularly obvious and where an interpretation in terms of directive meaning would be singularly implausible. These are sentences which formulate predictions. When my knowledgeable friend tells me "Tailwind ought to win the third race easily," he may well be suggesting that I put a little money on such a sure bet. However, the primary meaning of his utterance, since he is well aware of my philosophical skepticism and my moral reservations about gambling, is to inform me in advance about the outcome of the third race. When the plumber asserts "this valve ought to fix your hot water tank" he is simply predicting that I will have no more trouble with that particular bit of apparatus. In these sentences the word "ought" is used to emphasize the claim that the prediction being made is a reasonable one. We ordinarily substitute "ought to" for "will" either when the prediction being made is a particularly hazardous one, as in the case of horse racing, or when the predictor is a particularly competent one, as in the case of the plumber. Both factors are probably present when the experienced farmer gazes up at the evening sky, sniffs the breeze, and says "it ought to rain tomorrow." In such cases the word "ought" has much the same meaning as "probably." It serves to show both that the prediction claims to be somewhat less than certain knowledge and that it purports to be a reasonable conjecture rather than a blind guess.

This examination of a wide variety of the uses of the word "ought" suggests that as a rule its meaning is critical. The most frequent uses of this word are in circumstances where the claim to rationality might easily be overlooked. Where a prediction might be interpreted as a wild conjecture, one is apt to substitute "it ought to happen" for "it will happen." When a value judgment might easily be misinterpreted to be merely the expression of an idiosyncratic wish, one usually says something "ought to be" the case. Since the criticism of action is so closely associated with commanding and advising, the word "ought" occurs frequently in judgments of obligation. In all these cases the word is being used to underline a claim to rationality which is in danger of being forgotten. In most other cases as well, the expressions "ought" and "ought not" are used to modify, challenge, reaffirm, withdraw, concede, or reject this claim on behalf of some indicated object.

The fact that these expressions normally have predominantly critical meaning, however, does not exclude the possibility that they sometimes have other kinds of meaning as well. I have already pointed out that ought sentences can have directive or evaluative meaning. To tell someone what he ought to do amounts at times to telling him to do it, and to say that something ought to be is to say that it would be a good thing if it existed. Even here criticism remains in the back of the speaker's mind. It would be unusual to use these expressions where one was not prepared to defend his utterance with reasoning. This is probably why the word "ought" so rarely occurs in purely emotive utterances.

However, one might express his hurt feelings by saying "you ought not to have spoken to me in that tone of voice." Emotive and critical meaning are combined in such instances.

It remains only to look into the question of whether ought sentences can have descriptive meaning. It is often suggested that the causal ought is purely descriptive, but I think that this is a mistake. "If you want to be warm, you ought to close the window" is certainly closely related to "if you close the window, you will be warm"; but they do not have the same meaning. While the latter is merely a predictive description with implications for action, the former is a critical judgment which points out the irrationality of accepting an end and rejecting the means. The reason some ethicists have identified the two is that they have assumed that any real ought sentence must express a categorical imperative. But if the word "ought" is used to criticize rather than to issue a special form of a directive, one need not be especially perplexed over the causal ought. Sentences such as "if you long to be popular you ought to take baths" are simply critical sentences underlining the reasonableness of a specified course of action on the condition that one has a certain desire.

Although sentences involving the causal ought are not descriptive, it is quite possible that occasionally the word "ought" does function, at least in part, descriptively. Suppose I ask how hard John has been working and am told that he has not been working "as hard as he ought to be." No doubt evaluation or criticism are involved here; I am being told that John is a poor worker or that he ought to work harder. At the same time, I am being informed about how hard he has actually been working. The reply is descriptive in that it tells me what kind of a worker John is.

Moreover, this descriptive aspect is not just an inference from what I am told but precisely what the reply is meant to convey.

On the whole it seems that there is slightly less variety in the uses of the word "ought" than in the uses of the other words I have discussed, although there is still enough complexity to make the word epistemologically interesting. In most sentences the primary meaning of "ought" is critical. Often it emphasizes a claim to rationality which might be overlooked, but it also serves to challenge, reaffirm, withdraw, concede, or reject some claim to rationality. Although ought sentences frequently criticize action, they can be about assertions or emotions as well. The most important secondary uses of "ought" are directive and evaluative, but there are occasional emotive and descriptive uses as well.

4. *Summary*

I have attempted to distinguish and characterize the main uses of the words "good," "bad," "right," "wrong," and "ought." While these are only a minute sample of the vocabulary of ethics, they seem prima facie to be a fairly representative one. I have attempted to bring out the tremendous variety of meanings which these words can possess and to show how these various meanings can be interpreted in terms of five basic kinds of meaning. This, it seems to me, is the most effective way to gain some grasp of the significance of individual ethical sentences. But what can one say about the nature of ethical sentences in general? I cannot evade this final question any longer.

— XII —

Conclusion

I have tried to characterize the various meanings of some of the words which frequently occur in typically ethical sentences. Doubtless these characterizations were inaccurate at times, but I am fairly confident that they were substantially correct. While there are plenty of other words in our ethical vocabulary which might have been discussed as well, the sample presented seems sufficient to give us some grasp of the meaning of ethical sentences. What can we conclude about the nature of ethical language?

1. The Objective Validity of Ethical Language

For one thing, there is nothing in the meaning of most ethical sentences which would automatically rule out their objective validity. For the sake of convenience I have limited my investigation to two kinds of ethical sentences—value judgments and judgments of obligation. Obviously it would be rash for me to hazard any generalizations which would extend beyond these boundaries to whatever other kinds of ethical language there may be. However, there is no need to deny that these sentences, at least, possess a genuine claim to rationality.

Sometimes it is denied that either value judgments or judgments of obligation can possess objective validity on the grounds that neither has any cognitive meaning. If by cognitive meaning is meant descriptive meaning, the premise of this argument is correct. But why must it be assumed, usually by definition, that all cognitively respectable language is descriptive? Evaluative and critical sentences seem to fall along the assertion-denial dimension just as truly as descriptive ones do. Surely it is not safe to assume without considerable proof that only descriptive sentences can be rationally justified. It is hard to see what facts logical truths could be said to describe, yet one is loath to admit that such sentences are without cognitive significance.

Objective validity is often denied to evaluations because they seem to express attitudes rather than beliefs. I willingly grant, and even insist, that attitudes do stand at the heart of the meaning of our value sentences. At the same time, I have argued that evaluative meaning should not be confused with emotive meaning. Evaluations assert or deny our attitudes; they do not simply express our emotions. That it is quite possible for a mere attitude to have a genuine claim to rationality I have argued at length in my chapter on the emotive theory of ethics. Thus the fact that attitudes are central to the meaning of our value sentences does not by itself imply that evaluations are lacking in objectivity.

Judgments of obligation are often thought to be without objective validity because of their practical nature. It is imagined that the only way to explain their bearing upon action is to interpret them as being some sort of disguised imperative. That judgments of obligation are not imperatives in any form can be seen from the fact that they occur in the past tense and in all three persons as readily as in the second person present or future. It is because critical meaning has been generally ignored that many have thought that the only way to make judgments of obligation practical is to give them directive meaning.

There appears to be nothing in the nature of either value judgments or judgments of obligation to force one to deny their objective validity. Quite the contrary. That such sentences *claim* to be objectively valid can be seen by reflecting upon what is involved in asserting them. It seems unlikely that this claim to rationality is always mistaken. Even if it were, this would still provide a sort of objectivity, for they would all be objectively mistaken.

The crux of the matter is whether or not it is possible to give genuine reasons for and against judgments of value and obligation. I think that it is. To show that such sentences can be rationally justified would, I fear, require another book. For the moment I will limit myself to two contentions. First, these typical ethical sentences at least make a claim to rationality; this is part of their very meaning. Second, that this claim is out of place cannot be assumed without proof; prima facie it seems to be quite in order.

2. The Adequacy of Ethical Language

Another conclusion of some interest is that the language of ethics is reasonably adequate. We are able to discuss ethical questions and formulate ethical opinions fairly well in the existing vocabulary. This is not always recognized. Often, in fact, it is suggested that ethical language is particularly subject to linguistic ills such as ambiguity and vagueness. This dissatisfaction with the language of ethics probably comes from comparing it with the language of science. The natural and mathematical sciences suggest the ideal of a language free from all ambiguity, imprecision, vagueness, and emotional overtones. Certainly ethical language falls far short of this ideal. It does not follow, however, that the language of ethics is hopelessly inadequate to perform its task, for its task is not that of science. Hence it should not be judged by the scientific ideal.

It is natural to assume that each word stands for a single concept, but often one discovers that a single word has two or more distinct meanings. Such ambiguous words are frowned upon because of the confusion they create; one can never be sure which meaning is intended by any given use of the word. During the past half-century writers in ethics have tried to avoid such confusion by carefully distinguishing the different senses of ethical words. Hartmann, for example, distinguished between the ought-to-do and the ought-to-be. Broad noted that "right" may mean materially right, formally right, or perfectly right. Ewing conscientiously and painstakingly differentiated between ten distinct senses of the word "good." The conclusion seems obvious that our ethical vocabulary is highly ambiguous.

Such a conclusion would be out of place, however. The typical ambiguous word has two or more distinct senses only one of which is intended by any given occurrence of that word. In the case of ethical words the variety of meanings forms an almost continuous gradation; the multiplicity of uses cannot be collected into a few distinct senses. There are too many shades of meaning to say that the ethical words stand for a limited number of concepts, and differences of meaning are too slight to distinguish separate concepts anyway. One can distinguish the kinds of meaning an ethical word may have, but several of these can be present in the same occasion of use. Here the question is not which meaning the word has, but of how many kinds of meaning it has. Instead of thinking of an ethical word as standing for several discrete concepts, it is better to think of it as possessing a range of uses which vary along several dimensions. Perhaps we should say that the language of ethics is flexible rather than ambiguous. Like ambiguity, this flexibility may create a certain amount of confusion. It is hard to be sure which kinds of meaning a given ethical utterance possesses and in what degree it possesses each of them. This uncertainty is minimized, however, by our familiarity with ethical language which makes us sensitive to these shades of meaning. This flexibility is more of a help than a hindrance, moreover, for it enables us to compress evaluation, direction, and criticism into a very few words. This linguistic economy lends force to our conversation as well as saving us time and money.

A second respect in which ethical language might seem to be inadequate is precision. The physicist can compare the temperature of two objects to a fraction of a degree, but who can express the comparative degree of obligation to keep a promise and to tell the truth? The chemist can state the exact chemical composition of a diamond, but who can say exactly how good or beautiful it is? Certainly ethical sentences are lacking in precision.

It does not follow that this is the fault of the language in which they are formulated. What limits the precision of these statements is our ability to measure and compare, not the inaccuracy of the words we use. We have the words to describe the length of a piece of string to one millionth of a millionth of a millimeter. These words are useless, however, unless we can measure the string that accurately. If ethical language is imprecise, this is because of the limits of our ability to discriminate the various degrees of value and obligation. The vocabulary of ethics will express accurately every distinction of value and obligation we are capable of making. That is all one can ask of any language.

With regard to vagueness the situation is similar. A term is vague to the extent that there are actual or possible instances where it is impossible to tell whether or not it is applicable. Admittedly such borderline cases exist in plenty in ethics. One must recognize this vagueness in the language of ethics, but one cannot infer that the difficulty is linguistic. The situation is not one which could be remedied by introducing new words or by removing purely verbal confusion. Instead, our inability to decide when an ethical word correctly applies comes from the complexity and indefiniteness of the factors which determine value and obligation. If there were an ethical language which was less vague, we would be unable to make use of it; for we are incapable of reaching any definite judgments in these borderline cases. The language we do have is quite adequate to formulate the insight we actually possess.

Another objection sometimes made to ethical language is that it is laden with emotive meaning. Logicians and semanticists alike warn us of the dangers of emotive language. Language charged with emotion tends to excite us to the point where we become incapable of thinking clearly. Moreover, it can arouse attitudes and prejudices which lead to an unquestioning acceptance of the speaker's position. There can be little doubt that the strong emotions engendered by ethical discussion do make responsible and critical thinking difficult.

But once again it is misleading to lay the blame on the doorstep of our language. Is it the words themselves or the people who use them which are too emotional? The primary reason that ethical discussion is charged with emotion is that we feel strongly about most important ethical issues. If we introduced today a new vocabulary free of both emotive meaning and emotive force, tomorrow it would acquire emotional overtones by association with the situations in which it is used. The ideal of a nonemotive ethical language is pointless until those who are to use the language become completely unemotional. In addition, the elimination of all emotion from ethical discourse would have its disadvantages. Part of the job of ethical language is to mold attitudes and modify behavior. For these purposes an emotionally charged language is helpful and, until men become more rational, even indispensable.

On the whole, therefore, it seems to me that ethical language is quite adequate. To be sure, it is flexible, imprecise, vague, and emotional. However, the possibility of improvement is limited, not by linguistic failings, but by our capacity to judge clearly and accurately in the moral sphere. With the language at our disposal it is possible to express our judgments of value and obligation with ease and to convey them to others with very little loss of comprehension. Ethical discourse seems carried on with clumsy tools only when we misunderstand just what it is and judge it by standards which are appropriate to other areas. Ethical sentences are not very imperfect and confusing examples of scientific language; they are excellent examples of ethical language. When we have grasped the ways in which ethical words are intended to function, we will see that they perform their tasks very well.

3. The Heterogeneity of Ethical Language

Like many others, I have written at some length about ethical language. But to use the expression "ethical language" at all would seem to presuppose that there are several distinct species of the genus language and that one of these is peculiarly ethical. Can it really be said that ethical language forms a separate species of language? We have seen that many sentences seem to be both ethical and nonethical at once and that apparently ethical sentences can function in very different ways.

If ethical sentences are a species of language, they are so only in an extended sense of the term. Few would hesitate to say that dogs are a species of animal, for they seem to belong to a single natural kind. That is, dogs are similar to one another in various striking and biologically important ways and clearly different from all other kinds of animal. But, even ignoring the fact that some pets may not be animals, should one say that pets are a species of animal? At first one is tempted to think not. Many different species of animal (dogs, cats, rabbits, even mice and lions) belong to the class of pets. Pets are not *a* kind of animal, for many different kinds of animals can be pets. Yet in a broader sense, pets are a kind of animal; all pets share the characteristic of being domesticated animals kept for companionship. Pets are a kind of animal, even if not a natural kind. That is, they do have something in common, but not as much as classes such as dog or cat. Ethical sentences are a species of sentence only in this loose sense in which pets are a species of animal. They share the characteristic of being relevant to ethical problems, but this pretty well exhausts their similarity. Just as many different kinds of animals belong to the class of pets, so many different kinds of sentences belong to the class of ethical language.

At the very least one would wish to include judgments of moral value and judgments of moral obligation in ethical language. But, if my interpretation is correct, these are quite different kinds of sentences. One has evaluative meaning and the other critical meaning. Although these two kinds of meaning do share indication and assertion-denial, their differences are at least as striking. The heart of evaluation is to be for or against its object, while the heart of criticism is to make, modify, challenge, press, withdraw, reaffirm, or concede a claim to rationality. These two kinds of sentence are essentially dissimilar.

Why, then, do we group judgments of moral value and judgments of moral obligation together as ethical sentences? Because they both seem particularly relevant to the problems of ethics. But if this is the basis of our classification, there are many other kinds of sentence which it would be hard to exclude. Probably judgments of nonmoral value and obligation would be the first to be added. Psychological descriptions, such as reports of enjoyments, are relevant to the desirability of some object. Causal laws have a direct bearing upon judging the best means to achieve a desired end. Almost any rational choice must take account of many factual assertions. Ascriptions of responsibility are obviously related to the concerns of the ethicist. Statements about freedom of the will are thought by many to bear upon the reality of obligation. Theological statements about the existence of God and his inescapable justice make a real difference to the way we ought to live here on earth. Ascriptions of rights are not unrelated to our basic duties as citizens. Promises have moral implications if any utterances do. Even a groan of pain may be an invitation to moral action. It appears that many very different kinds of sentences have a strong claim to be included in the class of ethical language.

In itself, ethical language is most heterogeneous. It contains all those sentences which are relevant to ethical problems. Since there are many problems which have traditionally been considered ethical and many ways in which a sentence can be relevant to a given problem, many different kinds of sentence can be ethical in their various ways. It is not the kind of meaning which a sentence has but the context in which it occurs which determines whether or not it is ethical. Should one consider the sentence "That is a very beautiful painting" to be ethical on the grounds that it expresses a value judgment? Many would prefer to say that it belongs to the language of esthetics. But what if one is considering whether he ought to buy the painting? Then the very same sentence takes on an ethical flavor. There seems to be nothing particularly ethical in descriptive meaning, but descriptions have a direct bearing upon every moral choice. What unites ethical language is not its essential similarity but the context within which it occurs. My conclusion is that ethical language is basically heterogeneous.

4. *The Theory of Ethical Language*

Does this imply that it is useless to ask about the nature of ethical language? In the traditional sense of the word "nature," where the nature of anything is its essence, such a question would seem to be uninteresting. To know the essence of ethical language, that it is relevant to ethical problems, is to know very little about it. But in a looser sense of the word one can and should ask about the nature of ethical language. One should ask for a theory which will interpret ethical language in such a way that it resolves the many problems which arise from its misunderstanding.

Such a theory will not be too greatly concerned about whether or not this or that kind of sentence deserves to be labeled "ethical." Instead, it will take as its subject matter any kind of sentence which the practicing ethicist uses, for all of the sentences ordinarily used in the discussion of ethical problems must be clarified before the epistemologist of ethics can claim to have finished his job. The final theory must distinguish between the various kinds of sentences which the ethicist finds important, describe the important characteristics of each, and show how each compares with other kinds of sentences. Ethical language will be properly understood only when one has distinguished and described the various strands which make it up and has explained how they are interwoven in the fabric of ethical discussion.

It is quite possible that such a theory will include certain general conclusions about ethical language as a whole. In this chapter I have hazarded a few tentative generalizations. There is nothing in the meaning of ethical sentences which would automatically rule out their objective validity. Ethical language is, by and large, quite adequate to perform its tasks. Ethical language is basically heterogeneous.

If this last conclusion is correct, such generalizations will not take us very far. Any real grasp of ethical language requires a detailed but systematic characterization of the various kinds of ethical sentences. I have concentrated my attention primarily upon only two kinds of sentences, value judgments and judgments of obligation.

I have suggested that the former might well be said to have evaluative meaning, the main features of which are indication, partiality, and assertion-denial. Every value sentence indicates some object or objects to which it refers and in terms of which its correctness is to be judged. Evaluation always formulates some pro or con attitude; it is for or against its object. And the evaluation makes an implicit claim to rationality; to assert or deny an evaluation is to be prepared to defend it with reasons. Although evaluations share indication and assertion-denial with descriptions, they are not just a special class of descriptive sentences. The heart of description is quasi-comparison, classifying an obect in terms of its similarities and dissimilarities with other objects. Evaluations lack such quasi-comparison, just as descriptions are not characterized by partiality. But if evaluations do not have descriptive meaning, neither do they have emotive meaning. Emotive utterances express emotion, while evaluations assert or deny attitudes. Not only may the attitude which an evaluation formulates be unemotional, but the value sentence makes a claim to rationality which is quite lacking in emotive sentences.

I have contended that sentences which formulate judgments of obligation can best be interpreted as a species of critical judgment. They modify, press, challenge, reaffirm, withdraw, concede, or reject the claim to rationality implicit in human action. In addition to this explicit critical meaning, such sentences possess indication and assertion-denial. It is this feature of assertion-denial which primarily distinguishes critical sentences from emotive ones. Since critical sentences possess neither quasi-comparison nor partiality, they have neither descriptive nor evaluative meaning. Although they deal with action, their meaning is not directive. Directive sentences prescribe or prohibit; they attempt to get someone to engage in or leave undone some action. Critical sentences are not so much concerned with causing an action to be or not to be done as with passing judgment upon its implicit claim to rationality. Just as judgments of truth or falsity judge the claim to rationality implicit in some statement, so judgments of obligation judge the claim to rationality implicit in some action.

Even if my analysis is correct as far as it goes, it is obviously only a start. There are many other kinds of sentence, whether or not one chooses to label them "ethical," which remain to be discussed. Surely the epistemologist of ethics canot ignore ascriptions of responsibility, ascriptions of rights, promises, the metaphysical statements which provide the theoretical framework for most ethical systems, and the various kinds of statements to which we all appeal in justifying our ethical conclusions. At best, my own efforts have been only a first step. Whether they are a step in the right direction I must leave for the reader to judge.

BIBLIOGRAPHY

I. INTRODUCTION

A. J. Ayer. *Language, Truth and Logic*. London: Victor Gollancz, 1950, Pages 102–103. Distinguishing ethical from nonethical sentences.

R. B. Brandt. *Ethical Theory*. Englewood Cliffs: Prentice Hall, 1959. Pages 2–4, 158–166. On which sentences are ethical and how to decide what they mean.

W. K. Frankena, "Moral Philosophy at Mid-Century," *Philosophical Review*, 60:44–55 (January 1951). Summary of contemporary questions, answers, and approaches.

J. Ladd. *The Structure of a Moral Code*. Cambridge: Harvard University Press, 1957. Pages 82–85. On the range of ethical sentences.

II. ETHICAL NATURALISM

R. B. Brandt, "The Definition of an 'Ideal Observer' Theory in Ethics," *Philosophy and Phenomenological Research*, 15:407–413 (March 1955). A criticism of Firth's formulation.

R. B. Brandt. *Ethical Theory*. Englewood Cliffs: Prentice Hall, 1959. Chapter VII. Some considerations both for and against ethical naturalism.

R. B. Brandt, "The Status of Empirical Assertion Theories in Ethics," *Mind*, N. S., 61:458–479 (October 1952). A rebuttal of certain arguments against ethical naturalism.

C. D. Broad, "Certain Features in Moore's Ethical Doctrines," in P. Schlipp, ed., *The Philosophy of G. E. Moore*. Chicago: Northwestern University Press, 1942. Discusses

BIBLIOGRAPHY

the distinction between natural and nonnatural properties.

J. Dewey, "The Theory of Valuation," in *International Encyclopedia of Unified Science*. Chicago: University of Chicago Press, 1939. A qualified interest theory of value.

P. Edwards. *The Logic of Moral Discourse*. Glencoe: The Free Press, 1955. Chapter VII. A modified naturalism stressing the ambiguity of ethical words.

A. C. Ewing. *The Definition of Good*. New York: Macmillan, 1947. Chapter II. A criticism of ethical naturalism.

R. Firth, "Ethical Absolutism and the Ideal Observer," *Philosophy and Phenomenological Research*, 12:317–345 (March 1952). An analysis of ethical sentences in terms of an ideal observer.

R. Firth, "Reply to Professor Brandt," *Philosophy and Phenomenological Research*, 15:414–421 (March 1955). A defence of his original formulation.

W. K. Frankena, "Ewing's Case against Naturalistic Theories of Value," *Philosophical Review*, 57:481–492 (September 1948). A reply to Ewing's arguments.

W. K. Frankena, "The Naturalistic Fallacy," *Mind*, N. S., 48:467–477 (October 1939). An attempt to interpret and evaluate the naturalistic fallacy.

S. Hampshire. *Thought and Action*. London: Chatto and Windus, 1959. Chapter I. On the distinction between the theoretical and practical aspects of life.

R. M. Hare. *The Language of Morals*. Oxford: The Clarendon Press, 1952. Chapters V and VI. A criticism of ethical naturalism and a discussion of the teaching of ethical words.

J. Jarvis, "In Defense of Moral Absolutes," *Journal of Philosophy*, 55:1043–1053 (November 20, 1958). Another view of the teaching of ethical words.

C. I. Lewis. *An Analysis of Knowledge and Valuation*. La Salle: Open Court, 1946. Chapters XII–XVII. An analysis of value judgments in terms of a directly experienced dimension of value.

G. E. Moore. *Ethics*. London: Oxford University Press, 1912. Chapters III and IV. Arguments against subjective versions of naturalism.

G. E. Moore. *Principia Ethica*. Cambridge: Cambridge University Press, 1903. Chapters I–III. A refutation of ethical naturalism.

D. H. Parker, "Value as Any Object of Any Interest," *Ethics*, 40:465–473 (July 1930). A criticism of Perry and reformulation of the interest theory.

R. B. Perry. *General Theory of Value*. New York: Longmans, Green, 1926. Chapters V and XII. An analysis of value judgments in terms of interest.

R. B. Perry. *Realms of Value*. Cambridge: Harvard University Press, 1954. An application of the interest theory of value to various areas.

A. N. Prior. *Logic and the Basis of Ethics*. Oxford: The Clarendon Press, 1949. Chapters I–IV. The nature and import of the naturalistic fallacy.

P. B. Rice. *On the Knowledge of Good and Evil*. New York: Random House, 1955. Chapters V, VI, VII, XV. A modified naturalism which tries to come to terms with the naturalistic fallacy.

W. D. Ross. *The Foundations of Ethics*. Oxford: The Clarendon Press, 1949. Chapter II. A criticism of ethical naturalism.

W. Savery, "A Defence of Hedonism," *Ethics*, 45:1–26 (October 1934). Defines "good" in terms of pleasure.

M. Schlick. *Problems of Ethics*. New York: Prentice Hall, 1939. Chapters I and V. A form of hedonism and the claim that any theory of absolute values is practically empty.

F. C. Sharp. *Ethics*. New York: Appleton Century Crofts, 1928. Chapters VII and XIX. A form of naturalism in terms of desire.

S. Toulmin. *The Place of Reason in Ethics*. Cambridge: Cambridge University Press, 1950. Chapters II and III. A criticism of ethical naturalism.

E. Vivas. *The Moral Life and the Ethical Life*. Chicago: University of Chicago Press, 1950. Chapters I–XI. Detailed criticisms of several forms of naturalism.

E. Westermarck. *Ethical Relativity*. London: Kegan Paul, Trench, Truber, 1932. Chapter V. An analysis of moral words in terms of the emotions.

M. White, "Value and Obligation in Dewey and Lewis,"

Philosophical Review, 58:321–329 (September 1949). A criticism of two naturalistic analyses on the grounds that they miss the normativeness of ethical sentences.

D. C. Williams, "The Meaning of 'Good,' " *Philosophical Review*, 46:416–423 (July 1937). A kind of first-person interest theory.

III. ETHICAL INTUITIONISM

R. B. Brandt. *Ethical Theory*. Englewood Cliffs: Prentice Hall, 1959. Chapter VIII. Some puzzles for intuitionism.

C. D. Broad. *Five Types of Ethical Theory*. New York: Harcourt, Brace, 1944. An intuitionism centered on the notion of fittingness or suitability.

C. D. Broad, "Is 'Goodness' a Name of a Simple Non-Natural Quality?" *Aristotelian Society Proceedings*, 34:249–268 (1933–34). Criticism of Moore's interpretation of the word "good."

P. Edwards. *The Logic of Moral Discourse*. Glencoe: The Free Press, 1955. Chapter IV. A refutation of intuitionism.

A. C. Ewing. *The Definition of Good*. New York: Macmillan, 1947. Chapters IV and V. Analysis of ethical sentences in terms of the fittingness of certain attitudes.

N. Hartmann. *Ethics*. Translated by S. Coit. New York: Macmillan, 1932. Volume I, Chapters XIII and XIV. An intuitionism which does not exclude the emotions.

G. E. Moore. *Principia Ethica*. Cambridge: Cambridge University Press, 1903. Preface and Chapter I. Goodness as a simple characteristic known by intuition.

H. A. Prichard, "Does Moral Philosophy Rest on a Mistake?," *Mind*, N. S., 21:21–37 (January 1912). Intuitionism regarding judgments of obligation.

W. D. Ross. *The Foundations of Ethics*. Oxford: The Clarendon Press, 1949. Chapters III and VIII. Stresses the analogy between ethical and mathematical knowledge.

W. D. Ross. *The Right and the Good*. Oxford: The Clarendon Press, 1946. Chapters I and III. An intuitionism with regard to both value and obligation.

H. Sidgwick. *Methods of Ethics*. London: Macmillan, 1907.

Chapters III, VIII, and XIII. Asserts one form of intuitionism and rejects two others.

P. F. Strawson, "Ethical Intuitionism," *Philosophy*, 24:23–33 (January 1949). A criticism of ethical intuitionism.

M. White. *Towards Reunion in Philosophy*. Cambridge: Harvard University Press, 1956. Chapter X. A criticism of Moore.

IV. THE EMOTIVE THEORY OF ETHICS

H. D. Aiken, "Emotive 'Meanings' and Ethical Terms," *Journal of Philosophy*, 41:456–470 (August 17, 1944). Critical of the emotive theory.

A. J. Ayer. *Language, Truth and Logic*. London: Victor Gollancz, 1950. Chapter VI and pages 20–22. A pure emotive theory of ethics.

A. J. Ayer, "On the Analysis of Moral Judgments," *Horizon*, 20:171–184 (September 1939). Clarification of his stand on the emotive theory.

W. H. F. Barnes, "A Suggestion About Value," *Analysis*, 1:45–46 (March 1934). Early hint of an emotive theory.

R. B. Brandt. *Ethical Theory*. Englewood Cliffs: Prentice Hall, 1959. Pages 203–231. Arguments for and against the emotive theory.

R. B. Brandt, "Some Puzzles for Attitude Theories of Value," in R. Lepley, ed., *The Language of Value*. New York: Columbia University Press, 1957. A criticism of one emotive theory of ethics.

R. B. Brandt, "Stevenson's Defense of the Emotive Theory," *Philosophical Review*, 59:535–540 (October 1950). A criticism of Stevenson.

R. Carnap. *Philosophy and Logical Syntax*. London: Kegan Paul, Trench, Truber, 1935. Among other things an early statement of the emotive theory.

J. Dewey, "Ethical Subject-Matter and Language," *Journal of Philosophy*, 42:701–712 (December 20, 1945). Argues against the claim that ethical words are emotive instead of cognitive signs.

P. Edwards. *The Logic of Moral Discourse*. Glencoe: The Free Press, 1955. Chapter VIII. A restricted emotive theory.

BIBLIOGRAPHY

A. C. Ewing. *The Definition of Good*. New York: Macmillan, 1947. Pages 10–18. A criticism of the emotive theory.

J. N. Findlay, "Morality by Convention," *Mind*, N. S., 53:142–169 (April 1944). An emotive theory modified to avoid extreme subjectivism.

J. Harrison, "Can Ethics Do Without Propositions?" *Mind*, N. S., 59:358–371 (July 1950). With one small reservation a defence of the emotive theory.

A. Kaplan, "Are Moral Judgments Assertions?" *Philosophical Review*, 51:280–303 (May 1942). An emotive theory modified to allow for the rational criticism of ethical sentences.

J. Ladd, "Value Judgments, Emotive Meaning, and Attitudes," *Journal of Philosophy*, 46:119–128 (March 3, 1949). Argues that Stevenson misconstrues the moving appeal of value judgments.

J. E. Ledden, "On the Logical Status of Value," *Philosophical Review*, 59:354–369 (July 1950). Another statement and defence of emotivism.

C. K. Ogden and I. A. Richards. *The Meaning Of Meaning*. New York: Harcourt, Brace, 1948. Chapter VII. An early sketch of the emotive theory.

D. H. Parker. *The Philosophy of Value*. Ann Arbor: University of Michigan Press, 1957. Chapter III. A kind of emotive theory.

R. Robinson, "The Emotive Theory of Ethics," *Aristotelian Society*, Suppl. 22:79–106 (1948). Another statement of emotivism.

W. D. Ross. *The Foundations of Ethics*. Oxford: The Clarendon Press, 1949. Pages 30–42. Arguments against the pure emotive theory.

B. Russell. *Religion and Science*. New York: Henry Holt, 1935. Chapter X. An early statement of emotivism.

C. L. Stevenson, "The Emotive Conception of Ethics and its Cognitive Implications," *Philosophical Review*, 59:291–304 (July 1950). Argues that emotive theory does more, not less, than other theories to explain all relevant cognitive factors.

C. L. Stevenson, "The Emotive Meaning of Ethical Terms," *Mind*, N. S., 46:14–31 (January 1937). Reveals clearly the relation of the emotive theory to the interest theory of value.

C. L. Stevenson. *Ethics and Language.* New Haven: Yale University Press, 1944. The fullest exposition of the emotive theory.

V. Tomas, "Ethical Disagreements and the Emotive Theory of Values," *Mind*, N. S., 60:205–222 (April 1951). Critical of Stevenson.

S. Toulmin. *The Place of Reason in Ethics.* Cambridge: Cambridge University Press, 1950. Chapter IV. A criticism of an emotive theory of ethics.

M. White. *Towards Reunion in Philosophy.* Cambridge: Harvard University Press, 1956. Chapter XI. Critical of emotivism.

V. THE ORDINARY LANGUAGE APPROACH

H. D. Aiken, "The Authority of Moral Judgments," *Philosophy and Phenomenological Research,* 12:513–525 (June 1952). Criticism and extension of MacDonald.

K. Baier. *The Moral Point of View.* Ithaca: Cornell University Press, 1958. Analysis of ethical sentences in terms of reasons for action.

I. Berlin, "Logical Translation," *Aristotelian Society Proceedings,* 50:157–188 (1949–50). Argues against trying to reduce all sentences to one favored model.

R. B. Brandt. *Ethical Theory.* Englewood Cliffs: Prentice Hall, 1959. Pages 221–225, 231–239. Brief criticism of the ordinary language approach.

A. C. Ewing. *Second Thoughts in Moral Philosophy.* New York: Macmillan, 1959. A modification of his earlier view in the light of the ordinary language approach yet critical of their analyses.

S. Hampshire, "Fallacies in Moral Philosophy," *Mind*, N. S., 58:466–482 (October 1949). General statement of one ordinary language approach to ethics.

R. M. Hare. *The Language of Morals.* Oxford: The Clarendon Press, 1952. An analysis of ethical language by analogy with imperatives.

H. L. A. Hart, "The Ascription of Responsibility and Rights,"

BIBLIOGRAPHY

Aristotelian Society Proceedings, 49:171–194 (1948–49). Interpretation of two kinds of ascriptive sentences.

M. MacDonald, "Ethics and the Ceremonial Use of Language," in M. Black, ed., *Philosophical Analysis.* Ithaca: Cornell University Press, 1950. Compares ethical language to the language of rite and ritual.

P. H. Nowell-Smith. *Ethics.* Oxford: Basil Blackwell, 1957. An analysis which stresses the variety of uses which ethical sentences have.

S. Toulmin. *The Place of Reason in Ethics.* Cambridge: Cambridge University Press, 1950. Chapters IX–XII. The function of ethical sentences as harmonizing actions and attitudes.

J. O. Urmson, "Grading," *Mind,* N. S., 59:145–169 (April 1950). A comparison of value words to grading words.

L. Wittgenstein. *The Blue and Brown Books.* New York: Harper, 1958. The thinking behind the ordinary language approach.

L. Wittgenstein. *Philosophical Investigations.* Oxford: Basil Blackwell, 1953. The most fully developed reflections of the later Wittgenstein.

VI. DESCRIPTIVE MEANING

M. Black, "Vagueness: An Exercise in Logical Analysis," *Philosophy of Science,* 4:427–455 (October 1937). Contrasts vagueness with ambiguity and generality.

I. M. Copilowish, "Border-Line Cases, Vagueness, and Ambiguity," *Philosophy of Science,* 6:181–195 (April 1939). Argues that vagueness is just a special case of ambiguity.

C. Morris. *Signs, Language and Behavior.* New York: Prentice Hall, 1946. Pages 72–79. Discussion of descriptive sentences.

C. K. Ogden and I. A. Richards. *The Meaning of Meaning.* New York: Harcourt, Brace, 1948. Chapters I, III. On descriptive meaning.

R. B. Perry. *General Theory of Value.* New York: Longmans, Green, 1926. Chapter XI. Analysis of cognitive judgments.

B. Russell, "On Denoting," *Mind,* N. S., 14:479–493 (October 1905). On the meaning of denoting expressions.

BIBLIOGRAPHY

B. Russell. *An Inquiry into Meaning and Truth.* New York: W. W. Norton, 1940. Chapters II, III, VI. On descriptive sentences.

C. L. Stevenson. *Ethics and Language.* New Haven: Yale University Press, 1944. Chapter III. A characterization of descriptive meaning.

P. F. Strawson, "On Referring," *Mind*, N. S., 59:320–344 (July 1950). A criticism of Russell's theory of descriptions.

S. Toulmin. *The Place of Reason in Ethics.* Cambridge: Cambridge University Press, 1950. Discusses the nature of description.

S. Toulmin and K. Baier, "On Describing," *Mind*, N. S., 61:13–38 (January 1952). A discussion of what describing is and is not.

VII. EMOTIVE MEANING

M. Black, "Some Questions About Emotive Meaning," *Philosophical Review*, 57:111–126 (March 1948). Critical of the concept of emotive meaning.

W. K. Frankena, "Some Aspects of Language," and " 'Cognitive' and 'Noncognitive,' " in P. Henle, ed., *Language, Thought and Culture.* Ann Arbor: University of Michigan Press, 1958. A discussion of the relation between the emotive and cognitive aspects of language.

C. Morris. *Signs, Language and Behavior.* New York: Prentice Hall, 1946. Pages 67–72. On emotive meaning and expressiveness.

C. K. Ogden and I. A. Richards. *The Meaning of Meaning.* New York: Harcourt, Brace, 1948. Chapters VII, X. On the nature of emotive meaning.

B. Russell. *An Inquiry into Meaning and Truth.* New York: W. W. Norton, 1940. Chapter XIV. Deals with the expressive aspect of language.

C. L. Stevenson. *Ethics and Language.* New Haven: Yale University Press, 1944. Chapter III. A characterization of emotive meaning.

C. L. Stevenson, "Meaning: Descriptive and Emotive," *Philosophical Review*, 57:127–144 (March 1948). A clarification of his conception of emotive meaning.

BIBLIOGRAPHY
VIII. EVALUATIVE MEANING

R. B. Brandt, "An Emotional Theory of the Judgment of Moral Worth," *Ethics*, 52:41–79 (October 1941). Argues that emotions are basic to judgments of moral value.

R. B. Brandt, "Moral Valuation," *Ethics*, 56:106–121 (January 1946). An analysis of certain value predicates in terms of the emotions.

R. M. Hare. *The Language of Morals*. Oxford: The Clarendon Press, 1952. Chapter VII. Contrasts evaluative and descriptive language.

M. H. Mandelbaum. *The Phenomenology of Moral Experience*. Glencoe: The Free Press, 1955. Chapter IV. An analysis of specifically moral judgments of value.

C. Morris, "Significance, Signification, and Painting," in R. Lepley, ed., *The Language of Value*. New York: Columbia University Press, 1957. An attempt to apply the scientific method to the study of value terms.

C. Morris. *Signs, Language and Behavior*. New York: Prentice Hall, 1946. Pages 79–83. Brief discussion of appraisive meaning.

D. H. Parker. *The Philosophy of Value*. Ann Arbor: University of Michigan Press, 1957. Chapter IX. On specifically moral value.

R. B. Perry. *General Theory of Value*. New York: Longmans, Green, 1926. Chapters XX, XXI. On judgments of comparative value.

W. D. Ross. *The Foundations of Ethics*. Oxford: The Clarendon Press, 1949. Chapter XII. An analysis of specifically moral value.

W. D. Ross. *The Right and the Good*. Oxford: The Clarendon Press, 1946. Chapter VI. On judgments of comparative value.

IX. DIRECTIVE MEANING

E. Beardsley, "Imperative Sentences in Relation to Indicatives," *Philosophical Review*, 53:175–185 (March 1944). One interpretation of imperatives defended against other views.

H. G. Bohnert, "The Semiotic Status of Commands," *Philoso-*

phy of Science, 12:302–315 (October 1945). An analysis of commands stressing their similarities to descriptions.

P. Edwards. *The Logic of Moral Discourse.* Glencoe: The Free Press, 1955. Chapter VI. A discussion of imperatives.

E. W. Hall. *What Is Value?* New York: Humanities Press, 1952. Pages 113–154. On the logic of imperatives.

R. M. Hare, "Imperative Sentences," *Mind,* N. S., 58:21–39 (January 1949). Argues that imperatives are subject to the same logic as indicatives.

R. M. Hare. *The Language of Morals.* Oxford: The Clarendon Press, 1952. Chapter I. An analysis of prescriptive language.

B. Mayo, "Varieties of Imperative," *Aristotelian Society*, Suppl. 31:161–174 (1957). Discusses the nature of imperatives.

C. Morris. *Signs, Language and Behavior.* New York: Prentice Hall, 1946. Pages 83–86. A few words on prescriptors.

X. CRITICAL MEANING

J. L. Austin, "Other Minds," *Aristotelian Society*, Suppl. 24:148–187 (1950). On the use of "I know" as performatory.

A. J. Ayer. *Language, Truth and Logic.* London: Victor Gollancz, 1950. Chapter V. On the nature of truth and probability.

K. Baier. *The Moral Point of View.* Ithaca: Cornell University Press, 1958. Chapter III. Interprets ethical sentences as asserting the existence of reasons for action.

A. Castell, "Meanings: Emotive, Descriptive, and Critical," *Ethics,* 60:55–61 (October 1949). Argues that one use of words is "as a vehicle of criticism."

W. D. Falk, "Goading and Guiding," *Mind,* N. S., 62:145–171 (April 1953). Contrasts ought sentences with imperatives and descriptions.

A. C. Garnett, "The Indicative Element in Deontological Words," *Ethics,* 67:42–52 (October 1956). Argues that the claim to good reasons is the indicative element in ought sentences.

E. W. Hall. *What Is Value?* New York: Humanities Press, 1952. Pages 154–190. Discusses the relation between ought sentences and imperatives.

BIBLIOGRAPHY

S. Hampshire. *Thought and Action.* London: Chatto and Windus, 1959. Chapter IV. A discussion of criticism in terms of the criteria employed.

J. Ladd. *The Structure of a Moral Code.* Cambridge: Harvard University Press, 1957. Chapters V–VIII. An analysis of judgments of obligation in terms of the concept of a prescription.

C. I. Lewis. *The Ground and Nature of the Right.* New York: Columbia University Press, 1955. Places rational criticism at the heart of all judgments of right and wrong.

B. Russell. *An Inquiry Into Meaning and Truth.* New York: W. W. Norton, 1940. Chapters XVI, XVII, XXI. On truth and falsehood.

P. F. Strawson, "Truth," *Analysis,* 9:83–97 (June 1949). A criticism of the semantical theory of truth.

P. F. Strawson, "Truth," *Aristotelian Society,* Suppl. 24:129–156 (1950). A defense of his theory.

A. Tarski, "The Semantic Conception of Truth," *Philosophy and Phenomenological Research,* 4:341–375 (March 1944). On the meaning of the word "true."

S. Toulmin. *The Uses of Argument.* Cambridge: Cambridge University Press, 1958. Chapter I. An analysis of the meaning of critical words in terms of their force and criteria.

J. O. Urmson, "Parenthetical Verbs," *Mind,* N. S., 61:480–496 (October 1952). On the use of expressions such as "I think," "I know," and "I guess."

XI. THE VOCABULARY OF ETHICS

H. D. Aiken, "A Pluralistic Analysis of the Ethical 'Ought' " *Journal of Philosophy,* 58:497–505 (August 1951). An analysis of "ought" on an emotive theory modified in the light of Toulmin.

A. C. Ewing. *The Definition of Good.* New York: Macmillan, 1947. Chapter IV. Distinguishes various meanings of "good" and "ought."

R. M. Hare. *The Language of Morals.* Oxford: The Clarendon Press, 1952. Chapter XII. Presents models for the meanings of our basic ethical words.

N. Hartmann. *Ethics.* Tranlsated by S. Coit. New York: Macmillan, 1932. Volume I, Chapters XVIII, XIX. Distinguishes three senses of "ought."

P. H. Nowell-Smith. *Ethics*. Oxford: Basil Blackwell, 1957. Chapters XII, XIII. On various uses of various ethical words.

E. Westermarck. *Ethical Relativity*. London: Kegan Paul, Trench, Truber, 1932. Chapter V. Brief characterizations of many ethical words.

INDEX

Abstractness, 175, 223–224
Ambiguity, 204–205, 300–301
Applicability, 175–176, 222
Aristotle, 176
Assertion-denial: a synthesis, 160; nature of, 168–170; in evaluation, 211–214; in critical meaning, 251; implicit critical meaning, 264
Attitudes: and ethical sentences, 95; contrast with beliefs, 105; nature obscure, 109–110; causal relation to beliefs, 110; objective validity of, 117–127; caused, 118; not feelings, 118; not always agitations, 119; corrigible, 122; dependence on belief 122–124; irrationality, 126; subject to justification, 126–127; distinguishing one from another, 210–211; relevance to evaluations, 214–219
Austin, J., 250, 261–262
Ayer, A. J., 23–24, 90–91, 113

Baier, K., 63, 81, 128, 129
Bentham, J., 23
Berkeley, G., 31
Blindness, moral, 67–68, 80
Brandt, R. B., 51
Broad, C. D., (quoted) 21, 300

Castell, A., 250
Characteristics: confusing distinct, 46; and meaningfulness, 63
    empirical: defining ethical words by, 24–25; and meaningfulness, 30; teaching words that stand for, 37–39; ethical words do not stand for, 45

ethical: identifying, 34–37
natural: nature of, 21; contrasted with nonnatural, 47
nonnatural: and ethical words, 60–61; doubt as to existence of, 64; resultant, 70; existence questioned, 80; and objective validity in ethics, 80–81
Cognitive meaning, *see* Emotive-cognitive dichotomy
Commands, *see* Imperatives
Comparison: in description, 162–163; in evaluation, 209–210; limits in evaluation, 225–226
Contextual implication, 179–180
Critical meaning: samples of, 250; indication in, 251; assertion-denial in, 251; nature of, 251–252; nondescriptive, 253; varies with place in reasoning, 253–254; not justificatory, 254–255; compared to boasts and challenges, 255–258; claim involved, 258–260; compared with performatory meaning, 261–263; positive vs. negative, 263–264; explicitness, 264–266; strength, 266; width, 266–267; semantical presuppositions of, 267–270; in judgments of obligation, 270–276
Criticism: nature of, 251–252; not describing, 253; not justifying, 254–255; different grounds of, 266–267; proper objects of, 268–269

Definitions: presuppose grasp of language, 4; empirical, 25; hard